Victimhood Discourse in Comtemporary Israel

Victimhood Discourse in Contemporary Israel

Edited by Ilan Peleg

LEXINGTON BOOKS
Lanham • Boulder • New York • London

Published by Lexington Books
An imprint of The Rowman & Littlefield Publishing Group, Inc.
4501 Forbes Boulevard, Suite 200, Lanham, Maryland 20706
www.rowman.com

6 Tinworth Street, London SE11 5AL

British Library Cataloguing in Publication Information Available

Library of Congress Cataloging-in-Publication Data

Names: Peleg, Ilan, 1944- editor.
Title: Victimhood discourse in contemporary Israel / edited by Ilan Peleg.
Description: Lanham, Maryland : Lexington Books, 2019. | Includes bibliographical references and
    index.
Identifiers: LCCN 2019001053 (print) | LCCN 2019010946 (ebook) | ISBN 9781498553513 (elec-
    tronic) | ISBN 9781498553506 (cloth : alk. paper) | ISBN 9781498553520 (pbk. : alk. paper)
Subjects: LCSH: Victims--Israel. | Collective memory--Israel. | Group identity--Israel. | Holocaust,
    Jewish (1939-1945)--Influence. | Arab-Israeli conflict--Psychological aspects.
Classification: LCC DS113.3 (ebook) | LCC DS113.3 .V53 2019 (print) | DDC 362.88095694--dc23
LC record available at https://lccn.loc.gov/2019001053

Printed in the United States of America

Table of Contents

Chapter One

Hegemonic Victimhood Discourse in Contemporary Israel and Beyond

Conceptual Introduction and an Analytical Framework

Ilan Peleg

I am a man more sinned against than sinning.
(William Shakespeare, King Lear, 3.2.49–60)

No Longer are we necessarily 'a people that dwells alone'.
And no longer is it true that 'the whole world is against us'.
(Prime Minister Rabin's Knesset speech, July 13, 1992)

Victimhood is a rather universal theme among human beings, both individuals and groups. This edited book, focusing on victimhood, is the thought-product of eleven scholars representing a variety of disciplines in the humanities and the social sciences. The volume deals in a conceptual manner, but also empirically, with what might be defined as "collective victimhood." It applies its insights about this socio-psychological phenomenon to contemporary Israel as a fascinating case, noting the overall impact of victimhood on Israeli politics[1] but, at the same time, its broad implications to numerous other societies. In some ways, the current volume attempts to summarize the existing "State of the Field," while putting collective victimhood at the center of the stage as a way of promoting future research on the topic.[2] Victimhood is about the long shadow of the past and the even longer shadow of the present and future.

The volume is highly diverse. While some of the articles focus primarily on the politics of victimhood (e.g., the one by Ruth Amir), others deal with the ideological components of this important phenomenon, particularly from the perspective of the evolution of Zionism (e.g., the essay by Moshe Ber-

1

ent). Several of the articles dwell on the possibility of the political transformation of the Israeli victimhood discourse, particularly among leaders (see, for example, Yael Aronoff's paper on Israeli prime ministers who deserted victimhood), while others focus on specific events such as the 1967 war, events that might have led Israelis to "embrace" victimhood (e.g., Daniel Navon's paper in this volume). While some of the contributions offer a broad, historical Jewish perspectives on victimhood (e.g., Yechiel Klar's analysis), others look closely at the politics of victimhood within the Palestinian national movement (see, in particular, Ido Zelkovitz's essay). Most importantly, some of the articles, particularly Irit Keynan's, focus on new ways of progressing beyond victimhood. In brief, the spectrum offered by this volume is extremely broad: it covers politics, history, psychology, sociology, and literature in an intellectual effort to deal with the phenomenon of victimhood in its Israeli context.

Continuing the contribution of several books and numerous articles, the present volume notes that collective victimhood has been particularly a prevalent theme in societies embroiled in intergroup conflicts.[3] As such, the collective victimhood could be conceived of as a socio-psychological phenomenon and politically relevant condition that impacts numerous societies-in-conflict. Although the phenomenon of collective victimhood does not necessarily impact all societies, all the time or at the same level of intensity, it is quite common in many societies, particularly those in which nationalism is prevalent. As a concept that could be usefully applied to those societies, collective victimhood requires analytical, empirical and comparative perspectives. Such perspectives are offered in different parts of this volume.

In abstract theoretical terms, collective victimhood could be defined as a socially constructed paradigm or prism through which members of a particular group respond in a highly negative manner to the outside world, viewing the out-group as victimizers. More empirically, and therefore more applicable to any particular situation or society, collective victimhood is a shared belief system that combines five mutually supportive convictions characterizing a large number of people in a society (possibly even the national majority):

    a. a sense that the victimized group is the target of systematic and relentless persecution;

    b. the conviction that the persecution is permanent and unchangeable, a constant and not a variable (although its intensity may change across time and space);

    c. the belief that the persecution is completely unrelated to the actions of the targeted in-group and that it is exclusively the product of actions taken by the out-group (it is therefore assumed that the persecuted in-group cannot impact that victimization);

d. the notion that the persecutors include many, most or even all members of the out-group;
e. the perception that the persecuted group, the collective victim, is in a unique situation, different than any other group. In the eyes of the victim, its condition of victimhood is highly particularistic and definitely not universal.[4]

ISRAELI COLLECTIVE VICTIMHOOD

Empirically, the collection of analytical articles presented in this volume focuses on contemporary Israel, an interesting but not entirely unique case of collective victimhood. Popular culture sometimes captures fundamental socio-political reality such as Collective Victimhood earlier than academic scholarship. In the case of Israel's deep sense of collective victimhood, documented in this volume, this reality was brilliantly captured by Yoram Tehar-Lev in his popular song "Haolam kulo nedgeinu" (The Entire World Is against Us). In terms of collective victimhood against Israelis, the Tehar-Lev's simple but perceptive poem has three crucial elements that characterize collective victimhood in general (that is, it could be found also in other societies):

1. "Ha'olam Kulo" (the entire world) clearly means all non-Jews as such, a sense that all members of the constructed out-group are victimizers of the in-group.
2. The victimizers are against "us" (members of the in-group) permanently: the condition of victimization is temporally a given, a permanent condition that could not change. In the blunt words of Tehar-Lev's song, "we have learned it from our forefathers and we will teach it to our children and grandchildren." In other words, the collective victimhood is perceived as a timeless condition (Totemic time),[5] not as a phenomenon that might be reversible in the future.

    To put it crudely, there is a sense in Israeli collective victimhood that all the traditional enemies of the Jewish people are, in the final analysis, one and the same, regardless of the specific circumstances under which they have appeared on the stage of history and regardless of the specifics of their interactions with Jews: Pharaoh = Haman = Acashverosh (Ahasuerus) = Khmelnsytsky = Hitler = the Mufti of Jerusalem = Yasser Arafat. These historic figures are conceptually indistinguishable within the paradigm of Israeli collective victimhood. There is a frequent, dominant tendency to collapse these victimizers into one, symbolic, and simplistically a-historic anti-semetic "being."

3. The song by Tehar-Lev ends in the defiance of the collective victim: "Whoever is against us, can go to hell!" (Kol mi she'hu negdeinu, she'eyelech le'azazel!). The sense of collective victimhood leads quite naturally to defiance in the face of what is seen as continuous injustice by the out-group.

Since Tehar-Lev wrote his catchy song (in the 1970s), a lot has changed in regard to Israeli collective victimhood. In my opinion (and to a large extent the opinion of others such as Alon Gan[6] and Ruth Amir[7] who have written extensively about Israeli victimhood), over the last few decades Israelis' sense of collective victimhood has intensified and expanded as never before. Moreover, this volume argues that collective victimhood has now emerged in Israel as what might be called an "hegemonic discourse," that is, a great number of people, probably the national majority, and particularly the country's political leadership, assume it to be an existential condition that is, in principle, unchallengeable. In contemporary Israel, collective victimhood had emerged as a political and cultural dominant condition.

The historical dynamics of collective victimhood is a key for the appreciation of its strength in contemporary Israel.[8] Within the history of modern Zionism in the past, collective victimhood tended to characterize the more nationalist elements within the Zionist movement and (after 1948) the State of Israel. In a book published on Menachem Begin in 1987, I have noted Begin's strong, fundamentalist sense of Jewish victimhood.[9] This attitude has emerged from Begin's direct and personal encounter with anti-Semitism in his East European hometown of Brest-Litovsk, the tragic fate of his own immediate family during the Holocaust, and his ideological Revisionist up-bringing within the nationalist Betar organization in Poland (which Begin eventually headed). This life experience and ideological convictions led Menachem Begin to further radicalize the ideology established by Vladimir Jabotinsky (1880–1940).[10]

The overall thesis of this volume, reflected in several of the chapters, is that in contemporary Israel, as distinguishable from Israel in the first thirty years of its independent existence (1948–1977), the sense of collective victimhood has moved much beyond the Nationalist Right; it now occupies the ideological, political and perceptual center of the country. This argument has seven main elements:

1. Collective victimhood has become, in effect, the "hegemonic narrative" in Israel. The term "Hegemonic" is used here in the way it was offered by Antonio Gramsci,[11] namely as a prominent set of ideas in society that the vast majority of the people cannot even contemplate to challenge. Hegemonic condition is about the relative centrality of a concept in the public sphere of a particular society and collective

victimhood seemed to have emerged as a central component in Israel's public belief system.

2. Outsiders' criticisms of Israeli policies (in regard to the government's promotion of settlements in the West Bank, for example) or actions (such as large-scale military operations in Lebanon or in Gaza) are often interpreted by many or even most Israelis, particularly influential political leaders, as simply the continuation of the old, historic anti-Semitic persecution of the Jews. [12]

3. The "Victimhood" motif is used heavily and effectively by the Israeli leadership today. Prime Minister Benjamin Netanyahu, for example, is a "heavy user" of the victimhood-lingo. Every confrontation between his government and the increasingly critical world becomes part of the deepening victimhood narrative. The Holocaust is used as the "final proof" for the eternal victimhood of the Jewish people. Thus, collective victimhood has emerged not merely as politically instrumental but even as a culturally cultivated and psychologically internalized condition. Victimhood has emerged as the very core, the essence of the Israeli political discourse, particularly (albeit not exclusively) in terms of the relationships between Israel and the world.

4. Collective victimhood in Israel is based on a rather complicated combination of at least five mutually reinforcing elements, reflecting historical reality, contemporary political situation, and long-held traditional perceptions: (a) most importantly, the real history of the persecution of the Jews as a small minority (particularly in Europe) has been a long-standing condition, recognized by numerous scholars and other observers[13]; (b) Israeli-Jewish traditional holidays such as Pessach, Purim or Hanukah and much newer holidays such as Yom Ha'Atzmaut, Yom Hashoah and even Yom Yerushalaim, are variations (to a greater or lesser degree) of Jewish victimhood, resistance, and eventual redemption; (c) the unresolved Israeli-Palestinian conflict adds concrete, everyday reality, and reminder of Jewish victimhood, strengthening it beyond its deep historical memory; (d) the increasing political isolation of Israel in the world sharpens in the minds of numerous Israeli Jews the sense of victimhood; and (e) the analogy of any and all anti-Israeli critiques to the Shoah, a process that we might call the Holocaustization of the Israeli discourse. [14]

In explaining Israel's increasing political isolation, victimhood is frequently used and is increasingly accepted by many, as the one and only cause for that isolation. Alternative explanations to that isolation (such as the Israeli control of the West Bank and Gaza, the on-going settlement activity in those territories, and the persistence of human rights violations or at least wide perception thereof[15]) are automatically dismissed as reflecting the world's inherent anti-Israeli and anti-

Jewish bias. Such a reflexive reaction makes a real public debate in regard to the causes of Israel's isolation a virtual impossibility. A victimhood paradigm dominating the public sphere is unhelpful in promoting rational debate. Victimhood has emerged as an intellectual and psychological shield against serious political debate, a form of internalized censorship within the Israeli society.

5. Traditional Herzlian Zionism, and the original essence of "Israeliness" itself, reflecting the attitude of the Founding Father and his generation, were about an important duality: the elimination of the actual victimization of the Jews and (equally important!) the elimination of Jewish sense of collective victimhood.[16] From this perspective (at least), Herzl failed in transmitting his perception to future generations, as did Ben-Gurion and the other Founding Fathers of the State of Israel. It could be argued that collective victimhood is too deeply ingrained in Jewish history and psyche and that, in combination with the endless Middle East conflict, it might have simply become non-erasable.[17]

6. While certain historical events have contributed to the development of an ingrained sense of Israeli victimhood, this perception is much deeper than a consequence of a single or even a set of events; it is a historically and culturally determined reality. In this regard, I disagree with the conception that Israeli victimhood is rooted in the 1967 or the 1973 wars and the traumas that they entailed.[18] Specific events in Israeli history did not create collective victimhood; they have merely intensified it or confirmed it.

7. There is a real danger today that Israel's sense of collective victimhood will continue to *escalate* (especially facing increased and inevitable worldwide isolation) and that it will become the very core of Israeli identity itself. We are arguably already at that point.

BROADENING AND THEORIZING THE ANALYSIS OF ISRAELI VICTIMHOOD

In order to gain deeper understanding of the case of Israel, it has to be assessed within a broader analytical framework, a position adopted by the current volume. Two ideas are important in this regard: (a) the Israeli case must be *compared with other victimhood cases,* including the Palestinian one, in order to gain a more general, even universal perspective on the phenomenon of victimhood; (b) the case of Israeli Collective Victimhood could gain insight from *theoretical social science.*

There are several important points to be made in this context:

1. Victimhood is often related to "chosenness" (Bechira in Hebrew). In studying the Israeli Right, I have noticed that its strong sense of victimhood is complemented by an equally strong sense of "chosenness." Victimhood is often *compensated* (and frequently *overcompensated)* by a sense of chosenness, usually expressed in theological or semi-theological terms. The "Nation" is perceived not only as the permanent victim of its numerous persecutors, but also as having been chosen for some kind of larger universal mission. This phenomenon is not unique to the Jews or Israelis, although it may not be entirely universal among the nations of the world either.

   The great Polish poet Adam Mickiewicz described his nation as "The Christ among the Nations," the victim and savior at one and the same time. "Like Jesus, the Polish nation was killed and will rise to free the European people."[19] This complicated duality applies also to Israeli nationalists, although it is obviously not expressed by them in specific Christian terms. The nexus between Israeli right-wing politics and nationalist religion of self-renewal could often be found in the notion of "victimhood." Victimhood Israeli-style is about "a culture of resistance" as it is about martyrdom.[20]

2. A second useful term in dealing with collective victimhood is "exceptionalism." It is, to a large extent, the bedrock of collective victimhood: those who believe in victimhood, always perceive that their nation as entirely "exceptional," unique among the nations. While not all exceptionalisms lead to collective victimhood, all collective victimhoods lead to exceptionalism.

3. Victimhood leads often, and unavoidably, to the classical self-fulfilling prophecy, one of the most useful concepts in modern social science, added to our repertoire by Columbia sociologist Robert Merton. A nation that believes in "perpetual victimhood" is likely to behave as a perpetual victim, thus leading everyone else to treat it as a perpetual victim. Example: the behavior of Imperial Germany prior to World War I. The Germans behaved as if they were Europe's victims (allegedly "encircled" by all); their overly aggressive foreign policy caused the others eventually encircle Germany, leading to the War of 1914.[21]

The examples used here emphasize the conviction of several scholars represented in this volume that Israel is not a unique case of collective victimhood. Yet, given Israel's unique history and the long tradition of Jewish history from which Israel has emerged, it could and should be argued that Israel has become an extreme case of victimhood.

Victimhood is present in the perceptual lenses of many, although not all, nations and stateless national movements: it has been a dominant feature in the history of such diverse countries as Poland, Hungary, Ireland, China, Russia, the Arab states (especially the Palestinians), and many others.

A book by University of Toronto's scholar Alan Davies, *The Crucified Nation: A Motif in Modern Nationalism* (2008) brings out the tendency of some nations to view themselves as the ultimate victims, those who are crucified. Importantly, in Christian mythology the crucifixion is not only the ultimate victimization of the innocent, and therefore an invitation for victimhood; it is also the key for eventual redemption.

This complicated conceptual duality and those seemingly contradictory motifs are important for the understanding of victimhood in any national conversation, including the one in contemporary Israel. In Israel, the notion of victimhood has come to dominate large parts of the public conversation on major national issues. The danger is that political culture dominated by a strong sense of collective victimhood might lead to an emotional monologue devoid of rational rigor. This is especially the situation in regard to Israel's deteriorating relations with the rest of the world, particularly liberal public opinion in the West. There is a danger that the country might be transformed from its original vision of being an "Aspirational Culture"—a society trying to achieve values such as the equality for all of its members ("Chevrat Mofet")—into a "Victimhood Culture," a society mired in the ultimate apocalyptic struggle against a world perceived as inalterably hostile. Haolam kulo negdeinu. . . .

BEYOND VICTIMHOOD

Although Israel's victimhood has become dominant and even hegemonic within the Israeli society over the last several decades, particularly since the 1967 war, victimhood has been a distinct characteristic of much of the Palestinian national discourse as well, a phenomenon analyzed in this volume in detail by Ido Zelkovitz.[22] Interestingly, the historian Benny Morris titled his expansive volume on the Israeli-Palestinian conflict *Righteous Victims*, reflecting to a large extent the dominance of victimization and victimhood among both Israelis and Palestinians.[23] While a sense of victimization has emerged gradually among Zionists and Israeli Jews and came to dominate the discourse especially since the 1967 war,[24] "Palestinianism" itself was historically born out of a deep sense of collective victimhood (directed particularly toward the British mandatory regime and the Zionist Jews), and its final, validating "proof" since 1948 has been *al-Naqba.*

When two collective Victimhoods as meta-historical belief systems collide, as we have seen in Israel/Palestine over the last few generations,[25] the chances of breaking the vicious circle of mutual victimization and victimhood are rather low.

Maybe the only way of moving beyond victimhood is to reimagine the traditional historical narrative and even allow for the development of alternative narrative. Such narrative may include the shared legacy and common suffering of the victim and the victimizer.[26]

In some ways, the Israeli-Palestinian conflict has been transformed from a mostly violent encounter into an emotional, irrational competition over who is the Champion of Victimhood.[27] The only way toward a better future for both people is to abandon this Victimhood Olympics and deal with the conflict among them in a rational and humane manner where the interests, perceptions and, indeed, suffering of both peoples are taken into consideration.[28] In order to escape the hegemony of victimhood, it might be important to focus more on the future than on the past.[29] The essays included in this volume put the issue of Israeli victimhood into a broad historical context,[30] opening the gates for imagining a better future for all people involved.

The Structure of the Volume

This book is a comprehensive introduction, exposition and development of the topic of "collective victimhood." While it focuses on Israel, it introduces numerous theoretical concepts that could be used for the analysis of any society, polity or culture, particularly those involved in continuous conflict with other societies.

The opening chapter, written by the editor Ilan Peleg, is titled "Hegemonic Victimhood Discourse in Contemporary Israel and Beyond." Following a theoretical introduction in which fundamental concepts (particularly "collective victimhood") are defined, this chapter makes the argument that collective victimhood had become the hegemonic narrative in contemporary Israel, identifies its consequences, and points out the tensions between the current victimhood discourse and traditional Herzlian Zionism. The chapter points out that among the Palestinians victimhood has also become dominant, and it questions the possibility of moving toward a resolution of the Israeli-Palestinian conflict as long as this reality dominates the conflict.

Chapter 2, "Zionism and Victimization: From Rejection to Acceptance" is the work of historian Moshe Berent. It examines in detail the role of victimization and victimhood within traditional Zionist thought and politics (starting with the early Zionists and the historians of Zionism), pointing out that while Zionism's initial position rejected the traditional notion of Jewish victimhood, many in the post-independence era of Israel (after 1948) have, in fact, adopted this notion. Moreover, even friends and supporters of Israel have adopted the notion that the country is a victim and that its victimhood is an international norm; they see this victimhood as part of Israeli identity.

Chapter 3, written by Yael S. Aronoff, shifts the attention to Israeli politics on its highest level. It is titled "Israeli Prime Ministers: Transforming the

Victimhood Discourse." The chapter highlights six Israeli prime ministers and examines in some details the role of the victimhood discourse in their careers. While some of these leaders emphasized the permanence of hostility toward Israel, others deviated to at least some degree from that notion. By focusing on ideological factors, character and personality, Aronoff offers perceptive analysis of the role of victimhood in determining Israeli policies. This article demonstrates the usefulness and the relevance of the concept of victimhood.

Chapter 4 is written by sociologist Daniel Navon and is titled "Embracing Victimhood: How 1967 Transformed Holocaust Memory and Jewish Identity in Israel and the United States." It argues that the identity of both Israelis and American Jews changed as a result of the traumatic Six-Day War and that both have "embraced" victimhood. Using a variety of materials, Navon provides detailed description of the pre-War "narrative-identities" about Israel and analyzes the transformation in those, a dramatic change that had, in his opinion, major impact on Zionist and Jewish-American identity. The author concludes by discussing the implications of what he calls "the narrative-identity of Jewish victimhood" for the Israeli-Palestinian conflict.

Chapter 5, written by social psychologist Yechiel Klar, is titled "Historical Victimhood and the Israeli Collective Consciousness." Klar argues that not only there is a deep sense of historical victimhood in Israel—an argument that he establishes in great detail—but that it carries with it several contradictory legacies. He shows that the Holocaust has evolved from what was considered a major negation of Israeliness itself into a primary cornerstone of Israeli identity. He then examines what he calls "post-Holocaust obligations." The chapter presents several empirical studies that supports its theoretical argumentation and concludes by focusing on Israeli-Palestinian relations.

Chapter 6 moves from the Israeli victimhood discourse to the alternative or competing Palestinian victimhood narrative. Written by Ido Zelkovitz and titled "The Politics of Victimhood in the Palestinian National Identity," the author traces the evolvement of the victimhood narrative among Palestinians in Israel and particularly out of Israel in the post-1948 era. He uses materials such as literary works (memoirs, novels and poems) and political speeches in order to examine Palestinian thoughts about their national history and future. Zelkowitz focusses on important aspect of the Palestinian narrative by analyzing such aspect as women as symbolizing Palestine.

Chapter 7 is one of the two chapters in this volume that contemplate ways of moving beyond the hegemonic victimhood discourse in Israel and, particularly, in the context of Israeli-Palestinian relations. It is written by Irit Keynan and is titled "Transforming Victimhood: From Competitive Victimhood to Sharing Superordinate Identity." Noting the detrimental effects of competitive victimhood, Keynan describes the establishment of joint Israeli-

Palestinian organizations such as "The Parents Circle" and how they might transform the victimhood discourse into a more constructive dialogue. Keynan ends her paper by stating that victimhood can be defeated.

Chapter 8, "The Politics of Victimhood: A Vision of an Apocalypse" is written by Ruth Amir. It argues that victimhood is embedded in Israeli politics, identified the role that victimhood play, and points out that the victim status has traditionally been denied to a variety of "others," thus suppressing political, ethnic, religious and economic rivalries. The chapter deals with the construction of victimhood within the contemporary Israeli society, focusing on both its internal and external manifestation, and dwells on the implications of the victimhood discourse for human rights and universalist approaches. It concludes by proposing a "rights-based" rather than "pity-based" discourse as means of moving away from the politics of victimhood.

The concluding chapter (chapter 9) of this volume is written by three authors, Maya Kahanoff, Itamar Lurie and Shafiq Masalha. It is titled "Moving Beyond the Victim-Victimizer Dichotomy: Reflecting on Palestinian-Israeli Dialogue." The trio presents a few cases in which real transformation occurred in the discourse between Israeli Jews and Palestinian Arabs, transformation in which the exclusive perception of victimhood expanded and allowed a more nuanced approach to the "other." On a normative side, this highly empirical study, calls for moving beyond victimhood, recovering from personal and collective trauma, transforming the nature of intergroup conflict and adopting an alternate route toward a better future.

NOTES

1. Collective victimhood is invariably based on group cultural memory, although collective memory does not necessarily lead to collective victimhood. See also Gerhard Wagner, "Nationalism & Cultural Memory in Poland: The European Union Turns East," *International Journal of Politics, Culture & Society*, Winter 2003, Vol.17, No.2, pp. 191–202

2. Among the most important contributions on the subject of victimhood, particularly in Israel, are the many books and articles of Tel Aviv University professor Daniel Bar-Tal (see especially his volume, *Intractable Conflict: Socio-Psychological Foundations and Dynamics*, Cambridge University Press, 2013). Ruth Amir's book and Alon Gan's book (both in Hebrew) are also central for the understanding of victimhood as a cultural and political phenomenon in contemporary Israel.

3. Noa Schori-Eyal, Eran Halpern and Daniel Bar-Tal, "Three Layers of Collective Victimhood: Effects of Multileveled Victimhood on Intergroup Conflicts in the Israeli-Arab Context," *Journal of Applied Social Psychology*, Vol. 44, 2014, pp. 778–794 (quote is on p. 778).

4. Alternative and less specific definitions than my own definition are possible, but to make the study more applicable to real world situations, I am opting to offer the concrete characteristics of what I call "collective victimhood." One may also choose to focus on alternative but related concept to that of victimhood such as "trauma" (see, for example, Irit Keynan, *Psychological War Trauma & Society: Like a Hidden Wound*, Routledge, 2015). To me, while trauma might produce victimhood, it is a distinct phenomenon (and, in fact, may or may not lead to victimhood). The same applies to the condition of "anxiety" (see *AJS Perspective*, "The Anxiety Issue," Spring 2015, or Katie J. Chipman et al., in *Anxiety, Stress & Coping*, Vol. 24(3), May 2011, pp. 255–271

5. See Robert Paine, "Israel and Totemic Time?" *Royal Anthropological Institute of Great Britian & Ireland*, No.59, December 1983, pp.19–22.

6. See Alon Gan, *From Victimhood to Sovereignty: An Analysis of the Victimization Discourse in Israel*, Israel Democracy Institute, 2014 (in Hebrew)

7. Ruth Amir, *The Politics of Victimhood: The Redress of Historical Injustices in Israel*, Resling, 2012 (in Hebrew). The Amir book was also published in an English version.

8. Several articles in this volume analyze the notion of victimhood from a broad historical and ideological perspective. See, for example, the articles by Moshe Berent and Yechiel Klar.

9. Ilan Peleg, *Begin's Foreign Policy: Israel's Turn to the Right*, 1987.

10. Ilan Peleg, ibid

11. On Gramsci, see Antonio Gramsci, *Selections from the Prison Notebooks*, Lawrence& Wishart, 1971; James Joll, Antonio Gramsci, NY: Viking,1977; Antonio Santucci, *Antonio Gramsci*, Monthly Review Press, 2010; Walter L. Adamson, *Hegemony & Revolution: Antonio Gramsci's Political & Cultural Theory*, University of California Press, 1983.

12. Juliana Ochs talks about "allusive victimhood" where there is discourse based on analogy to past victims (see her "The Politics of Victimhood & its Internal Exegets: Terror Victims in Israel," *History and Anthropology*, Vol 17, No.4, December 2006, pp. 355–368)

13. On the long history of anti-Semitism, see for example, Jerome A. Chanes, *Antisemitism: A Reference Handbook*, ABC-CLIO, 2004; on the history of the papacy and antisemitism see David Kertzer, *The Popes against the Jews: The Vatican's Role in the Rise of Modern Anti-Semitism*, Knopf, 2001

14. Even a moderate political figure such as Abba Eban, Israel's foreign minister, referred to Israel's 1967 borders as "Aushwitz borders."

15. Ilan Peleg, *Human Rights in the West Bank and Gaza: Legacy and Politics*, Syracuse University Press, 1995.

16. See Moshe Berent's article in this volume.

17. At this stage of reflecting on the permanence of the victimhood discourse, it is best to hypothesize that it might be non-eraseable. As several of the articles in this volume indicate, such a conclusion might be too pessimistic.

18. See Daniel Navon, "We are a People, One People: How 1967 Transformed Holocaust Memory and Jewish Identity in Israel and the United States," *Journal of Historical Sociology* 28(3), September 2015, 343–337.

19. G. Wagner, ibid., p. 205; Ziol Kowski, 2012, pp. 147–156.

20. Norman Davies, "Polish National Mythologies," in Geoffrey Hosking & George Schoepflin, eds., *Myths & Nationhood*, NY: Routledge, 1997, pp. 141–157

21. Collective victimhood is but one type of "representation" in international relations. See Donald A. Sylvan & J.F Voss, eds., *Problem Representation in Foreign Policy Decision Making*, NY: Cambridge University Press, 1998.

22. See Neil Caplan, "Victimhood in Israeli & Palestinian National Narratives," *Bustan: The Middle East Book Review* 3, 2012, pp.1–19 and "Victimhood & Identity: Psychological Obstacles to Israeli Reconciliation with the Palestinians" in Kamal Abdel-Malek and David Jacobson, eds., *Israeli & Palestinian Identity in History & Literature* (NY:St. Martin's Press,1999, pp.63–86). On the United States see Conor Freiderdorf, "The Rise of Victimhood Culture," *The Atlantic*, September 11, 2015 and "Is 'Victimhood Culture' a Fair Description?" *The Atlantic*, September 19, 2015 as well as Arthur C. Brooks, "The Real Victims of Victimhood," *NYT*, December 26, 2015.

23. Benny Morris, *Righteous Victims: A History of the Zionist-Arab Conflict, 1981–2001*, Vintage Books, 2001.

24. See in this context the article by Navon in this volume.

25. See Alan Dowty, *Israel/Palestine*, Third Edition, especially chapters 2–3.

26. See the Keynan article in this volume for the idea of developing shared identities by groups in conflicts. For historical examples look at the philosophies of Martin Luther Kink, Nelson Mandela, and M. Ghandi.

27. See Daniel Barenboim, in the *Economist*, November 17, 2011.

28. I totally agree with Caplan, ibid., p. 1: "Overcoming these [Israeli & Palestinian] narratives of victimhood A decreasing the level of self-righteousness which both sides embrace is a prerequisite for making some of the tough compromises involved.

29. See the Aronoff article in this book.

30. Klar et al. in this volume. See also Shlomo Sand's books.

BIBLIOGRAPHY

Abdel-Malek, Kamal, and David C. Jacobson, eds. *Israeli and Palestinian identities in history and literature*. Macmillan, 1999

Adamson, Walter L. *Hegemony and revolution: A study of Antonio Gramsci's political and cultural theory*. University of California Press, 1983.

Amir, Ruth. *The politics of victimhood: The redress of historical injustice in Israel*. Resling, 2012 (in Hebrew).

Antonio, Gramsci. "Selections from Prison Notebooks, edited and translated by Quintin Hoare & Geoffrey N. Smith." (1971)

Bar-Tal, Daniel. *Intractable conflicts: Socio-psychological foundations and dynamics*. Cambridge University Press, 2013

Bar-Tal, Daniel, and Y. Teichman. *Stereotypes and Prejudice in Conflict Representation of Arabs in Israeli Jewish Society*. Cambridge University Press, 2005.

Caplan, Neil. "Victimhood in Israeli and Palestinian National Narratives." *Bustan: The Middle East Book Review* 3, no. 1 (2012): 1–19.

Chanes, Jerome A. *Antisemitism: a reference handbook*. Abc-clio, 2004

Chipman, Katie J., Patrick A. Palmieri, Daphna Canetti, Robert J. Johnson, and Stevan E. Hobfoll. "Predictors of posttraumatic stress-related impairment in victims of terrorism and ongoing conflict in Israel." *Anxiety, Stress, & Coping* 24, no. 3 (2011): 255–271.

Davies, Norman. *Polish national mythologies*. Polish Studies Program, Central Connecticut State University, 1998.

Dowty, Alan. *Israel/Palestine*. Polity, 2012.

Friedersdorf, Conor. "The rise of victimhood culture." *The Atlantic* 11 (2015).

Gan, Alon. *From Victimhood to Sovereignty: An Analysis of the Victimization Discourse in Israel*. Israel Democracy Institute, 2014 (in Hebrew).

Joll, James. *Antonio Gramsci*. Penguin (Non-Classics), 1978.

Schori-Eyal, Noa, Eran Halperin, and Daniel Bar-Tal. "Three layers of collective victimhood: effects of multileveled victimhood on intergroup conflicts in the Israeli–Arab context." *Journal of Applied Social Psychology* 44, no. 12 (2014): 778–794.

Kertzer, David I. "The popes against the Jews. New York: Alfred A." (2001).

Keynan, Irit. *Psychological war trauma and society: Like a hidden wound*. Routledge, 2015.

Morris, Benny. *Righteous victims: a history of the Zionist-Arab conflict, 1881–1998*. Vintage, 2011.

Navon, Daniel. "'We are a people, one people': How 1967 Transformed Holocaust Memory and Jewish Identity in Israel and the US." *Journal of Historical Sociology* 28, no. 3 (2015): 342–373.

Ochs, Juliana. "The politics of victimhood and its internal exegetes: terror victims in Israel." *History and Anthropology* 17, no. 4 (2006): 355–368

Paine, Robert. "Israel and totemic time?" *Rain* 59 (1983): 19–22.

Peleg, Ilan. *Begin's Foreign Policy, 1977–1983: Israel's Move to the Right*. No. 164. Greenwood Press, 1987.

Peleg, Ilan. *Human Rights in the West Bank and Gaza: legacy and politics*. Syracuse University Press, 1995.

Santucci, Antonio A. *Antonio Gramsci*. NYU Press, 2010.

Sylvan, Donald A., and James F. Voss, eds. *Problem representation in foreign policy decision-making*. Cambridge University Press, 1998.

Wagner, Gerhard. "Nationalism and cultural memory in Poland: The European Union turns east." *International Journal of Politics, Culture, and Society* 17, no. 2 (2003): 191–212.

Ziolkowski, Eric. "Christ, National Images of," in *Encyclopedia of the Bible and Its Reception, vol. 5: Charisma–Czaczkes* (Berlin: DeGruyter, 2012, Cols 147–156).

Chapter Two

Zionism and Victimization

From Rejection to Acceptance

Moshe Berent

In a breakthrough paper published in 1926 Salo Baron had set himself against what he had termed as "the lachrymose conception of Jewish history" which, according to him, was dominant in his times. This conception considered the history of the Jews as one of victimization, persecution, and violence, as living from one pogrom to another. According to Baron, this misconception of Jewish history was a post-emancipation, or a post-revolutionary, myth, created mainly by two currents within Judaism: one was the reform movement which considered the post-revolutionary liberal values as a basis for integration into the general society. This current sought to negate pre-revolutionary Jewish history, that is the Middle Ages' "victimization," with the post-revolutionary status of the Jews, or at least the opportunities offered by the emancipation. The second current was Zionism, which sought to negate the diaspora altogether and consequently applied the lachrymose concept of Jewish history also to the modern era.

It seems as if Baron's warning, which was directed mainly toward historians, has become the accepted norm in Jewish historiography. Nevertheless, to the extent that the lachrymosian conception of Jewish history had been wrong from a historiographical point of view, whether in the Middle Ages, or in modern time, it had been still the traditional view of the Jewish masses themselves. As Adam Teller[1] says, "pre-modern Jews seem to have viewed their own recent history simply as a series of catastrophes." Thus, notwithstanding Baron, Zionism (or to that extent liberalism) had not invented victimization as a constant factor in Jewish life but rather inherited it from traditional Judaism. Further, while Baron accused Zionism of stereotyping the history of Judaism, he seemed to have been doing the same to Zionism, that is, stereotyping it as advocating the lachrymose concept of Jewish history. There is no doubt that the victimization of the Jews played an important role in Zionism, yet whether it amounted to a lachrymosity in the Baronian sense is questionable.

The purpose of the present paper is to examine the role of victimization in Zionism. Zionism's initial position was the rejection of the traditional notion of victimization as a law of history about which nothing could be done: the establishment of a Jewish nation-state was supposed to solve the "Jewish Problem" and to put an end to the victimization of the Jews. Yet, according to the post-independence Zionist ethos it seems that the establishment of a Jewish nation-state not only did not solve the Jewish Problem, but the Jewish State itself had become the successor of the problem and the main object of victimization. Though this ethos is often criticized as a myth created by Israeli governments for nation-building purposes and to justify Israeli policies, it is not unfounded: Israel is perhaps the only member state of the United Nations whose existence has been constantly threatened since its establishment. Furthermore, the victimization of Israel had turned into an international norm accepted also by its friends. Yet, unlike its original position, the current Zionist ethos considers victimization as a law of history about which nothing could be done, on the one hand, and endorses it as a part of Israeli identity, on the other.

POLITICAL ZIONISM AND THE VICTIMIZATION OF THE JEWS

There is no doubt that the victimization of the Jews played a central role in Herzl's ideas and in what had been known as Political Zionism, yet it is rather questionable whether their approach amounted to lachrymosity in the sense that Baron had spoken of. Zionism was meant to solve the Jewish Problem of Europe by the establishment of a Jewish nation-state. The Jewish Problem meant the victimization of the Jews which amounted to pogroms, persecutions, and poverty. Baron's theory is sometimes interpreted as if it identifies the victimization of the Jews mainly with violence which had been created by antisemitism and Jewish persecution. Yet, as Baron himself had noted, in modern Eastern Europe it would be very difficult to separate the socio-economic status of the Jews from the limitations imposed on them by the government. Anyway, political Zionism had a much wider view of victimization which included also the socio-economic status of the Jews, their pauperization, and the lack of national identity which had complemented their victimization.

Political Zionists were less concerned with the Jewish past and more with the present and the future. Thus their approach was more practical rather than philosophical or historiographical. It was not important whether the Jews were persecuted in the Middle Ages, and there was no need for "lachrymose conception of History"—Jews were persecuted at their times and, at least in Eastern Europe, they considered themselves as being persecuted.

Yet there were important differences between the notion of victimization employed by Political Zionists, on the one hand, and the Jewish traditional concept of victimization, on the other. The first difference from the traditional lachrymose concept of history was that according to political Zionism not all Jews were persecuted and not in all places. Zionism was not intended for all Jews but mainly for persecuted Jews. Persecutions and pauperization characterized East European rather than West European Jewry. Further, the solution for victimization was the creation of a Jewish nation-state, thus consequently victimization and persecutions were linked to the question of the national identity of the Jews, or more accurately to its absence. Thus Zionism was meant for Jews without a clear national identity. In a communication circulated on the behalf of the Preparatory Committee of the First Zionist Congress it was said that the purpose of the congress was to establish an executive committee which would aspire "to establish a safe and endurable national home for those Jews who can not or would not assimilate in their local countries."[2] Thus there was not an identity between Herzl's "Jewish Nation," on the one hand, and traditional Judaism, on the other. The inability and lack of wish on behalf of the Jews to assimilate in their local countries characterized Eastern rather than Western Europe. Notwithstanding antisemitism, in the West, which had retained a "civic" concept of nationalism, Judaism was perceived as a religion and the Jews as members of their local nations. In Eastern Europe, on the other hand, which retained an "ethnic" concept of nationalism, Judaism, or the Jews, were perceived as nationality, on the one hand, and there had not been at that time developed nation-states into which the Jews could assimilate, on the other. Furthermore, industrialism and capitalism which had created the basis for Jewish integration in the modern era were much more advanced in the west. And of course, democracy was much more secured in the west, where the Jews enjoyed equal rights, while in the east the limitations imposed by the government upon the Jews prevented them from utilizing the new horizons opened by capitalism and industrialism and eventually led to their pauperization.

Thus, Political Zionism considered itself as a solution mainly for Eastern European Jews and notwithstanding Baron, had not negated life in diaspora altogether. After his first encounter with the Russian Jews during the First Congress, Herzl says: "I have often been told in the beginning, 'The only Jews you'll win will be the Russian Jews'. Today I say, 'They would be enough!'"[3]

This doesn't mean that some Political Zionist had not entertained a lachrymose concept of Jewish history in the Baronian sense; nevertheless this was not translated into a political scheme. Thus, for instance, in his "Auto

Emancipation" Pinsker expressed a clearly lachrymosian concept of Jewish history when he said that "Judeophobia is a psychic disorder. As such it is hereditary and, as a disease transmitted for two thousand years, it is incurable." Nevertheless, he did not think that Jewish emigration to the homeland would comprise of all the Jewish communities in the world. Western Jewry will not emigrate, because they are relatively secured and free. Pinsker singled out Russia (which included areas of Poland), Romania, and Morocco as the main reservoirs of mass immigration to Palestine, and, as Avineri remarks, this was a striking forecast of the eventual structure of Israel.[4]

Indeed, the Jews of the emancipation played an important role in Herzl's scheme: they would help the Zionists not only because of Jewish solidarity, but mainly because Zionism would divert the mass immigration to the west of the Jews from the east. The latter carried with it the dangers of invoking antisemitism and thus threatened the assimilation of western Jews into their local nations.

There were other important differences between the notion of victimization employed by Political Zionism and that of the Jewish tradition. Thus, Political Zionism added to the traditional concept of lachrymose a sense of urgency. The traditional concept of victimization meant that Jews were living in the past from pogrom to pogrom and were intended to live like that in the future (and in fact until "The End of Days"), and consequently it still considered the life in the diaspora as bearable. Political Zionism added to the traditional notion of victimization a sense of urgency: things were going to get worst and the Jews were going to face catastrophic disasters in the immediate future, if not "the last pogrom."

The third deviation from the traditional lachrymosity was, of course, the solution or the way out of it. Thus while the traditional concept of lachrymosity considered the alleviation of the victimization of the Jews in the "End of Days," Political Zionism offered an immediate solution: the creation of a Jewish nation-state. The Jewish State was supposed to create a safe space for the Jews free from victimization. Yet, the creation of the Jewish nation-state would affect also the victimization of the Jews who will remain in the diaspora. The Jewish state would not only alleviate the pressures of Jewish immigration westward, but it would "normalize" the Jewish condition. The Jews in Eastern Europe and in the rest of the world, who would not immigrate to the national home would turn at once into a "normal" national minority, one which had a country of origins.[5] Thus the establishment of the Jewish State would lead to the termination of the Jewish Problem.

The forth difference between Political Zionism's notion of victimization and the traditional one was the politicization of victimization: to the extent that the Jewish tradition offered a solution, this would be achieved at the End of the Days when all the Jews would follow the laws of the Torah. This solution rest in the personal or communal level. Political Zionism's politicization of victimization was very much in the Social Contract tradition. As far as the Jews were concerned they were in the "State of Nature" and the way out of it was by the regulation of violence in the form of a state. Thus, the victimization of the Jews was not only the reason for which the Zionist movement was established, but also "the engine" of Zionism. It was supposed to motivate the Jews and to make them join the Zionist movement and immigrate to their homeland. Yet, unlike the Social Contract tradition, the Jews' "State of Nature" was not a theoretical abstraction, but rather a real one which had been manifested in those times by the great Jewish emigration movement westward, especially to the United States. Thus, as in case of the Social Contract, victimization, or the desire for security, served as a source for the movement's legitimization among the Jews, and also in the international community. In the case of the international community the victimization of the Jews had served not only to back a moral claim. Political Zionists insisted that the "Jewish Problem" was indeed also a "European Problem" and that it threatens the stability of Europe in general and of the emerging nation-states in Eastern Europe in particular. Consequently, political Zionists insisted that it had been in the interest of the European states and the international community to solve the Jewish problem. All this point out that for political Zionists victimization was real rather then derived from an abstract law of history: real enough to motivate the Jews, on the one hand, and to play an important role in the real-politics of the international arena, on the other.

PRACTICAL ZIONISM AND THE VICTIMIZATION OF THE JEWS

With the decline of Political Zionism following the death of Herzl and the ascendance of Practical Zionism there had been a change of both the role and the meaning of victimization in the Zionist ideology.

The differences between Practical Zionism on the one hand, and Political Zionism, on the other laid mainly in two important elements.[6] The first was a disagreement on the purpose of Zionism, at least in the foreseeable future. Unlike Political Zionism, Practical Zionism did not consider the solution to the Jewish Problem to be the first aim of Zionism. At least in the short and intermediate range it aspired for the establishment of elite utopian community in Palestine: be it Ahad Ha'am's "Spiritual Center," on the one hand, or Labor's utopian socialist society, on the other, or both. For some, like Ahad Ha'am and his followers, this utopian society was a purpose of its own, for others, it was a necessity needed to create the conditions for statehood and the following mass Jewish immigration. Yet, as the latter had not introduced any timetable, statehood and mass immigration were postponed to a remote indefinite future, and what might have been seen as a tactical purpose—the establishment of "The Perfect Society"—had practically turned out to be

absolute.[7] In this sense post-Herzlian Zionism had been essentially a movement for a Jewish cultural revival rather than a movement for the solution of
the Jewish problem.

The second important disagreement between Political Zionism and Practical Zionism was on the nature of politics. Practical Zionists mistrusted grand
political actions or initiatives, the sort which were advocated by Herzl, and
preferred an incremental evolutionary process toward the establishment of
the national home, what had been known as the policy of "a Dunham here
and a Dunham there, a cow here and a cow there." Thus one disagreement
between Herzl and the Practical Zionists was about the nature of immigration
and settlement in the homeland. Herzl objected to "infiltration" to the homeland and wanted a mass immigration in the short-range once the Charter
would be granted. The Practical Zionists, on the other hand, wanted a gradual
settlement of carefully selected individuals, not necessarily under Jewish
sovereignty. Hence, the important difference concerning sovereignty and
statehood. The Political Zionists demanded an immediate Jewish sovereignty, which was necessary for both, the organization of the mass Jewish immigration, on the one hand, and the wide measures of colonization which were
needed to settle them, on the other. The Practical Zionists, though, preferred
a slow development even without Jewish sovereignty, while postponing the
question of statehood and mass immigration to an indefinite future.

Complementary to abandoning or postponing the solution to the Jewish
Problem to indefinite future, post-Herzlian Zionism also adopted the "Work
of the Present" (*avodat hahove*) as a nation-building program. It had started
with what has been known as the Helsingfors Program. The latter, which had
been adopted in the aftermath of the Uganda Affair, suggested that Zionists
should fight also for securing Jewish rights as individuals and minorities in
the diaspora and aspire to establish Hebrew cultural autonomies especially in
the emerging Eastern European nation-states. Thus between the two world
wars post-Herzlian Zionism had been formaly a dual-facet or even multi-
facet movement for national self-determination, aiming to establish Jewish
"homes" in Palestine, on the one hand, and in Eastern Europe countries, on
the other.[8]

Notwithstanding the apparent contradiction between the existence of Jewish autonomies in Eastern Europe and Jewish national home in Palestine the
Zionist ideology considered them complementary. The Jews of the diaspora
were not up to the mission of rebuilding Palestine. For those, like Ahad
Ha'am, who rejected the notion of mass immigration altogether, *avodat hahove* was supposed to unite the diaspora nation around the "Spiritual Center"
in Palestine, for others, in the long-range, *avodat hahove*, through the cultural and political revival in those autonomies, was supposed to prepare the
Jews for future life in Palestine. In the immediate range *avodat hahove* in the
diaspora was supposed to supply Palestine with budgets and with a small

influx of selected individuals which were needed for the building of the "Perfect Society." All in all, Practical Zionists had inverted the nation-building process of the Political Zionists. While for the latter immigration came first and then nation-building in the homeland, for the former the Jews had turn into a "diaspora nation" and nation-building was mainly to be done in the diaspora.

The spirit of Helsingfors Program and that of *avodat hahove* was that the fight for Jewish rights in the diaspora, on the one hand, and the rebuilding of Palestine as a Jewish national home, on the other, had been equal components of Zionism. Yet, from the point of view of the Zionist leadership the issue of Palestine had taken an immediate precedence. Further, the Zionist leadership insisted on the complete separation of the two tasks, at least in the foreseeable future. In the discussions after the Balfour declaration and toward the formation of the Mandate of Palestine, the Zionist leadership had insisted to separate the issue of Palestine from that of the Jewish Problem in Eastern Europe. Thus, it was possible, then, to see the creation of a Jewish national home in Palestine as part of the mosaic of new nation-states in Eastern Europe. The existence of large Jewish minorities in those countries threatened their stability and nation-building process. In this context, the removal of the large Jewish minorities to Palestine was indeed a direct European interest. Furthermore, in the aftermath of World War I there had been unprecedented pogroms in Ukraine, and hundreds of thousands of Jewish refugees could have been evacuated immediately. Thus during the Peace Conference, the French had suggested that the question of Palestine would be delivered to a committee which will be established in order to give attention also to the interests of the Jews in Poland, Galicia, Romania, etc. Yet, Sokolow, who was the chief Zionist negotiator for the Jewish rights in East Europe, insisted that these were two separated issues and that it is important "to prevent Zionism to be included in other Jewish questions."[9]

Under this "New Zionism" the victimization of the Jews could not have meant what it had meant under Political Zionism. Its alleviation had lost its urgency, which meant that the Zionists thought that victimization had become bearable, on the one hand, and that it no longer served as a guidance and source for political action, on the other. Consequently, for most of the nation, victimization had returned back to its traditional form before Zionism, that is a law of history about which nothing could be done, on the one hand, and which existed for thousands of years in the past and would continue to exist for many years in the future, on the other.

Nevertheless, the victimization of the Jews was not denied and also did not lose its centrality in post-Herzlian Zionist ideology. For once, as Vital noted, the Jewish Problem was the essence of Zionism, and as noted above, it had been a source of legitimization both among the Jews and in the international community. As Ahad Ha'am had noted with satisfaction after the

Tenth Zionist Congress (Basel, 5–9 August 1911) "You can hear the old slogans on the stage but only from habit and as empty names," and nobody really believes that "buying a small piece of land from time to time, or the establishment of a small settlement with an endless effort . . . a school here, a gymnasium there and so on—that these are the means to achieve this 'safe haven' that the 'Zionist Tradition' speaks of, a haven which will end all our troubles by putting an end to our diaspora."[10]

In the international community the Zionists had never hesitated to use the "Jewish Problem" to back their claim for Palestine. Thus in his testimony before "The Council of Ten" in the Peace Conference after the First Word War Weizmann said that "a million Jews are waiting for the order to march to Palestine," an order which he did not give and had never intended to give.[11]

Yet, while depoliticizing victimization, on the one hand, Herzl's successors had widened the concept in two important ways. First, while for political Zionists victimization was "real" and applied mainly to Eastern European Jews, his successors applied it to all Jews in all places. In other words, the definition of the "Jewish Nation" had changed. In political Zionism victimization served also as major nation building element and practically defined the nation in the diaspora. Herzl's Jewish Nation was not identical with the traditional Am Israel but was composed mainly of persecuted Jews. According to Political Zionism, eventually when the process of mass immigration was over, the Jewish state, which would alleviate the Jews from victimization, would take the place of victimization and define the Jewish nation and there would be an identity between the Jewish state and the Jewish nation. Herzl successors, on the other hand, considered the Jews to be a "diaspora nation," consequently it was ethnicity or religion rather than victimization which defined the nation in the diaspora. Furthermore, viewing the Jews as a "diaspora nation," the danger that the nation faced now was that of assimilation. In fact, that would become the main concern. The "dangers" of assimilation had been recognized also by Political Zionists. Indeed, though some of them believed that the Jews could not live in the diaspora, and that the diaspora meant extinction whether physical or spiritual, they had never made assimilation a Zionist concern, on the one hand, and recognized the right of the Jews to assimilate, on the other.

Though officially victimization was still there, in the post-Herzlian ideology it was actually looked down as a source of legitimization. Thus another important difference between the role of victimization in Practical Zionism when compared to its role in Political Zionism was that for the former victimization ceased to be "the engine of Zionism." Aiming at the immediate establishment of a "perfect" elite community in Palestine, post-Herzlian Zionism abhorred the idea of the Jewish masses pushed toward Palestine by persecutions. What Zionism needed, at least at that stage, were carefully selected individuals, motivated by spiritual desires of sacrifice for the ideal of the Perfect Society. Thus the main source of legitimization had shifted from the "Jewish Problem" to the materialization of Jewish authenticity, on the one hand, and the "undeniable" connection between Palestine and the Jews, on the other. Here, Leon Simon, one of the devoted disciples of Ahad Ha'am, reprimanded another devoted disciple, Chaim Weizmann, on a memorandum the latter had published on the needs of Zionism (1915) in which Weizmann was repeating the "old Herzlian slogans":

> I find it necessary to indicate that you have really weakened rather than strengthen our position. You are repeating Herzl's fatal mistake—that of turning anti-Semitism to the pillar stone of your building. Palestine enter your program incidentally and not as something essential. In my opinion, the claim a Jew has to Palestine, which for him is an internal need—as he approaches the problem as an inheritor of the Jewish tradition—is much stronger than the demand of the Jew who asks the world to get rid of a burden for the interest of the world. . . . It was absolutely natural for Herzl to adopt to point of view of the Gentiles (*goim*) for he himself was a Gentile (*goi*). But you, as one who had come from Pinsk, what are you doing in this gallery? . . . In this time of crisis I am so much longing to see a Jew form Pinsk who stands before the world "I demand the option to become a Jew![12]

Reinharz, who brings these words, emphasized that Leon Simon fears of Weizmann's adoption of Herzlian heresies had no foundations. Indeed, Weizmann's use of the Jewish Problem had always been tactical. As a devoted disciple of Ahad Ha'am he had never aimed to a state which would have solved the Jewish Problem. The purpose remained the establishment of a Perfect Society or a Spiritual Center in Palestine.

THE DEPOLITICIZATION OF VICTIMIZATION

In as far as victimization was concerned, there was a difference between the national homes which were supposed to be built in Europe, on the one hand, and Palestine, on the other. While in the first victimization would still exist, though bearable, the latter would be free of it but not been necessarily "safe." On the contrary, the hardships of Palestine were emphasized alongside with the demand that only the best abled Jews could have made an *Aliya*. In other words, to the extent that Palestine offered a solution to victimization in the immediate range, it was not by the creation of state in which will create a safe space where the Jews would not be victimized, but because in Palestine the Jews, each one of them and as a community of pioneers (*Halutzim*) could fight back or protect themselves. Yet, to join this community, a transfer of character was needed. The Jew had to elevate himself into the status of *Halutz,* or he had to transform himself from an "Old Jew" to a "New Jew."

Further, unlike in Political Zionism where alleviation of victimization was singled out, here it had been only one aspect of many equally and even more important tasks and skills the New Jew had to acquire (like the return to agriculture). Indeed, here we can see a shift from Political Zionism's social contract liberal worldview which singles out violence to a holistic romanticist worldview about the nature and the purpose of the state.

Thus, Practical Zionism had depoliticized victimization, first by making into a law of history about which nothing could be done, and second by turning it into a moral and personal issue. The escape from victimization was by the (self)-transformation of the Jewish character.

One of the sources for the depoliticization of victimization was the writer Micha Yosef Berdichevsky, who had a great influence upon pre-independence labor movement. Though Berdichevsky had been considered as Ahad Ha'am's greatest opponent, he shared with him the idea that Zionism had been essentially a movement for cultural revival rather than for the solution of the Jewish Problem. Yet, while Ahad Ha'am considered the Hebrew culture as a modern secular reform of Judaism, Berdichevsky considered is as the negation of traditional Judaism. The purpose of Zionism was to create a "New Jew" which would be antithetical to the "Old Jew." Further, in his famous saying "There is no Judaism, there are only Jews," Berdichevsky rejected not only the notion of the Jews as a diaspora nation, but also the existence of any Jewish collectivity, even the one which was suggested by Political Zionism and which was separated from traditional Judaism. Berdichevsky's nation had been an assemblage of individuals and the national liberation was an assemblage of personal liberations. In the spirit of Nietzschean philosophy emphasis was laid upon voluntarism or the "self-redemption" of the Jew. Thus only few self-redeemed individuals, those who had seen the light, would come and build the national home, while the rest were doomed to extinction (physical or spiritual or both). Berdichensky had a great influence on members of the Second *Aliya*, who were to form the leadership of the labor movement and the *Yishuv* before independence, and had influenced directly the creation of the myth of the Halutz, that is of the *Yishuv* in Palestine as a community of pioneers. [13]

Though Ahad Ha'am disagreed with Berdichesky about the desired characteristics of the New Jew, his position was the same. In his article "Moshe" he explained why the Israelites were prevented from entering Palestine. The sins of the Israelites ("The Golden Calf" and "The Story of the Spies") showed that The alleviation of Pharos's rule was not the end but rather the beginning of the story. Indeed,

> the master was no longer master but the slave still remained a slave. A people who had been educated for generations in a slave-house, cannot uproot from they heart the influence of this education and be really free.

Yet, while in the biblical story the Israelites were prevented by God from entering the promised land in Ahad Ha'am's allegory they were sentenced to wander in the desert by Moses (that is by Ahad Ha'am, or to that extent by "Zionism").[14] Thus, Anita Shapira[15] points to the poems of Chaim Nachman Bialik which dealt with "metei midbar" (The Dead of the Desert): the myth of the Exodus, where the People of Israel were found as unworthy of entering the Promised Land. According to Shapira, this myth suited the worldview of the Zionists, as the doctrine of the revival of the individual Jew in his historical homeland tacitly presupposed the existing generation (that is the current *Am Yisrael*) is "the generation of the desert."

Zionism's depoliticization of victimization had other sources within the Jewish history. One source was the Jewish non-political tradition. For according to the tradition the Jews will be saved when each and one of them will follow the laws of the Torah. The return to the Laws of the Torah, though inspired by the community, had been a personal rather than political or collective action. Further, according the tradition, the Jews went to exile also because real politics did not fit and corrupted Judaism. Strangely, post-Herzlian Zionism adopted this premise by adopting the idea of the Perfect Society. It was presented clearly in the ideas of Ahad Ha'am and Spiritual Zionism (see below). The return of the Jews to history should not be a return to real-politics, which corrupted Judaism, but rather to the sublime one, the one which characterized the Perfect Society. Here a sort of materialistic explanation, which was present also in the traditional explanation for the exile, was added: Jews should not engage in real-politics not only because it corrupted Judaism, but also because, since they were weak, it would be disadvantageous for them. Only in a morally purified world the Jews could completely escape their lachrymosian destiny.

Here this traditional Jewish view had found another strange ally in socialist utopian ideas entertained by the labor sector of Practical Zionism. Socialism in general tended to belittle politics as a "foam on the water." Politics was an infrastructure, a reflection of materialistic power relations. In this sense politics could not offer solutions, but since it reflected power relations, it could only mean the continuation of the status quo. In other words, since the Jews were (materialistically) weak, there had been no point for them to advance political solutions for their miseries. Further, the type of socialism adopted by labor's Zionism, that is of Utopian Socialism, rejected real-politics altogether, not only as one which does not befit Judaism or as one which is not suitable for the weak, but rather as one which does not befit mankind.

The outcome was that any large political schemes which intended to break the status quo (such as were offered by Herzl) were treated with suspicion. The solution rested either in an endless accumulation of small actions with the hope that in the future the sum of those actions would create a "real" or "materialistic" basis for the desired solution, on the one hand, or the adoption of utopianism or sublime politics, on the other, and in fact of both.

The depoliticization of victimization meant also the depoliticization of the Jewish problem. It meant that the responsibility for the alleviation of victimization rested directly upon the Jews rather than on the Zionist movement. Perhaps the most conspicuous example here would be the criticism directed toward the Jews during the Holocaust, that they went like sheep to the slaughter. Thus Itzhak Gruenbaum who headed the "Rescue Committee"—a body created by the Jewish Agency in Palestine to coordinate the rescue efforts in Nazi-occupied Europe—said in a speech on January 18, 1943, after the official announcement was made by the American State-Department and also by the Jewish Agency on the existence of the "Final Solution":

> There is one thing in this picture, that I cannot get rid of the bitter pain and sorrow which it invokes in me . . . that the Jews went to the slaughter while in none of them was invoked any desire to defend himself. . . . (This behavior invokes in him) . . . a feeling of shame and disgrace . . . people had turned to rags rather than human . . . I did not think that Poland's Jews would not defend themselves in these cases, that one leader could not be found among them that will inspire them to die while defending themselves. [16]

Before that, in 1942 when the danger of Nazi occupation threatened Palestine, Gruenbaum said: "The afflictions of the Jews (*tsarat hayehudim*) in the diaspora is that they preferred the life of a beaten dog over honorable death . . . we, at least, have to make sure that the legend of Masada will remain after us." [17]

In the first decades after independence the notion that during the Holocaust the Jews went to their death like "sheep to the slaughter" had been part of what Liebmen and Don Yehiya call Israel's "civil religion" (see below). Yet, in recent decades, also because of the decline of this civil religion, this phrase had lost its grace and arose a sharp criticism. The debate focused upon such questions as whether it was the correct way (factually and morally) to describe the behavior of the Jews during the Holocaust. Yet, what have been usually missed in this criticism was the relation between the theory of the "slaughtered sheep," on the one hand, and the removal of responsibility from the Zionist movement for the fate of the Jews in general and during the Holocaust in particular, on the other. As one kibbutz at the time published in its (reformed) *haggadah*: "Hitler alone is not responsible for the death of the six million—but all of us and above all the six million. If they knew that the Jew had power, they would not be butchered." [18]

THE SUBLIME POLITICS

Within Pracitcal Zionism's worldview of politics there were two possible solutions to the Jewish Problem. The first was by piecemeal politics and the second by the sublime one, or in fact by both. According to the first world view, politics was an infinite accumulation of small actions. It tended to view itself as "realistic," "pragmatic," or "practical" and thus divorced from both moral issues, on the one hand, and big political schemes, on the other. Yet, there had been another important expression of the depoliticization of Zionism, that is the demand for a sublime or a moral politics. As noted above, the idea that real-politics corrupts Judaism had been a constant theme in the traditional explanation of the diaspora. This notion of real-politics was shared by Ahad Ha'am and Spiritual Zionism. Thus the Jews could not engage in real-politics but only in the utopian one. Here victimization had acquired an important though somewhat opposite stance than it usually had in Zionism. Spiritual Zionism had not considered the alleviation of victimization to be the purpose of Zionism, but rather the creation of a "Spiritual Centre" for a small elite in Palestine. Yet in rebuilding the national home in Palestine Zionists had to be aware not to victimize non-Jews. In other words, the main concern was not to alleviate the victimization of the Jews, but rather to prevent them from victimizing others. Here victimization could have acquired even a positive value. For the fact that the Jews were victimized and powerless was an indication of their moral and political purity. In this sense the victimization of the Jews was preferable to any "political" solution which would probably mean the victimization of others. This world-view came to be dominant among a special group within "Spiritual Zionism" centered around "Brit Shalom," which included Martin Buber, Shmuel Hugo Bergman, Gershom Shalom, Chaim Yehuda Roth, Hans Kohn and other important figures of the intellectual elite of the pre-independence *yishuv*. Hans Kohn was a good demonstration of this group. Indeed, Kohn was aware of the fact that Political Zionism, which aspired to create a state, had been the last resort of the millions of Jews of Eastern Europe:

> I assume that millions of the east [Europe] Jews will be pushed to Palestine, because they have no home in another place. They cannot live in the European countries, not only because of the hard economic conditions but also because the feeling of inferiority, contempt and enslavement of Jews, therefore they are looking for a place in which they could become masters. And then they entangle a tragedy, as in the land which they desire for life of freedom and justice sit others, who are also reluctant to give it up because of the same national aspirations.[19]

Hagit Lavsky says that from Kohn's point of view this "was a tragic reality which would jeopardize the realization of Zionism as a Jewish mission. This leads him to abandon his original position and to consider Zionism as element which corrupts Judaism." Thus, "the most difficult tragedy is that the Jews had not learned to reconcile with their fate and want to escape it, if by Zionism if by assimilation." Political Zionism is a tragedy, as it requires irreconciliation with the fact "the people of Israel were chosen to suffer." Buber also made similar statements. [20] Akiva Ernst Simon, another member of Brit Shalom, suggested in a memorandum to the Jewish Agency—after 1929 Palestine riots (*meoraot tarpat*)—to declare that it would settle for a "spiritual center" in Palestine and the guarantee of its safety. According to Simon, if the revival of Israel is connected with injustice, (which means a spiritual deterioration) then it is better "that the Jewish people would cease to exist while just Judaism would exist, than that the Jewish people would continue its existence, while completely distorting and faking its image and constantly undermining the order of its historical influence." [21] As Luz [22] phrases it, one can find in Buber (and to that matter in Brit Shalom) a "martyr-like think." Though Buber, Simon, and Kohn could have not known it at that time, the meaning of their position was that Auschwitz was preferable to the "distortion of the image." Hedva Ben Israel notes that the dedication of this "group of intellectuals" to the absolute justice had been to the extent that they were willing to compromise the immigration of the refugees of Nazi persecution in Germany, before the Second World War, and of those refugees who survived the Holocaust. [23]

It should be noted that though this notion of the sublime politics employed by Brit Shalom or to that matter "Spiritual Zionism" is usually considered as antithetical to the one which was employed the mainstream of Practical Zionism, the "martyr-like think" had been constant theme in Practical Zionism and it was Golda Meir who said: "We can forgive the Arabs for killing our children, but we cannot forgive them for forcing us to kill their children." Or in other words, we could forgive the Arabs for victimizing us, but we cannot forgive them for making us victimizing them. [24]

POST-INDEPENDENCE ZIONISM AND VICTIMIZATION

Movements for national self-determination usually dissolve after independence, making place for the new state. To the extent that Zionism was a movement for national self-determination, this did not happen. Formally the Zionist institutions continued their existence after independence, and the so called "Zionist Ideology" is still considered to be the national ethos in Israel. Indeed, the justification for the existence of post-independence Zionism had been that victimization still existed and that the Jewish Problem had not been solved.

In their already canonical paper on civil religion in Israel, Liebman and Don Yehiya pointed out that starting from the early nineteen fifteens a new civil religion has emerged in Israel which actually meant the full adoption of the lachrymose concept of Jewish history. It included the notion of the isolation and persecution of the Jews in the diaspora yet it enlarged this concept to include also the isolation and persecution of Israel:

> This is the most ethno-centric of all civil religions. It affirms all Jewish history and culture and gives special emphasis to the isolation of the Jews and hostility of the Gentiles. The characteristic slogan of this period is the biblical metaphor "a people that dwell alone" or the rabbinic metaphor "Esau hates Jacob." It is needless to say, a civil religion especially suited to masses who are familiar with and attached to traditional symbols and unsophisticated concerning their explicit meaning.[25]

As Liebman and Don Yehiya rightly viewed, this approach to Jewish history was antithetical to the view that Practical Zionists, especially the Labor Movement, entertained before independence. The latter worldview, which they call Berdichevskian, had been confrontational toward the Jewish tradition, and, as noted above, put the "blame" of victimization on the Jewish traditional character. The New Civil Religion marked, then, a shift: Victimization had turned into a constant unchangeable element of the Gentile character. Thus, unlike pre-independence Zionist ethos, which projected that the establishment of a "Jewish State" would end the abnormality of the Jews victimization of the Jews, post-independence Zionist ideology considered it eternal.

As a part this "New Civil Religion" had emerged what Agassi called "The New Zionist Myth" which identified the Jewish Problem with the existence of Jews in the diaspora and considered relocation to Israel of all the Jews, wherever they are and whatever they wish, as the supreme target of the Zionist State.[26]

There were important differences between the notion of victimization in the "New Civil Religion" on the one hand, and the pre-independence one, on the other. The first was the sense of urgency which was applied to the "New Zionist Myth." While pre-independence Practical Zionism postpone the mass immigration to an indefinite future, now Jews were called, in fact demanded, to make an immediate *Aliya*. The second difference was that the demand was directed toward all the Jews. As noted above, Herzl and political Zionism's had distinguished between the "Jewish Nation," on the one hand, and the historical "Am Israel," on the other. The Jewish Nation was mainly comprised of persecuted Jews. Practical Zionism, on the other hand, had an ethnic concept of the Jewish Nation and identified it with the historical "Am Israel." Yet, as Practical Zionism objected to mass immigration the demand to make an immediate Aliya had never been issued to the Jewish masses.

Thus, the New Zionist Myth, for the first time, identified the Zionist "gathering of the exiles" with the biblical one.

What might seem to be a return to Political Zionism, the reappearance of idea of mass immigration, had not been necessarily inspired by a Herzlian worldview, but rather by the needs of the newly established state. The Holocaust created a new situation for the newly emerged state, for it desperately needed a nation, and the nation, that is, Eastern European Jewry, was exterminated. Thus Ben-Gurion observed in September 1944, "We are facing now the end of the war, when most of the Jews were exterminated . . . everyone asks himself the question: Where from will we take people for Palestine?" And later on he wrote "More than Hitler injured the Jewish People which he knew and hated, he had injured the Jewish State, which he had not foreseen its coming. The State was established yet it had not found the people who had been waiting for it."[27]

It is said that the principle of national self-determination pushes nations to seek statehood. Yet, sometimes it is the other way around and states are looking for nations. The newly created state was in a desperate need of a nation, and the myth of the "Jewish people" seemed a way to answer this need. Further, the notion of the Jewish State as a solution for the Jewish plight had always been the basis for the international legitimacy of Zionism. Though the Holocaust might have "proved" that Zionism was right, its consequences, that is the annihilation of European Jewry, could have been interpreted as if it was no longer needed. Hence, in the struggle for statehood and during the first decades of nation building, there was a need to emphasis not only the relation between Israel and the diaspora Jews, but also the constant hostility and dangers that the Jews were facing in the diaspora.

That this new call for Jews to make an Aliya was not inspired by Herzlian world view was reflected also by the fact that it was in fact a demand rather than a call or an invitation. The New Zionist Myth considered it not only a Jewish need to make an Aliya but actually a Jewish duty, mainly to Judaism or to Israel which symbolized it. In other words, more than Israel or Zionism offered to help the Jews, it was a demand from the Jews to help "Zionism" or Israel. Thus, in the very spirit of the *Haluts*, western Jews were required to abandon the comfortable life they were enjoying (*sir ha'basar*) and make an *alyia*. Of course, the fact that Western Jews were not victimized, on the one hand, and considered themselves and were considered by their neighbors as members of their local nations, was considered as temporary. The Jews were still considered potentially unsafe.

Yet, what had made the notion of victimization more applicable to western Jews was its enlargement to include also assimilation. As noted above, this trait was also visible in pre-independence concept of the Jews as a "diaspora nation," yet now it had become central: the dangers the Jews were facing were not only those of persecutions, but also, and perhaps mainly, those of assimilation. This notion of victimization had been expressed by the phrase "The Silent Holocaust," which was attributed to the "problem" of Jewish assimilation especially in the United States.

The New Zionist Myth was characterized by its religious overtones. These included the identity between the Zionist total gathering of the exiles and the biblical one, but also a shift from emphasis on victimization, on the one hand, and the creation of the Perfect Society, on the other, as the "engine of Zionism" and as reasons to make an *aliya*, to the thousands years of Jewish yearning to *Erez Israel*. These religious overtones were not intended only for Western Jews, where Judaism was perceived as a religion, but also to appeal to the mass immigration from Middle Eastern countries which had been comprised predominantly of traditional Jews. Ben-Gurion claimed that "for the Jews of Muslim countries the verse '*vetechezena einenu be'shuvcha le'tsion be'rachamim*' ('May our eyes behold Thy return to Zion in mercy') means more than any Zionist literature, that most of them, have never heard of."[28] This new affirmation of traditional Judaism meant also that of the Jewish traditional concept of victimization.

Perhaps the most significant change in post-independence notion of victimization was that it included also, and perhaps mainly, Israel itself. Indeed, in both Political and Practical Zionism, the Jewish State was offered as a solution to Jewish Problem and to victimization, and now, once statehood was achieved, the state had appeared as the successor of the Jewish Problem and the object of victimization. Oddly, it seems as if this "New Civil Religion" applied the notion of victimization more to Israel than to the Jews in general.

Thus in the 1950s emerged what Pedhazur[29] had called the "Defense Culture" (*tarbut habitachon*) of Israel. The latter, originated with Ben-Gurion, had two important premises: The first was that Israel is engaged in a constant "dormant war" which at any moment could erupt to open hostilities, and the second was that the purpose of the enemies was the annihilation of Israel. In a sense this world view continued the traditional conception of victimization: As the Jews lived from one pogrom to another the Israelis were going to live from one war to another. Yet, there was a crucial difference: in the traditional concept there was no "last pogrom," yet in the modern Israeli conception the "last pogrom" was immanent in every war, that is in case Israel would lose. There is a famous Israeli saying attributed to many leaders: "The last war will be the war which Israel will lose." The metaphor of the Holocaust was constantly used: in case of a defeat the fate of the Israelis would be the same as the fate of the Jews during the Holocaust.

CONCLUSION

It is a rather curious fact that the most severe notion of the victimization of the Jews was born with the Jewish state which was supposed to end victimization, yet it had become the main object of victimization. In the recent decades the post-independence civil religion had been on the decline and so the notion of the victimization of Israel. It has been argued that essentially the victimization of Israel was a myth created by Ben-Gurion and the elite as a means for nation-building on the one hand, and to justify Israeli policies, on the other.

Yet, as in the case of Baron, who attributed the lachrymose conception of Jewish history to a myth created by liberals and Zionists, we have to be careful not to attribute post-independence notion of victimization only to a myth created by the elite which sought to exploit popular feelings for mobilization, nation building and justification of its actions. It is true that Zionism, both Political and Practical, identified the establishment of the Jewish State with the end of victimization, yet it is also possible that in this respect the forefathers of Zionism were wrong, and the Jewish State was established in conditions unforeseen by them and in fact contrary to their original plans.

Thus, the emergence of the grim outlook of the Israeli elite in the 1950s and its prevalence until now could not be attributed to political expediency only. First, there was, of course, the Holocaust: a "pogrom" of this magnitude had not been imagined even by Herzl's Catastrophic Zionism. The Holocaust was not just a matter between the Germans and the Jews, but rather between western civilization and the Jews. On the eve of the Second World War the Western World was tainted with antisemitism, and the magnitude of the Holocaust could not be understood, unless we understand the reaction or to be more precise the non-action of the Allies. It is rather naïve to argue that the background that enabled such a catastrophic event had just vanished within a generation or even few generations because the world repented.

Indeed, the accepted wisdom among many Israelis nowadays, and not only among them, is that Israel "was given" to the Jews by the Gentiles as a compensation or repentance for the Holocaust. But this was not necessarily the view entertained by the Zionist elite right after independence and consequently there was another important reason for the Zionist's mistrust of the international community in the early decades. The Zionist movement, from its inception, had put its trust in the international community and in the international law. Israel and Zionism are often portrayed as non-legitimate, yet the truth is in as much as international law is concerned Zionism had been sanctioned perhaps more than any other movement for national self-determination, at least twice: first by the Mandate of the League of Nation, and second by the 1947 United Nation Partition Plan. In both cases the international community had failed the Zionists. First, the British had betrayed the Mandate, and then the international community had failed to impose the Partition Plan and Israel had been established, though according to international law, not by international law, but rather by bloody war of independence in which almost two percent of the Jewish population of the *Yishuv* was killed, and its Jewish population had faced, three years after the Holocaust, if not total extermination, then certainly a kind of a "last pogrom." It is perhaps rather a curious fact, yet the Zionists, because of naivety or weakness, had never conceived that they would have to fight for their independence. The "Charter" which they had sought, or to that extent the British Mandate, meant, at least for them, that statehood would be granted to them by the international community. There is no doubt that the Holocaust added to their expectations.

Indeed, it seems that the Holocaust had made direct antisemitism not politically correct, but it could be argued, as Schwarz-Friesel and Reinharz[30] among many others, that there had been an "Israelization of anti-Semitism." Further, the prevalence of the notion of victimization among the Israelis until now should be seen also in the light that Israel is perhaps the only country in the world that, since its establishment, has been constantly threatened with annihilation by its enemies: it had been a constant theme in the Arab countries' propaganda, and Iran is the very last example. Though the removal of the "Zionist Regime" perhaps does not amount to extermination, it certainly means a sort of Last Pogrom. Further, it certainly means a denial of a collective right. Thus post-Holocaust "Israelization of victimization" perhaps means that that the Jews are not victimized as individuals, but they are victimized as a collective. To all of these one must add the constant universal unprecedented unanimity of anti-Israeli votes in the United Nations.

The problem with the Israeli notion of victimization, then, is not necessarily that it is not true, but rather that it accepts the victimization of Israel as an international norm about which nothing could be done and in a sense it legitimizes it. Let us take the last debate on the Iran deal as an example. All the ingredients of Israeli notion or victimization were there: a hostile country making death threats toward Israel and seeking to acquire an atomic weapon which is a "Last Pogrom" type of weapon. The interesting thing about this debate is that in as much as the Israeli government had used the rhetoric of victimization to oppose the deal, it had never raised the demand to the international community that a precondition to any deal should be that Iran should openly retract its death threats toward Israel. This is interesting because it is very difficult to see how the international community could have ignored such a demand, on the one hand, and that the raise of the demand by the international community could indeed have killed the deal, on the other. Further, the fact that such a demand was not initiated by the international community perhaps shows that the latter also accepts the victimization of

Israel as a norm and considers it legitimate to do business with a country which issues death threats against a member of the United Nations.

Indeed, the victimization of Israel is accepted by both its governments, on the one hand, and the international community, on the other. Thus Israel had not participated in the various international coalitions which were created to fight either Iraq or ISIS. This was accepted as natural by both the Israelis and the International community, though Israel is a Middle Eastern country and these coalitions were formed against its sworn enemies. Further, during the First Gulf War Israel was attacked directly by Iraqi missiles, yet it did not respond. Here the victimization of Israel acquired a sort of "positive" value: those coalitions were not formed out of hostility or indifference to the Israeli cause, and it could even be interpreted as if the international community shielded and protected Israel. But it was still a victimization, as the Jews, or Israel, were conceived as an obstacle for international unity and Israel not a regular member of the international community. As for the Israelis, not only that they have accepted it, but also seemed to be pleased that the job, which included the direct protection of Israel, was done by others. The isolation of Israel is demonstrated further by the fact that Israeli soldiers had never participated in any United Nation's peace-keeping forces around the world. Here, also, the various Israeli governments had never protested or offered to send Israeli soldiers to U.N. peace-keeping forces and the Israelis seem to be pleased by this norm which prevents them from endangering Israeli life. This emergence of Israel as a non-regular nation runs contrary to the original aim of Zionism, that is to become a nation like all nations.

Indeed, it seems that while Israel could be seen as if it fights its victimizers, it does not really fight victimization. The latter had been incorporated into the Israeli world-view and identity to the extent that it had become indispensable. Yet, it is still questionable whether Israel could effectively fight its victimizers without fighting victimization.

NOTES

1. See Adam Teller (2014, 431–39).
2. See Elon 1975, p. 251.
3. Ibid 246.
4. See Avineri 1981, 80.
5. See Ben Yehuda 1905, 38.
6. For a detailed discussion on the differences between Political Zionism and Practical Zionism see Berent 2015, 253–263.
7. See Vital 1984, 10.
8. See Vital 1982, 467–486.
9. See Vital 1991, 300.
10. Vital 1991, 60.
11. Reinharz 1996, 279.
12. Ibid 403.
13. Shapira 1997, 163–171.

14. Kariv 1984.
15. 1997, 156–157.
16. Beit Zvi 1977, 109.
17. Segev 1991, p.62.
18. Liebman and Don Yehyia 1983, 64.
19. Lavsky 2002, 207.
20. Ben Israel 2000.
21. Dotan 1992, 60.
22. 2003, 176.
23. Ben Israel 2002, 17.
24. See also Berent 2015, 335–368.
25. Liebman and Don Yehiya 1983, 62.
26. Agassi 2015.
27. Friedlander 2009, 583–584.
28. Adler and Kahana 1975, p. 14.
29. 2003.
30. 2017.

BIBLIOGRAPHY

Agassi, Joseph. *Liberal Nationalism for Israel: Towards an Israeli National Identity*. Jerusalem and New York: Gefen, 1999.

Avineri, Shlomo. *The Making of Modern Zionism: The Intellectual Origins of the Jewish State*. New York: Basic Books, 1981.

Baron, Salo."Ghetto and Emancipation." In *The Menorah Treasury: Harvest of Half a Century*, edited by Leo W. Schwarz, 50–63. Philadelphia: Jewish Publication Society, 1964.

Beit-Zvi, Shabtai. *Post-Ugandian Zionism in the Crucible of the Holocaust*. Tel Aviv: Bronfman Publishers, 1977.

Ben Israel, Hedva. "Zionism and European Nationalism." In *The Age of Zionism*, edited by Anita Shapira, Jehuda Reinharz & Jacob Harris, 19–36. Jerusalem: Shazar Center. 2000

Ben Israel, Hedva. "National Identity of the Scholar and the Study of Nationalism." *Academia* 11(2002): 13–17.

Ben Yehuda, Eliezer. *The Jewish State: Papers on the East African Plan*. Warsaw,1905.

Berent, Moshe. *A Nation Like All Nations: Towards an Establishment of an Israeli Republic*. New York: Israel Academic Press, 2015.

Dotan, Shmuel. *The Struggle for Eretz Israel*. Tel Aviv: Ministry of Defense, 1992.

Elon, Amos. *Herzl*. London: Weidenfeld and Nicolson, 1975.

Friedlander, Saul. *1939–1945 The Years of Extermination*. Translated by Yossi Milo. Tel Aviv: Am Oved, 2009.

Kariv, Avraham. "Ahad Ha'am in the Maze of Positivism" *devarim ve'tsidei devarim*, 1984.

Lavsky, Hagit. "Nationalism Between Theory and Praxis: Hans Kohn and Zionism." *Zion* 57, no.2 (2002): 189–212.

Liebman, Charles S. and Eliezer Don Yehiya. "The Dilemma of Reconciling Traditional Culture and Political Needs: Civil Religion in Israel." *Comparative Politics* 16, No. 1(1983): 53–66.

Luz, Ehud. *Wrestling with an Angel: Power, Morality, Jewish Identity*. Translated by Michael Swirsky. New Haven: Yale University Press, 2003.

Pedhazur, Reuven. "Israel Defense Culture, Its Origins and Influences on the Israeli Democracy." *Politika* 11 (2003): 87–111.

Reinharz, Jehuda. *Chaim Weizmann: The Making of a Statesman*. Translated by Devora Barzilai-Yagar. Jerusalem: Hasifriyah Hazionit, 1996.

Schwarz Friesel, Monika and Jehuda Reinharz. "The Israelization of Antisemitism." *Jerusalem Post*, February 16, 2017. http://www.jpost.com/Opinion/The-Israelization-of-antisemitism-481835

Segev, Tom. *The Seventh Million*. Jerusalem: Keter, 1991.

Shapira, Anita. *New Jews Old Jews*. Tel Aviv: Am Oved, 1997

Teller, Adam. "Revisiting Baron's 'Lachrymose Conception': The Meaning of Violence in Jewish History." *AJS Review* 38, no. 2 (2014): 431–439.

Vital, David. *Zionism: The Formative Years*. Oxford, Clarendon Press, 1982.

Vital, David. "The Afflictions of the Jews and the Afflictions of Zionism." *Ha-Tzionut* 9 (1984): 7–17.

Vital, David. *Zionism: The Crucial Phase*. Tel Aviv: Am Oved, 1991.

Chapter Three

Israeli Prime Ministers

Transforming the Victimhood Discourse

Yael S. Aronoff

While a deep sense of victimhood shapes the identities of many Israelis and Palestinians and contributes to their skepticism of peaceful intentions of the other, these conceptions of victimhood are not shared by all citizens to the same degree. Many Israelis realize that they are unique in still having non-state actors, backed by a major regional power, formally calling for their state's destruction, at its borders. They also see the United Nations—as both the former and current Secretary Generals have acknowledged—disproportionately targeting Israel for criticism and investigation.[1] Israel is relatively unique both in the threats to its survival and in the double standard that leads international organizations and actors to single it out for condemnation. However, Israel is also the strongest military in the region, is strengthened by its democratic institutions and values, is backed by the world superpower, and has some ability to shape its acceptance in the region and in the world.

The physical threats and delegitimization, and its strength and degree of control over its acceptance, are not mutually exclusive phenomena.[2] Israelis and their leaders share these simultaneous perceptions of powerlessness and power but differ in the degree to which they focus on one side of the coin rather than the other, and the degree to which and how best they believe this hostile environment can be changed. Most Israelis simultaneously support a two-state solution and fear that the Palestinians have not accepted Israel's existence and would destroy it if they could.[3] Some Israeli leaders have hardly ever dwelled on victimhood discourse, or if they have, have not necessarily been stuck statically in this identity. Other Israeli leaders have often represented and reflected the victimhood discourse that is embedded in particular Israeli political cultures and have shaped and reinforced that worldview.

This chapter will highlight six Israeli prime ministers, each of whom drew to varying degrees on victimhood discourse in their careers, and several of whom shifted their reliance on victimhood discourse over time. I argue that the ideologies and personalities of these leaders help explain why some emphasized the permanence of the hostility toward Israel while others did not, and why some were more able to adjust their perceptions over time than others.[4] Two main factors that influence the degree to which a prime minister focused on victimhood over time are ideology and individual time orientation. The more a prime minister was committed to a particular ideology, and the more that ideology focused on a sense of perpetual victimhood across time, the more this shaped their worldview. Ilan Peleg has analyzed how Likud ideology has traditionally viewed the world as "actively involved in efforts to destroy Israel and the Jewish people."[5] This ideological stance also shapes hard-line perceptions that an enemy is monolithic and has ambitious, aggressive motives, and that concessions will therefore be taken advantage of rather than reciprocated.

These perceptions of victimhood are magnified by those leaders who have an individual time orientation in which they are emotionally tied to a past, and in particular a past which they view as cyclical and informing the present. These individuals focus on eternal victimhood, in which the enemy takes a different shape in each generation. Individual time orientation is an aspect of personality that describes the relative amount of time each leader devotes to thinking about the past, present, or future. As Rose McDermott put it, "some people remain preoccupied with the past, others manage to stay focused in the present, while still others concentrate on the future."[6] An individual's perception of time is a core element of cognitive style.[7] Ilona Boniwel and Philip Zombardo assert that time perspective "is one of the most powerful influences on virtually all aspects of human behavior" and that each individual's time perspective varies and influences individual choices.[8] Scholars such as Yaakov Vertzberger and Robert Jervis have particularly focused on individuals who have a greater propensity to assess present conditions through the lens of the past, using the "the representativeness heuristic" to find similarities between present and past events and make "often misplaced" generalizations.[9] In the Israeli context, Jacob Lassner and Ilan Troen argue that Jews have assessed present and future relations through varied interpretations of the past.[10] I have argued that leaders who are emotionally attached to and focused on a violent, conflict-ridden past, who view that violent history as repeating itself, and who view this past as a living reality, will be less likely to expect change and therefore recognize change in an adversary. When an individual has an archaic or totemic notion of time, he or she associates the present enemy with all other enemies, even in the ancient past.[11]

On the other hand, those prime ministers who had a present or future orientation were able to move away from a fixed image of an adversary as bent on Israel's destruction. They made far fewer analogies to past instances of victimization, and those having a present orientation generally changed perceptions gradually in small increments. This builds on Jervis's notion that information arriving gradually will be more likely to be dismissed, focusing on immediate events made changes seem less significant.[12] Leaders who focus on the future as being distinct from the past are more likely to be influenced by perceptions of future trends than dramatic events and are more likely to expect and initiate change.[13]

The following chapter will examine six Israeli prime ministers, holding differing political ideologies and varying time orientations, in order to examine the influence of these factors on their emphasis on past and present victimization. In particular, I will focus on the relative emphasis of the Holocaust as lens through which to read current threats, in particular with regard to Iran and to the Palestinian leaders.

YITZHAK SHAMIR: THE SEA IS THE SAME SEA AND THE ARABS ARE THE SAME ARABS

Yitzhak Shamir was prime minister from 1983–1984 and from 1986–1992. He was a self-described ideologue who adhered to ideology dogmatically and for whom ideology was the sole basis of evaluation. "From ideology," he said, "there are no retreats."[14] He also had a past orientation that led him to emphasize those in the past who wanted to destroy Jews and conflate those past enemies with current enemies who he perceived as sharing the same goals.

Shamir's ideology was based on revisionist Zionism founded by Vladimir Jabotinksy in the 1920s and 1930s. Shamir left Poland for Palestine in 1935 at age twenty and two years later joined the Irgun Zvai Leumi (IZL, Hebrew for the National Military Organization), a pre-state defense organization commanded by Jabotinksy; he later joined the Herut L'Israel (Israel Freedom Fighters), or Lehi, which split off from the Irgun to engage in an underground war against the British in Palestine. Post-independence the Herut "Freedom" Party emerged, adopting the basic philosophies of the Irgun, and that party in turn became the Likud Party in 1973. According to Shamir, members of Lehi were "well aware that our enemies vastly outnumbered our friends" and in 1979 Shamir continued to believe that "the whole world is against us."[15] In 1998 he stated that Israel had more enemies than friends.[16] He therefore did not believe that Israeli concessions would change the aims of Palestinians which he believed to continue to be the annihilation of Israel after the Oslo Accords, and he also did not believe that it would earn Israel greater acceptance around the world. He called US Secretary of State James Baker a new "hangman" for the Jewish people, and argued that Netanyahu's eventual acceptance of the Oslo Accords when he became prime minister "didn't help him at all. No one is for him. He is in conflict with the United States, with Europe, with the Arabs of course, and with part of the Jews."[17]

Shamir was haunted by the fact that his parents and siblings were murdered by the Nazis, and that haunting past informed his present. Shamir writes that he and Menachem Begin had "our adult lives, and many of our attitudes, permanently affected by the Holocaust . . . in Poland . . . among the millions who were abandoned, tormented, and slaughtered was my entire family. I cannot forget and will not forgive."[18] Shamir wrote,

> I had long followed, with horror and pain, the communist attempt to finish off what the Tsars had begun. . . . The persecution of Jews, the accusations and mock trials that led to execution of hundreds of thousands, the Government-directed anti-Jewish campaigns that let hooligans loose to pillage, desecrate, torture and kill, the murder of Jewish leaders, writers, doctors and poets sent to their deaths on absurd charges or imprisoned and subjected to brutality, were not items I merely read in the paper and signed over. They were wounds within me."[19]

Shamir criticized other leaders for not focusing enough on the past. He visited Dachau as foreign minister and he "cried, pierced by sorrow for the perished multitudes—and my family—feeling for a moment that the weight of the memories was almost too much to bear. But the brief ceremony over, the inadequate acknowledgment to history made, we went on to Bonn." He laments that for Chancellor Helmut Kohl "the Holocaust is history, long over, an enormity that happened when he and his generation were young or not yet born and thus not guilty, not to be blamed, not emotionally involved."[20]

Shamir used analogies to the Holocaust in order to explain why he thought that the Palestinians would never accept the state of Israel in any part of the territory, even after Yasser Arafat signed the 1993 Oslo Accords recognizing Israel in the 1967 borders. In 1994 he affirmed that he still believed his assertions two decades earlier that:

> the dominant element in the Israel-Arab Relationship is that those Arab groupings which do not recognize our right to live in the Land of Israel [i.e., the entire historic area] also do not recognize our right live in part of the Land of Israel . . . it was time we learned to believe our enemies when they say that they wish to destroy us. Who, after all, believed Hitler when he wrote in *Mein Kampf* that he would destroy all the Jews of Europe if he ever got the chance? Not enough has changed since then, how tragic.[21]

Shamir's past orientation and ideological conviction that the world was permanently hostile and that adversaries in each generation wish to destroy the Jewish people, both served to magnify threats and reject change on the part of an adversary.

BENJAMIN NETANYAHU: THE PRESENCE OF PAST VICTIMHOOD

Benjamin Netanyahu is Israel's longest continuously serving prime minister, having been prime minister from 1996–1999, from 2009–2013, and again since 2013. Unlike Shamir, Netanyahu is not an ideologue and is capable of being pragmatic and making tactical policy changes due to internal and external pressures in order to attain or remain in power, and also reaches out to strengthen relations with some African, Asian, and Eastern European countries. However, like Shamir, both his ideology and past time orientation emphasize the idea that there are enemies that wish to destroy Israel and victimize Israelis. Netanyahu's continuous focus on these themes limits his expectation that peace is possible, and prevents him from expecting change on the part of adversaries—and thereby limits his ability to recognize change if and when it occurs.

Netanyahu's parents and grandparents were supporters of Jabotinsky's revisionist Zionism. His father Ben-Zion joined the Revisionist party in 1928 and in 1939 worked in the United States as Jabotinsky's personal assistant until Jabotinsky's death in 1940. He was co-editor of the Revisionists' daily newspaper. Netanyahu keeps several volumes of Jabotinsky's works in his office and frequently consulted with his father until his father passed away in 2012.[22] Thus Jabotinsky's Revisionist Zionism, as championed by his father, constitutes Netanyahu's strongest ideological influence.

Dennis Ross argues that the strongest ideological influence on Netanyahu is that the world is filled with enemies. According to Ross, Netanyahu feels that "Israel has to constantly look over her shoulder because it is constantly being threatened. The world is shaped with enemies and one has to safeguard against them."[23] This view is confirmed for Netanyahu by what he sees as the Palestinian Authority's statements and actions that support terror, such as naming public squares after terrorists and making payments to their families. These all confirm his belief that he does not have genuine partners for peace. In this context, he sees the concessions he has made—signing the Hebron and Wye Accords during his first term; largely freezing West Bank settlements for nine months in his second term, and favoring a two-state solution since 2009—as having not been reciprocated or appreciated, but rather that the world condemns him anyway.

Netanyahu's past orientation reinforces his ideological expectation that every generation will produce adversaries seeking Israel's destruction and that accommodation will not be reciprocated. In *A Place among the Nations* he laments the "fashionable ahistorisicism prevalent today," and mocked Peres in the Knesset for his optimism: "You wrote a book about the new Middle East," Netanyahu said, "but what can be done, the old Middle East is exploding in your face."[24]

The ultimate example of Jewish victimhood is of course the Holocaust. However, different leaders focus on this to various degrees. Netanyahu, who has a past orientation, references Hitler twenty times in his book *A Durable Peace: Israel and Its Place among the Nations*. In this context he writes that "Israel, still the object of genocidal designs by some of the Arab world, has become in the view of many Western opinion-leaders the intransigent party, the obstacle to peace; Arabs who seek Israel's destruction and say so openly within the Arab world are often presented as reasoned and moderate."[25] In the context of talking about Hitler, Netanyahu also claims that the PLO's goal according to its charter is the liberation of Palestine through the liquidation of the Zionist presence. He continues

> there is hardly a case in modern history in which an antagonist has sought to completely annihilate a rival nation. Not even World War II, the most terrible of wars, resulted in such an outcome. The defeat of Hitler and the capitulation of Hirohito were nowhere understood as opportunities to eradicate Germany and Japan. Yet it is precisely this most extraordinary goal, the erasure of an entire nation and its people, that the PLO had chosen to emblazon on its banner (For this reason I insisted on the charter's annulment as part of the Wye Accords).[26]

He focuses on Haj Amin Al Husseini, the Mufti of Jerusalem, meeting with Hitler in Berlin in 1941 and making his base in Berlin in 1942–1944; Netanyahu quotes him as saying "I declare a Holy War. Murder the Jews, Murder them All!"[27] In arguing against a Palestinian state (before changing his position in 2009), he again uses Germany as a reference to argue that demilitarization does not last, as it did not after World War I when the German Rhineland was supposed to be demilitarized.[28] Another lesson that Netanyahu takes from the Holocaust is that Israel should not bend to international pressure and that in the "realm of political power, the habits of passivity and submissiveness acquired in exile are still very much with us."[29]

Netanyahu's emphasis on the danger of Iran acquiring nuclear weapons (a danger feared by the vast majority of Israelis) has often been framed by and filtered through the specter of genocide. This was one of his main themes in his multiple annual addresses to the United Nations. Netanyahu's past orientation leads him to claim that "for in every generation, there were those who rose up to destroy our people. In antiquity, we faced destruction from the ancient empires of Babylon and Rome. In the Middle Ages, we faced inquisition and expulsion. And in modern times, we faced pogroms and the Holocaust. Yet the Jewish people persevered. And now another regime has arisen."[30] In explaining his opposition to the Iran deal, he refers to the lessons of the Holocaust:

> Ladies and Gentlemen," he intoned, "it's not easy to oppose something that is embraced by the greatest powers in the world. Believe me, it would be far easier to remain silent. But throughout our history, the Jewish people have learned the heavy price of silence. And as the Prime Minister of the Jewish State, as someone who knows that history, I refuse to be silent. I'll say it again: The days when the Jewish people remained passive in the face of genocidal enemies – those days are over. . . . Seventy years after the murder of six million Jews, Iran's rulers promise to destroy my country. Murder my people. And the response from this body, the response from nearly every one of the governments represented here, has been absolutely nothing! [31]

Netanyahu's sense of victimhood not only frames the way he sees regional actors as enemies, but also frames the way he sees himself as a victim of the establishment, the media, and the justice system in Israel. His father always maintained that he had been the victim in his career of the academic establishment that excluded those on the political right, and Netanyahu throughout his life has railed against the establishment and media that attacks him. As investigations into corruption on his part proliferate, he has become fiercer in his condemnation of the media as enemies of the people.[32]

ARIEL SHARON: WARY BUT WILLING

Ariel Sharon was prime minister of Israel from 2001 until 2006, when he suffered a debilitating stroke that eventually took his life. He was no ideologue, and although he helped create the Likud Party, he claims that "I was not eager to put myself in the position of having to accept party discipline and a party line."[33] He left Likud in 2005 and established the centrist Kadima party in order to continue to implement his unilateral disengagement plan from Gaza and from most of the West Bank. Although Ariel Sharon had grown up in a Labor party community and therefore was not raised within the ideology of the Likud party that he himself helped found; at the same time, he shared a perception that the world was hostile to Israel and that its enemies desired its destruction. While, as I will argue below, he had a present time orientation and did not make as many analogies to the Holocaust and to Hitler as did Netanyahu and Shamir, he often asserted that "I don't know anyone [besides Arafat] who has so much civilian Jewish blood on his hands since Hitler."[34] Sharon believed that no other nation had so many enemies: in his view, 25 percent of the world wanted to see Israel dead, and the rest did not care—except for the United States.[35] He also bemoaned that "nowhere else do four million people carry on their lives in the midst of a hundred million hostile people."[36]

Sharon was skeptical about the urgency for, or the proximity of, peace and did not trust Mahmoud Abbas as a genuine peace partner.[37] At the same time, however, like Rabin he was oriented in the present and therefore was not confined to think that past instances of Jewish victimization were destined to repeat themselves. Sharon made plans for the immediate time frame and realized that day-to-day changes influence how one attempts to achieve a goal.[38] Having grown up in a Labor party community, he never believed that Judea and Samaria needed to be retained as an article of faith, and therefore was amenable to changing his mind about whether these territories were necessary for security. Sharon also grew in terms of his belief that one could not ignore the United States and its pressures. In that respect the Bush Roadmap, among other factors, also contributed to Sharon's own unilateral plan to withdraw all settlers and soldiers from the Gaza strip (accomplished in 2005), and eventually most from the West Bank (which he was not able to implement due to his stroke).

YITZCHAK RABIN: NO LONGER IS IT TRUE THAT THE WHOLE WORLD IS AGAINST US

Yitzhak Rabin was prime minister from 1974–1977 and again from 1992 to 1995 when he was assassinated. Rabin was the first Israeli prime minister to be born in Israel, and he grew up steeped in Labor ideology. His sister recounts that "our school reflected the worldview of my parents, a special school for young workers. Our home, our school, and our youth group, the Working Youth, were circles of the same thing, the values of pioneers."[39] Both the nature of his Labor ideology and his present time orientation enabled him to perceive that Israel's acceptance in the world could change and that an adversary's goals and tactics could change, meriting political solutions. Rabin was obsessed with details and looked at information about the political and military environment coming incrementally, neither focusing on the past, nor thinking that the present or future would replicate the past, nor being immersed in a more distant future.[40] When he was told for instance that Nixon would be bad for Israel in the long run, he responded that "Israel lives in the short run."[41] This meant that he did not dwell in historical persecution nor did he think that these analogies were necessarily relevant to the present.

Rabin, in contrast to Shamir and Netanyahu, did not habitually make analogies between current enemies and Hitler, and in his writings only mentions his own participation in the rescue of Jewish refugees in the context of

British detention of those refugees as they attempted to enter Palestine.[42] Labor ideology did not view the world as permanently hostile, and its proponents anticipated that Israel would become a normal nation in the world. Moshe Sharrett, Israel's first foreign minister and member of the Labor party claimed that Israel's admission into the United Nations brought Israel back into the community of nations and closed the dark chapter of persecution.[43] Likewise, Rabin already in 1964 stated that "Arab hostility is not an eternal factor. Even today when the situation looks hopeless, we have to remember that nations, hostile to each other for tens of years, found avenues to each other's heart, when the political circumstances changed."[44] The Labor Party perceived less hostility toward Israel after the peace treaty with Egypt in 1978, and Rabin was very much influenced by lessons he drew from the first intifada 1986–1992 and the first Gulf War. The Palestinian national movement had earned his respect, he recognized that the use of force was not ending the intifada and that political solutions were needed, and that the Israeli public was becoming more war weary. Both his ideology and his present time orientation enabled him to expect that circumstances can change. This recognition that a past of victimization did not determine the present and future was highlighted in his first speech to the Knesset upon becoming prime minister in July 13, 1992:

> It is our duty, to ourselves and to our children, to see the new world as it is now—to discern its perils, explore its process, and do everything necessary for the integration of the State of Israel in this changing world. We are no longer of necessity 'a people that dwelleth apart,' and no longer is it true that 'the whole world is against us.' We must cast off the sense of isolation that has held us captive for nearly half a century. We must join in the international campaign for peace, reconciliation, and cooperation that is currently sweeping the globe. Otherwise we shall be left behind, all alone.[45]

Yitzhak Rabin's assessment that Israel could shape its acceptance in the world through urgent and serious peace initiatives bore fruit. In the three years that he was prime minister, the number of countries recognizing Israel almost doubled from 91 to 160.

EHUD BARAK: CRITIQUING THE VICTIMHOOD MINDSET

Ehud Barak, Yitzhak Rabin's protégé, won the 1999 election by a landslide on a platform of continuing Yitzhak Rabin's legacy and reaching a peace agreement within a year, only to have his government fall a mere eighteen months later. Like all the prime ministers, he had originally been against a Palestinian state or recognizing the PLO and had focused on military force as a deterrent, but like Rabin, he recognized changes on the part of the PLO that culminated in their recognition of Israel in 1993, their abandonment of their earlier goal of destroying Israel, and their declared abandonment of terror tactics to achieve that goal. His Labor ideology and present time orientation enabled these changes, as they had for Rabin. Ehud Barak grew up on kibbutz Mishmar HaSharon, which was affiliated with the left wing of the socialist parties that formed the precursors of the Labor Party, and he joined the youth group HaShomer Hatsair at age sixteen and represented the Labor Party as prime minister.

Like his fellow Labor party members, Barak did not think that hostility toward Israel from the world and from its neighbors was permanent. In fact, he recalls believing peace was a strong possibility in the near future. He initially retired from the military after only six years, believing that Israel would soon be at peace with its neighbors. The PLO had been formed, but he did not perceive it as an existential threat. He thought that, in another thirteen years, Israel would not be dependent on its military and he could take his son to Lebanon as a tourist.[46] Although he acknowledges that the Arab world had completely rejected Israel in the past, "today Arab states are competing among themselves in arguing over which peace initiative will be adopted by the international community."[47] However, he also thinks that the improved situation for Israel regionally and globally will be stilted and possibly deteriorate without an urgent effort to reach a peace agreement with the Palestinians. As Netanyahu's defense minister, he repeatedly implored Netanyahu to present the United States with a peace initiative to improve relations between the two countries, strengthen the moderates in the Arab world, and to end attempts to isolate Israel internationally.[48]

Barak, like the other Israeli prime ministers, believes that Iran poses a grave threat to Israel, and as defense minister in Netanyahu's government he contemplated using force to try to destroy Iran's nascent nuclear capabilities, at least as a threatened deterrent or way for the international community to exert pressure on Iran. However, unlike Netanyahu, Barak never perceived the Iranian threat as an existential one, and thought it highly problematic to compare it to the Holocaust. He criticized Netanyahu for cheapening the Holocaust by doing so: "With all . . . due respect to the Iranians – and I was probably more hawkish than Netanyahu about this issue – none of the threats that are described as the Hitler du jour is an existential threat to Israel anymore."[49] Barak's present orientation led him to deal with current threats rather than worse case scenarios of future threats. He preferred not to speculate on whether Iran could be an existential threat in the future, but rather to deal with the fact that it currently was not an existential threat.[50] Rather, Barak defined the threat of Iranian nuclear weapons as having more to do with the dangers of wider nuclear proliferation in the Middle East, and the effects it would have on its growing sponsorship of terror.[51] Barak chastises Netanyahu for not being more proactive about trying to reach a peace agreement with the Palestinians and argues that the Netanyahu government "drifted into a mindset of pessimism, passivity, fear, and victimhood."[52]

SHIMON PERES: ENVISIONING A NEW MIDDLE EAST

Nearly all of Shimon Peres's family was killed in the Holocaust, including his grandparents who were burned alive in their synagogue in Vinshneva in today's Belarus, and then buried in a mass grave. Despite this trauma he was firmly oriented toward the future rather than the past. While Netanyahu refers twenty times to Hitler in his book, *A Durable Peace,* Shimon Peres has one reference in his book, *Battling for Peace,* and never conflates current enemies with those of the past.[53] In his address to the German Parliament on Holocaust Day in 2010 he proclaimed that "while we can't forget, we can look forward to a new future."[54]

"Peres has done more for the cause of peace in the Middle East than just about anybody alive" said President Obama in 2012 upon bestowing Shimon Peres the Medal of Freedom. Shimon Peres, former president, prime minister, and foreign minister of Israel, had been a hawk who was one of the initiators of Israel's nuclear military facility in Dimona in the 1950s but he ultimately received a Nobel peace prize for signing the Oslo accords with Yasser Arafat in 1993. Peres moved from relying on deterrence alone, to believing that creating mutual shared interests were vital to peace and security. He established the Peres Center for Peace to foster that vision of peace. Peres's transformation is reflected in the titles of his books: in 1970 he wrote *David's Sling,* in which he emphasizing Israel's defense buildup. After Israel's withdrawal from Lebanon in 1982, Peres perceived Israel to be sufficiently strong to negotiate Palestinian issues. In the late 1980s and early 1990s, he wrote books with titles like *Battling for Peace* and *The New Middle East*, emphasizing Israel's need to take the initiative in making peace with its neighbors. Peres believed that the world had changed and that territory was no longer as important for strategic depth. Whereas previously more land would afford more time for preparation and lessen risks during a tank attack, he concluded that land no longer fully protects one from nuclear weapons, missiles, and terrorism and that therefore diplomacy was the best way to achieve national security. Shimon Peres was an open-minded visionary who adapted his worldview and policy preferences to perceived future trends and to new ideas. He privately made a decision in the early 1980s that eventually Israel would have to negotiate with the Palestine Liberation Organization, ten years before Yitzhak Rabin reached that conclusion.

Shimon Peres enthusiastically propelled the Oslo peace process forward and believed that a peace agreement was an urgent Israeli priority. He consistently and passionately spoke of the need for peace. He kept this sense of urgency during the violent years of the second intifada from 2000–2005 that had caused scars of mistrust on both sides. Peres's determination to reach an agreement remained constant despite his disapproval of Arafat's role in inciting the violence. He still emphasized forging ahead with the peace process, which was "as necessary as air was to breathe." In 2008, in the aftermath of the second intifada and the Palestinian leadership's disarray after the violent Hamas coup in Gaza, Peres remained optimistic: "Never in the past 100 years," he intoned, "have we been closer to peace than we are today. We will not cease to negotiate with the Palestinians and help them with all our might in order to establish an independent Palestinian state with a real economy."[55] He repeatedly referred to Mahmoud Abbas as a partner for peace and complemented his bravery in recognizing that although he was born in Safed in pre-1967 borders of Israel that he would not return there, and that there is a future in which resolution of the conflict is possible.[56]

The upheavals in the Middle East in the past several years strengthened current Israeli Prime Minister Benjamin Netanyahu's sense of caution and risk aversion regarding peace negotiations, while for Peres they strengthened his sense of urgency to pursue peace. Peres reportedly said, "We're about to crash into the wall. We're galloping at full speed toward a situation where we will lose the State of Israel as a Jewish State."[57] Despite his criticisms—of Netanyahu for his intransigence, as well as of the Palestinian Authority for reconciling with Hamas without demanding any changes to Hamas's stance against Israel—he was unable to reach peace during his life time. However, he has made his one-time radical assumption—that there will be a peace agreement between Israel and Palestine and that there will be two states—the accepted, conventional wisdom of the international community, the United Nations, the Arab League, the EU, the United States, and of most Israelis and Palestinians since Oslo.

Although vocal about the dangers of Iran acquiring nuclear weapons, and assertive about the unique and problematic call on the part of the Iranian government to destroy Israel, Peres never conflated the Iranian government with that of Hitler and was adamant that Israel could not strike Iran first without the approval of the United States, in order to prevent such a development. Peres argued that he was influential in stopping Netanyahu from doing so.[58] He also affirmed that the past is not cyclical and static, and that he would be ready to have direct negotiations with Iran as "the Iranians are not our enemies. . . . The great king of Iran was the first Zionist in the world. King Cyrus called for the Jewish people in Iran to go and settle in Israel and build a second temple."[59]

While Peres was not naïve to Israel's historical and current enemies, he believed that the world had been transformed and that peace was a necessity. He admitted that "Israel was a tiny island that, for most of its existence, was surrounded by a sea of enemies" and that some enemies still hope for Israel's destruction, but that when Israel was sufficiently strong, he devoted himself to peace. Peres recognized that the Oslo process has opened up peace between Israel and Jordan and he claimed that the effort to bring business leaders from around the world to Morocco for the Middle East/North Africa Economic Summit was intended to build peace economically. At that conference he proclaimed that "the entire world is gradually evolving from a universe of enemies into an arena of opportunities and challenges."[60] He argued that the Arab League's expression of its willingness to live alongside Israel on borders based on the 1967 borders represents a dramatic transformation, and that "countries can no longer afford to divide the world into friend and foe. Our foes are now universal – poverty and famine, radicalization and terror" and "so we must act swiftly to build the bonds of peace . . . so that we can together confront the challenges and seize the opportunities of a new era."[61]

PAST LESSONS AND FUTURE PROSPECTS FOR PEACE

This chapter shows that not all Israeli leaders, or the different ideologies they represent, focus on victimization to the same degree or are static in their perception of a hostile world. Of the several factors that influence a leader's capacity for changed perceptions, ideology, and individual time orientation are among those that made the difference between those who remained focused on analogies to the past and those who believed they could reshape the present prospects for peace to a greater degree. There is hope for current and future leaders and their constituents to be able to forge a growing set of relationships in the region that can in turn alter threat perceptions.

Indeed, recent developments point to the way perceptions of past victimization and their relation to current stances toward Israeli-Palestinian peace negotiations have taken unexpected permutations. While in past decades Labor leaders were more likely to perceive changes in the environment and Israel's ability to change, ironically, it is now leaders from the right that are more likely to emphasize Israel's improving relations around the world, which then translate into arguments that peace with the Palestinians is less urgent, while maintaining high threat perceptions of Iran and the Palestinians based on past experiences of victimization; those on the center-left, on the other hand, are more likely to focus on Israel's increasing isolation in the world which will get worse if a peace agreement is not reached. They acknowledged the gains that were made on Israel's acceptance, but fear that will deteriorate with an impasse in the peace process.

Benjamin Netanyahu's recent emphasis on relations with Gulf and other Arab states is a case in point. In Netanyahu's address to the United Nations on September 19, 2017, he proclaimed "We're in the midst of a great revolution, a revolution in Israel's standing among the nations. This is happening because so many countries around the world have finally woken up to what Israel can do for them . . . in one year: hundreds of presidents, prime ministers, foreign ministers and other leaders have visited Israel, many for the first time." He talked about how he visited six continents, and concluded that, "after 70 years, the world is embracing Israel, and Israel is embracing the world."[62] He does not yet sense an embrace from the UN, which he thinks is still largely biased against Israel, but he recognizes some signs of positive change in the organization.[63]

While Netanyahu emphasized his efforts to improve Israel's relations with countries around the world, he devoted only a very small portion of the speech to prospects for peace, and seemingly does not think that peace with the Palestinians will have a significant or determining influence on improving relations with other countries around the world and in the region. There is no urgency in his call for peace, and he does not directly talk to Mahmoud Abbas or the Palestinian people. Rather, he spends the bulk of the time warning the world about the dangers from Iran. The turmoil in the Middle East—turmoil that is threatening regimes, state boundaries, and hundreds of thousands of lives—only magnifies the sense, in leaders like Netanyahu, that a peace agreement with the Palestinians raises the risk of potential victimization; for others like Ehud Barak and the late Shimon Peres, on the other hand, the same regional turmoil magnified the urgency of achieving an Israeli-Palestinian peace.

As this speech suggests, Netanyahu hopes to forge improved relations with Arab states in the region even without a peace agreement with the Palestinians. He boasted in September 2017 that Israel is enjoying "the best-ever relations with the Arab world." There have been many reports of intelligence cooperation and trade relations among Israel and Gulf states, and even an unsubstantiated report that the Saudi Arabia's Crown Prince Mohammed bin Salman visited Tel Aviv in early September, 2017 in order to discuss prospects for regional peace.[64] Likewise, in September 2017 the King of Bahrain Hamad bin Isa al Khalifa publicly condemned Arab boycotts against Israel, claimed that his citizens are free to travel to Israel, and Bahrain's National Orchestra played the Israeli national anthem, *Hatikva*, in Los Angeles.[65] The King also suggests that Israel and Bahrain might announce normalized ties with mutual embassies in the next year.[66] These solidifying interests have been represented by the Arab League's repeated reaffirmation of the Arab Peace Initiative, which in 2013 accepted that the borders would be based on 1967 borders with swaps. The growing mutual interests between Israel and other Arab states who are concerned about Iran's influence in the region, were also exemplified, after the outbreak of the Israeli war with Hezbollah in July 2006, when the Arab League meeting on July 15 condemned the "unexpected, inappropriate and irresponsible acts" of Hezbollah.

The Arab states did not have much of a response to Israeli actions in the Gaza wars with Hamas at the end of 2008, and again in 2012 (Egypt, instead, criticized Hamas).[67]

While Netanyahu has recently emphasized Israel's greater acceptance in the world, Peres in 2016 warned of Israel's unprecedented isolation, and emphasized the urgency of reaching peace with the Palestinians in order for Israel to assure its place among the nations, along with enhancing security and reinforcing democracy.[68] Therefore, while Labor leaders felt that reaching peace with the Palestinians would pave the way for Israel's greater acceptance in the world—an idea that came to fruition in the Oslo period in the 1990s—it is Likud leaders who more recently emphasize Israel's greater acceptance in the world which is not contingent on the Palestinian track. For them, Israel's acceptance rests on economic success and strengthening ties with India and China, as well as with Arab states feeling threatened by Iran and ISIS, rather than by reaching peace with the Palestinians. It is Left and Centrist leaders who fear to a greater degree that Israel will eventually lose the good relationships it has forged and that true normalization in the region will not be reached if peace is postponed. However, it is still the past orientation of some leaders, combined with ideological emphasis on victimhood, that continues to magnify threats and impede more urgent overtures to the Palestinians.

NOTES

1. UN Secretary General Ban Ki Moon argued before the UN Security Council that "we cannot have a bias against Israel at the UN." "Decades of political maneuvering," he admitted, "have created a disproportionate number of resolutions, reports and committees against Israel" (May Bulman, "Ban Ki Moon Says UN Has Disproportionate Focus on Israel," *Independent ,* December 17, 2017). Likewise, UN Secretary General Antonio Guterres has said that he would fight anti-Israel bias at the UN, asked a UN official to withdraw a report accusing Israel of apartheid, and said that "a modern form of anti-Semitism is the denial of the right of the state of Israel to exist" (Anne Gearn, "All 100 Senators Sign Letter Asking for Equal Treatment of Israel at the U.N," *The Washington Post,* April 27, 2017).

2. See David Biale's, *Power and Powerlessness in Jewish History* (New York: Knopf Doubleday Publishing Group, 1986).

3. Alan Dowty, *Israel/Palestine Third Edition* (Cambridge, Polity Press, 2012) 218–19, 252.

4. For a more in-depth exploration that engages multiple personality and ideological factors, and examines how these shaped perceptions and policies toward the Palestinians, see Yael Aronoff, *The Political Psychology of Israeli Ministers: When Hard-Liners Opt for Peace* (New York: Cambridge University Press, 2014).

5. Ilan Peleg, *Begin's Foreign Policy, 1977–1983* (New York: Greenwood Press, 1987), 53; Ilan Peleg, "Israel's Foreign Policy Under Right-Wing Governments: A Constructivist Interpretation," *Israel Studies Forum* 19, no. 3 (2004): 111.

6. Rose McDermott, *Presidential Leadership, Illness, and Decision Making* (New York: Cambridge University Press, 2008), 10.

7. Milton Rockeach and Richard Bonier, "Time Perspective, Dogmatism, and Anxiety," in *The Open and Closed Mind: Investigation into the Nature of Belief Systems and Personlaity Systems,* ed. Milton Rokeach (New York: Basic Books, 1960).

8. Ilona Boniwell and Philip Zimbardo, "Time to Find the Right Balance," *The Psychologist* 16, no. 3 (2004): 129–31; Ilona Boniwell and Philp G. Zimbardo, "Balancing Time Perspective in Pursuit Optimal Functioning," in *Positive Psychology in Practice* eds. P. Alex Linley and Stephen Joseph (Hoboken, NJ: John Wiley & Sons, 2004), 165.

9. Yaacov Vertzberger, *The World in Their Minds: Information Processing, Cognition, and Perception in Foreign Policy Decisionmaking* (Stanford, CA: Stanford University Press, 1990), and Robert Jervis, *Perception and Misperception in International Relations* (Princeton: Princeton University Press, 1976), 145, 203, 331.

10. Jacob Lassner and S. Ilan Troen, *Jews and Muslims in the Arab World: Haunted by Pasts Real and Imagined* (New York: Rowman & Littlefield Publishers, 2007) 325.

11. Myron J. Aronoff, "The Politics of Collective Identity: Contested Israeli Nationalisms" in *Terrorism, Identity and Legitimacy,* ed. Jean Resefel (Oxford: Routledge, 2010) 168–87; Myron J. Aronoff, *Israeli Visions and Divisions, Cultural Change and Political Conflict* (New Brunswick, NJ: Transaction Publishers, 1989) 137.

12. Jervis, *Perception and Misperception,* 217.

13. Yael Aronoff, *The Political Psychology of Israeli Prime Ministers,* 12.

14. Haim Misgav, *Sichot Im Yitzhak Shamir [Conversations with Yitzhak Shamir]* (Tel Aviv: Sifriat Poalim Publishing House, Ltd., 1997), 164.

15. Shamir, *Summing Up,* 38.

16. Misgav, *Conversations with Yitzhak Shamir,* 57; interview with Yitzhak Shamir, July 5, 1998, Tel Aviv.

17. Interview with Yitzhak Shamir, July 5, 1998, Tel Aviv.

18. Shamir, *Summing Up,* 5, 7,8 6.

19. Ibid., 83, 69.

20. Ibid., 114.

21. Interview with Yitzhak Shamir, July 5, 1998, Tel Aviv; Shamir, *Summing Up,* 93.

22. Ben Caspit and Ilan Kafir, *Netanyahu: The Road to Power* (Secaucus, NJ: Carol Publishing Group, 1998), 14–31; Ronit Vardi, *Mi Ata Adoni Rosh Hamimshala? [Benjamin Netanyahu?: Who Are You, Mr. Prime Minister?]* (Jerusalem: Keter Publishing House Ltd., 1997), 52, 54, 70, 85; David Remnick, "The Outsider," *The New Yorker,* February 5, 1998, 86 ; Yossi Kelien Halevi, "His Father's Son," *The Jerusalem Report,* February 5, 1998, 12.

23. Interview with Dennis Ross, August 6, 1999, Washington D.C.

24. Netanyahu, *A Place Among the Nations,* 25, 29; Benjamin Netanyahu, *Knesset Minutes* April 18, 1994, 6248.

25. Benjamin Netanyahu, *A Durable Peace: Israel and Its Place among the Nations* (New York: Warner Books, 2000), 174.

26. Ibid., *204.*

27. Ibid., *212.*

28. Ibid., 305.

29. Ibid., 373.

30. "Full Netanyahu 2015 address to the UN General Assembly," *The Times of Israel,* October 1, 2015.

31. Ibid.

32. Yossi Verter, "From Settlements to 'Fake News,' Netanyahu Stops at Nothing to Shore Up His Base," *Haaretz,* September 2, 2017.

33. Ariel Sharon, *Warrior* (New York: Simon and Schuster, 2001), 11, 224, 279, 285.

34. Serge Schmemann, "Hawkish Talons as Sharp as Ever," *The New York Times,* May 25, 1996.

35. Interview with Dov Weisglass, August 6, 2010, Ramat Hasharon. Director of Sharon's Bureau 2001–2005, previously his lawyer for twenty-four years.

36. Ariel Sharon, *Warrior,* 451.

37. For further discussion of the reasons for Sharon's lack of trust in Mahmoud Abbas see Robert Freedman, "George W. Bush, Barak Obama, and the Arab-Israeli Conflict," in *Israel*

and the United States: Six Decades of US-Israeli Relations, ed. Robert Freedman (Boulder: Westview Press, 2012), 49–51.

38. Sharon, *Warrior*, 554.

39. Interview with Rachel Rabin, July 7, 1998, Kibbutz Menarah, Israel.

40. Aaron S. Klieman, *Israel & the World, Israel & the World After 40 Years* (Washington, DC: Pergamon-Brassey's International Defense Publishers, 1990), 54; Peri, "Afterword," *the Rabin Memoirs*, 360; Dan Kurzman, *Soldier of Peace: the Life of Yitzhak Rabin 1922–1995* (New York: Harper Collins, 1998) 30.

41. David Philip Horovitz, *Yitzhak Rabin: Soldier of Peace* (London: Peter Halban, 1996), 57; Labor Party Leadership Bureau, September 4, 1974, 6, 52.

42. Yitzhak Rabin, *The Rabin Memoirs* (Berkeley: University of California Press, 1979), 13–14. Rabin's memoir, in fact, does not even have an entry for "Hitler" or "Holocaust" in the index.

43. Klieman, *Israel & the World, Israel & the World After 40 Years.* 30, 87.

44. As quoted by Ephraim Inbar, *Rabin and Israel's National Security,* from *Bamahane,* January 9, 1964, 4.

45. Yitzhak Rabin, "Not a Peace Process: But Peacemaking," Address to the Knesset by Prime Minister Yitzhak Rabin Introducing His Government, Jerusalem July 13, 1992, Appendix B in *Yitzhak Rabin: The Rabin Memoirs* (Berkeley: University of California Press, 1996).

46. I. Kafir, *Barak: the Biography* (Israel: Alpha Communications, 1999), 60.

47. Ari Shavit, "Barak to Haaretz: Israel Ready to Cede Parts of Jerusalem in Peace Deal," *Haaretz,* September 1, 2010.

48. Rebecca Anna Stoil, "Barak: We Must Give U.S. Clear Peace Initiative," *Haaretz,* July 6, 2010; Hillary Leila Krieger, "Barak: US Wants Israel to Risk Assertive Peace Process," *The Jerusalem Post,* June 27, 2010.

49. Herb Keinon and Daniel J. Roth, "Barak: Israel's True Threat is One-State Option," *The Jerusalem Post,* July 217, 2017.

50. Mike Mullen, "Barak: Iran Poses no Immediate Existential Threat to Israel," *Haaretz,* April 19, 2010.

51. https://www.youtube.com/wathc?v+y4c7_aLit24

52. Keinon and Roth, "Barak: Israel's True Threat is One-State Option," *The Jerusalem Post,* July 27, 2017.

53. Shimon Peres, *Battling for Peace: Memoirs* (London: Orion Books, 1995), 43–47.

54. "Peres to Address German Parliament on Holocaust Day," *Haaretz,* January 25, 2010.

55. Tovah Lazaroff, "Peres and Guests Debate Peace Prospects," *Haaretz,* October 28, 2008.

56. Avner Avrahami and Reli Avrahami, "Peres's Post-Presidency Vision: Hamas-Free Gaza, Peaceful Israel," *YNET,* August 31, 2014.

57. Akiva Eldar, "Why Are We Not Hearing From President Peres?" *Haaretz,* August 8, 2011.

58. Natasha Bertrand, "Shimon Peres 2 Years Ago: I Stopped Netanyahu from Attacking Iran, and You Can Talk about It When I'm Dead," *Business Insider,* September 30, 2016; Ari Shavit, "How Shimon Peres Stopped Israel From Bombing Iran," *Haaretz,* October 31, 2013.

59. Robert Tait, "Shimon Peres: Israel and Iran could Negotiate," *The Telegraph,* June 18, 2013.

60. Shimon Peres, *No Room for Small Dreams: Courage, Imagination, and the Making of Modern Israel,* (New York: Harper Collins, 2017), 173, 204.

61. Peres, *No Room for Small Dreams,* 218.

62. "Full Text of Prime Minister Benjamin Netanyahu's UN Speech," *The Jerusalem Post,* April 19, 2017.

63. Ibid.

64. Yasser Okbi and Maariv Hashavua, "Did the Saudi Prince Make a Covert Visit to Israel?" *The Jerusalem Post,* September 11, 2017.

65. Tom Tugend, "Bahrain King Denounces Arab Boycott of Israel, Says Countrymen Can Visit," *The Jerusalem Post,* September 17, 2017.

66. Toi Staff and Dov Lieber, "Israel, Bahrain Could Announce Normalization Ties by Next Year," *The Times of Israel,* September 23, 2017.

67. Joel S. Migdal, *Shifting Sands: The United States in the Middle East* (New York: Columbia University Press, 2014) 349–57.

68. Uri Savir, "Peres' Secret Plan for a Two-State Solution," *Al Monitor,* September 24, 2017.

BIBLIOGRAPHY

Aronoff, Myron. *Israeli Visions and Divisions, Cultural Change and Political Conflict.* New Brunswick, NJ: Transaction Publishers, 1989.

Aronoff, Myron, "The Politics of Collective Identity: Contested Israeli Nationalisms" in *Terrorism, Identity and Legitimacy,* ed. Jean Resefel. Oxford: Routledge, 2010.

Aronoff, Yael. *The Political Psychology of Israeli Ministers: When Hard-Liners Opt for Peace.* New York: Cambridge University Press, 2014

Aronoff, Yael. "Predicting Peace: The Contingent Nature of Leadership and Domestic Politics in Israel." Eds. Miriam Fendius Elman, Oded Haklai, and Hendrik Spruyt. Syracuse: Syracuse University Press, 2014.

Biale, David. *Power and Powerlessness in Jewish History.* New York: Knopf Doubleday Publishing Group, 1986.

Boniwell, Ilona and Philip Zimbardo. "Time to Find the Right Balance," *The Psychologist* 16, no. 3 (2003): 129–31.

Boniwell, Ilona and Philip Zimbardo. "Balancing Time Perspective in Pursuit Optimal Functioning." In *Positive Psychology in Practice,* edited by P. Alex Linley and Stephen Joseph, 165–78. Hoboken, NJ: John Wiley & Sons, 2004.

Bulman, May. "Ban Ki Moon Says UN Has Disproportionate Focus on Israel," *Independent,* December 17, 2016.

Caspit, Ben and Ilan Kafir. *Netanyahu: The Road to Power.* Secaucus, NJ: Carol Publishing Group, 1998.

Dowty, Alan. *Israel/Palestine Third Edition.* Cambridge: Polity Press, 2012.

Eytan, Freddy. *Ariel Sharon: A Life in Times of Turmoil.* Montreal: Studio 9 Books, 2006.

Freedman, Robert. "George W. Bush, Barack Obama, and the Arab-Israeli Conflict from 2001–2011." In *Israel and the United States: Six Decades of US-Israeli Relations,* edited by Robert Freedman, 36–78. Boulder: Westview Press, 2012.

"Full Text of Prime Minister Benjamin Netanyahu's UN Speech." *The Jerusalem Post,* April 19, 2017.

Gearn, Anne. "All 100 Senators Sign Letter Asking for Equal Treatment of Israel at the U.N." *The Washington Post,* April 27, 2017.

Horovitz, Philip David. *Yitzhak Rabin: Soldier of Peace.* London: Peter Halban, 1996.

Inbar, E. *Rabin and Israel's National Security.* Baltimore, MD. The Johns Hopkins University Press. 1999.

Interview with Dennis Ross, August 6, 1999, Washington D.C.

Interview with Dov Weisglass, August 6, 2010, Ramat Hasharon. Director of Sharon's Bureau 2001–2005, previously his lawyer for twenty-four years.

Interview with Meir Shetrit, June 13, 2012, Jerusalem.

Interview with Rachel Rabin, July 7, 1998, Kibbutz Menarah, Israel.

Interview with Yitzhak Shamir, July 5, 1998, Tel Aviv.

Jervis, Robert. *Perception and Misperception in International Relations.* Princeton: Princeton University Press, 1976.

Kafir I. *Barak: the Biography.* Israel: Alpha Communications, 1999.

Keinon and Roth. "Barak: Israel's True Threat Is One-State Option." *The Jerusalem Post,* July 27, 2017.

Klieman, S. Aaron. *Israel & the World after 40 Years.* Washington, DC: Pergamon-Brassey's International Defense Publishers, 1990.

Kurzman, Dan. *Soldier of Peace: the Life of Yitzhak Rabin 1922–1995.* New York: Harper Collins, 1998.

Lassner, Jacob and S. Ilan Troen. *Jews and Muslims in the Arab World: Haunted by Pasts Real and Imagined.* New York: Rowman & Littlefield Publishers, 2007.

McDermott, Rose. *Presidential Leadership, Illness, and Decision Making.* New York: Cambridge University Press, 2008.

Migdal, S. Joel. *Shifting Sands: The United States in the Middle East.* New York: Columbia University Press, 2014.

Netanyahu, Benjamin. *A Durable Peace: Israel and Its Place among the Nations.* New York: Warner Books, 2000.

Okbi, Yasser, and Maariv Hashavua. "Did the Saudi Prince Make a Covert Visit to Israel?" *Jerusalem Post,* September 11, 2017

Peleg, Ilan. *Begin's Foreign Policy, 1977–1983.* New York: Greenwood Press, 1987.

Peleg, Ilan. "Israel's Foreign Policy under Right-Wing Governments: A Constructivist Interpretation," *Israel Studies Forum 19,* no. 3 (2004): 1–14.

Peres, Shimon. *Battling for Peace: Memoirs.* London: Orion Books, 1995.

Peres, Shimon. *No Room for Small Dreams: Courage, Imagination, and the Making of Modern Israel.* New York: Harper Collins, 2017.

Rabin, Yitzhak. *The Rabin Memoirs.* Berkeley: University of California Press, 1979.

Rokeach, Milton and Richard Bonier. "Time Perspective, Dogmatism, and Anxiety." In *The Open and Closed Mind: Investigation into the Nature of Belief Systems and Personality Systems,* edited by Milton Rocheach. New York: Basic Books, 1960.

Schmemann, Serge. "Hawkish Talons as Sharp as Ever." *The New York Times,* May 25, 1996.

Sharon, A. & Chanoff, D. *Warrior: An Autobiography.* New York: Simon & Schuster, 1989.

Verter, Yossi. "From Settlements to 'Fake News,' Netanyahu Stops at Nothing to Shore Up His Base." *Haaretz,* September 2, 2017.

Chapter Four

Embracing Victimhood

How 1967 Transformed Holocaust Memory and Jewish Identity in Israel and the United States[1]

Daniel Navon

Just over fifty years ago, with Israel on the brink of war, Jewish American leaders from around the country gathered for a march in Washington DC. They were united by the idea that Israel faced an existential threat and a conviction that American Jews had a duty to help forestall a second Holocaust just a generation after the horrors of Nazi genocide. Above all, they declared a newfound sense of identity with Jews in Israel. The president of the major Jewish women's group, Hadassah, delivered a "Proclamation" on behalf of the Conference of Presidents of Major American Jewish Organizations. It began with the simple declaration: "We are a people, one people." She continued, "We proclaim our one-ness with our brethren in Israel. With them we suffer the wounds they have borne in their brave struggle to live in their own land, in peace and freedom. With them we vow that the victories won on the fields of battle shall not be lost at the tables of diplomacy." In Israel, this outpouring of solidarity and support from the Diaspora was deeply felt, leading to the common refrain that the 1967 war was "a Jewish battle, not just an Israeli one."

This collective response to a major military crisis in the Middle East hardly seems surprising to us today. Yet it was actually a striking rupture. As we will see, some at the time even thought this new sentiment would be fleeting. After 1967, however, both Israeli and American Jewish identity would never be the same again.

Over twenty years later, against the backdrop of the first Palestinian *Intifada*,[2] then-prime minister Yitzhak Shamir spoke of the "eternal hatred for the eternal people" at Israel's central Holocaust commemoration ceremony. Shamir's 1989 speech encapsulated key elements of Jewish identity in both Israel and the United States. "Even today as we dwell in our own land," he said, "evil-hearted and unfeeling people shoot poison arrows at our young-sters as they wander the countryside, turning it into a valley of death. We again face the phenomenon of eternal hatred for the eternal people."[3] Fast-forward another twenty years to the 2009 Yom HaShoah ceremony, and we find Prime Minister Netanyahu arguing: "Anti-Semitism is an age-old histor-ic phenomenon. However, if anyone thought that after the horrors of the Holocaust, this malignant phenomenon will vanish from the world, today it is clear that they were, unfortunately, mistaken. . . . In our generation, only a few dozen years after the Holocaust, new forces arise, clearly and openly stating their intention to wipe the Jewish State off the face of the earth."[4] Similar themes have been invoked consistently at the ceremony for the last half-century. More broadly, when it comes to Israeli and Jewish American identity politics, scholars have long recognized that "it is an axiom of their narrative that Israel is the innocent victim."[5]

But how did this come to pass? Although the persecution of Jews is now said to be eternal, the sentiment is actually much newer to Zionist representa-tions of Jewish life in the State of Israel. In order to truly grasp the "axiom of their narrative," we therefore need to trace its historical development. Doing so reveals a rapid transformation of Holocaust memory and Jewish identity in Israel and the United States during and following the military crisis of 1967. In that year, in the course of events surrounding Israel's crushing victory over Egypt, Jordan, and Syria and occupation of East Jerusalem, the West Bank, Gaza Strip, and the Golan Heights, Jews in both Israel and in the United States moved to embrace a Holocaust-laden narrative of axiomatic victimhood that condemns Jews, and ipso facto Israelis, to perennial enmity.

Using a range of primary and secondary materials, this chapter provides a detailed description of the shifting Zionist and Jewish American narrative-identities[6] about Israel, the Holocaust and victimhood before, during and after 1967. I discuss the long-term developments that predisposed both com-munities to identity change, the contingent events that precipitated the trans-formation of 1967, and the factors contributing to its durability. In order to chart the narrative in Israel, and especially the transition of 1967–1968, I make recourse to ministers' speeches and other records from Yad Vashem (Israel's Holocaust commemoration authority), *Jerusalem Post* coverage of Israel's Holocaust memorial day, coverage from other papers in more recent years, and a substantial secondary literature. Turning to a less well-docu-mented sphere, I also analyze several American newspapers—both national and local, generalist and Jewish—alongside archival material from the American Jewish Historical Society's "Near-East Crisis Collection" as well as other sources in order to outline American Jewish narratives about Israel and the Holocaust. This material allows for the first account that traces the 1967 transformation of Jewish narratives in both Israel and the United States.

The transformation of Jewish narratives about Israel, the Holocaust, and victimhood that took place in 1967 had a major impact on Zionist and Jewish American identity, as well as both communities' political representations over the past half-century. The new, Holocaust-centered narrative that emerged in 1967 radically rearranged elements of what came before, displacing both communities' faith in their respective national situations to end Jewish victimization and enabling qualitatively new levels of co-identification, political coordination and exchange between Israeli and American Jews. Furthermore, I argue that this dual transformation allowed American Jews to become partial members of Zionism's "imagined community."[7] By way of conclusion, I discuss the implications of this narrative-identity of Jewish victimhood for the conflict over Israel/Palestine today.

JEWISH NARRATIVES IN ISRAEL AND THE UNITED STATES BEFORE 1967

In the years following the liberation of Europe, the Holocaust was marginal in Israeli and Jewish-American identity representations. The tenor when the Holocaust was discussed or commemorated can seem shocking to contemporary sensibilities.[8] Meanwhile, the two communities' leaderships and dominant organizations pursued divergent national goals through to at least the early 1960s. American Jewish organizations sought, on the whole, the complete integration of the Jewish community into American society. The dominant Zionist ideology in Israel, by contrast, focused on national rebirth through the reclamation of the land and the rehabilitation of the Jew from his Diasporic pathologies.[9] This all changed in 1967.

Consider the American situation first. Throughout this period, Jews and Jewish organizations were notable for their involvement in the Civil Rights movement and for making remarkable progress toward their goal of full and equal citizenship as Americans. Indeed, they had too much success at "assimilation" for some.[10] World War II was remembered primarily for the heroic actions of Jews as Americans under arms, in keeping with the association of the major Jewish organizations with American causes abroad more generally. The Holocaust—a term that was yet to achieve widespread usage—was not the subject of many large-scale organizational undertakings, with commemorations largely limited to the participation of survivors. Even the Anne Frank story was "deJudaized."[11] Thus while Hasia Diner has convincingly challenged the received wisdom about American-Jewish "forgetfulness" about the Shoah prior to the 1960s—showing how there was widespread communal remembrance and that Jews involved in the civil rights movement made frequent recourse to Nazi atrocities—even she agrees that Holocaust commemoration differed both qualitatively and quantitatively from what was to follow.[12] Most importantly, the Holocaust was not treated as a core element of American-Jewish identity or widely mobilized in support of Israel.

Support for Israel was much more guarded during this period as well. In 1950, the head of the American Jewish Committee (AJC) forced Israeli PM David Ben-Gurion into a public "understanding" affirming that American (and Diaspora Jewry more broadly) were not living in exile and recognizing: "The Jews in the United States, as a community and as individuals, have only one political attachment and that is to the United States of America. They owe no political allegiance to Israel." This "Blaustein-Ben Gurion Understanding" was forcibly reaffirmed by both leaders as late as 1961 and stands as a striking illustration of American Jewry's concern with maintaining their independence from Israel and their status as unadulterated Americans.[13]

Turning to the Israeli case, previous scholars have outlined the marginality of Holocaust survivors in early-state Israel and the widespread, bemused and derogatory notion that they had "gone as sheep to the slaughter."[14] Underlying this less-than-sympathetic understanding of European Jewry's fate was the prevailing ideology: Zionism's historical role was to "cure" the Jew of his Diaspora-borne afflictions, most notably victimhood. Indeed, the contrast drawn between the new Zionist nation and Diaspora Jewry has been plausibly described as "a rejection sometimes so strong that, paradoxically, it resembled anti-Semitic characterization of Jews."[15]

This line of thought had deep roots in the Zionist movement. Theodore Herzl, who founded modern Zionism, wrote about victimhood arising necessarily from the historical conditions of Diasporic existence, and especially the ghetto's tendency to drive Jews toward bourgeois lifestyles and finance. He even noted that anti-Semitism was inevitable and, in part, "legitimate self-defense" on the part of the Gentile. This situation—for Herzl nothing less than the "Jewish Question" itself—was deemed to be soluble only on a "political," i.e. national basis. While there was a religious basis for mutual identification among world Jewry, when Theodore Herzl spoke of the "Jewish People" he delineated a group bound not only by religious and cultural traditions and a language (of sorts),[16] but also a political history of otherness and vulnerability. What made Herzl's work notable was his secular ascription of nationhood to the Jews, his pronouncement that the nation was in need of a state and his skillful advocacy toward that end. In short, Herzl founded modern Zionism, arguing, to the consternation of most of his Jewish contemporaries from across the religious spectrum, that the "universal idea . . . old as the people . . . is the restoration of the Jewish State." Not only would a Jewish state provide a homeland and a refuge, it would bring about a social and spiritual transformation of the Jew: "A wondrous generation of Jews will spring into existence. The Maccabeans will rise again," allowing

Jews to "live at last, as free men . . . and die peacefully in our own house." Only then, Herzl argued, would the Jewish Question be put to rest. [17]

In this respect, there was a deep continuity in the dominant Zionist narrative from Herzl all the way through the early years of Israeli statehood. The idea of the *Sabra*—the Israeli-born Jew who was at once strong and connected to the land as well as sensitive and literary—was defined primarily in opposition to the Diasporic Jew rather than the Palestinian. In the first popular account of the transformation awaiting those Jews who would be raised as Hebrews to employ the term "Sabra," Uri Avnery wrote, "This is the most glorious victory of the Israeli generation—to see the sons of the Diaspora cured and made upright as they are absorbed and assimilated into [the Sabra] way of life." [18] Although they did not represent a large proportion of the Jewish population in Palestine, the Sabra were accorded an almost mythical status in Zionist discourse in the pre- and early-state years. At stake was nothing less than a national rebirth, with the Sabras cast as heirs to the valiant Hebrews of Antiquity. By contrast, Zionists tended to characterize the experience of Exile by a longing for the homeland alongside weakness, corruption, national alienation and, crucially, the inherent vulnerability and persecution of the Jews as a minority community wherever they went. [19]

The ideal of national rebirth reigned supreme even when it came to the state's inauguration of a Holocaust memorial center, *Yad Vashem*, and national memorial day, *Yom HaZikaron laShoah ve-laGvura* or "Holocaust Martyrs' and Heroes' Remembrance Day." Usually referred to as simply "*Yom HaShoah*," this national holiday, established in 1951 and publicly commemorated since 1959, marked the inauguration of the Holocaust into the official state narrative. Indeed, the ordering of *Yom HaShoah* alongside Israel's day for fallen soldiers and Independence Day evoked poignant narrative parallels with the Passover story. [20] The initiation of the Shoah into state memory was undoubtedly a key event in the history of Israeli Holocaust commemoration. That said, *Yom HaShoa* remained something of a secondary national holiday for its first few years, with no prime ministerial speakers at the central state ceremony and little interest from the media or, it seems, the population as a whole. More importantly, rather than subvert the prevailing narrative, *Yom HaShoah* served to bolster it. The annual theme was almost invariably about armed resistance to the Nazis, rather than the victims themselves. Ben-Gurion even used his first speech at the Yad Vashem ceremony, in 1963, to argue:

> we must ask ourselves a bitter question, a question which perhaps most Diaspora Jews find intolerable: Do we ourselves not bear a whit of responsibility for this tragic, this wretched fate? Do we not have it within our power to avert these perils – by a *fundamental transformation* which we must make in order to cease being a people dependent on the mercies of others?

As late as May 7, 1967, the *Jerusalem Post* could remark, "Memorial Day is usually devoted to a particular theme, and this year it is the armed struggle against the Nazis. This, in one form or another, has been the emphasis in recent years."[21]

Even the capture and trial of Adolf Eichmann, which was certainly a watershed in terms of Israeli engagement with the Holocaust,[22] did not subvert the prevailing meanings ascribed to the Holocaust. Ministers' *Yom Ha-Shoah* speeches and media coverage from the period, just like Mooli Brog's analysis of physical commemoration at Yad Vashem,[23] suggest that Holocaust commemoration continued to focus on Jewish resistance and heroism, rather than victimhood. Lipstadt further notes that the Eichmann trial had even less impact on American-Jewish discourse surrounding the Holocaust than it did in Israel. She points out that increased coverage of the Holocaust in Jewish publications was short-lived, the debate around Hanna Arendt's famous 1963 account notwithstanding. Meanwhile no commemorations, memorials and virtually no university courses were inaugurated in the aftermath of the trial. "Even among American Jewish intellectuals and religious leaders," Lipstadt argues, "the tenor of the conversation among Jews did not change dramatically."[24] Throughout the early 1960s, it seems that little attention was paid to ceremonies, organized largely by survivors, focusing on the Holocaust per se. Meanwhile, public memorialization of anything but the resistance remained rare. Finally, one is hard-pressed to find political activism in the name of Jews or Israel making recourse to the Holocaust.[25]

In sum, the Eichmann trial and a host of other developments—among them Israel's first recession and disillusionment with the post-Ben-Gurion governments, increased American-Jewish security and success, coverage of Soviet Anti-Semitism and the rise of "identity politics" in the United States[26]—may have predisposed Jews in both countries toward a more intense engagement with the Holocaust as an episode of Jewish victimhood. However, it is also clear that those factors did not determine the form that shift would take during the crisis of 1967 or the decades to follow.

THE TRANSFORMATION OF 1967

This is far from the first study to address the impact of the 1967 crisis and war on Jewish-American or Israeli identity.[27] However, it is the first to engage with both communities simultaneously, and I will argue that you cannot understand them in isolation from one another. While a thorough survey is beyond the scope of this paper, a few pertinent points from the extensive secondary literature and available primary sources are worth outlining.

First, the crisis was precipitated by a series of tactical blunders by UAR/ Egyptian president Nasser who moved two divisions into the demilitarized Sinai and indulged in bellicose rhetoric about "driving the Jews into the sea." Yet, both he and his Israeli adversaries knew that Egypt was in no position to threaten Israel militarily.[28] Thus a series of miscalculations would lead to a death-blow to Arab nationalism,[29] a new territorial/demographic framework to the Israel/Palestine issue, and, I will argue, a new narrative-identity among both Israeli and American Jewry that would profoundly shape the dynamics of conflict through to the present.

Second, Idith Zertal has outlined how a campaign by one faction of Israel's Labor movement seeking to displace Levi Eshkol, if not as prime minister then at least from the defense portfolio he also held, made extensive recourse to the Holocaust in the Israeli press from mid-May. This group of politicians and journalists was ultimately successful when one of their own, Moshe Dayan, was appointed defense minister. However, they also brought about a remarkable secondary effect: a widespread panic based on the idea of an imminent second Holocaust. A paradoxical fervor emerged in Israel during the run-up to war. From the relaxed and confident mood that obtained until at least mid-May, arose an existential fear for the State of Israel. On the one hand, there was a confidence in the Israel Defense Force's (IDF) ability to achieve a quick and decisive victory, while on the other there arose an existential fear of a "second Holocaust" that saw rabbis sanctifying mass graves.[30] Thus a propagandistic use of the Holocaust for short-term political gain ended up having sweeping, unintended consequences.

The 1967 crisis also precipitated a sea change in Jewish attitudes in the United States, and to a lesser degree elsewhere, toward both Israel and the Holocaust.[31] American Jewry responded, both organizationally and individually, with fundraising, activism, volunteering, and general interest and support on a wholly unprecedented scale. As one person cited in the American Jewish Committee yearbook article on the war and the American Jewish response put it, "Two weeks ago, Israel was they; now Israel is we."[32] The relatively passive ideological and philanthropic support of previous years gave way to *identification* with Zionism and with Israelis. Lipstadt argues, in a review of American-Jewish memory of the Holocaust, "in order for a broad range of American Jews to feel empowered to address the *Shoah* and to see its own fate in terms of the history of this event [i]t would take a cataclysmic event within the Jewish community, in the form of the Six Day War."[33] The 1968 AJC Yearbook postulates a similar progression, noting: "The conflict aroused in American Jewry unpredictedly [sic] intense feelings regarding Israel, Jewish survival and of their own sense of Jewish identity." It continues: the "trauma, perhaps best diagnosed as a reliving of the Holocaust," was, quoting Arthur Herzberg, "far more intense and widespread than anyone could have foreseen." While no detailed study was undertaken, the Yearbook avers, *"it is generally agreed that the Holocaust was the underlying catalyst"* (my emphasis). The author, Deborah Dawidowicz, summarizes:

> As the Arabs began to close in on Israel in the second half of May, American Jews, so frequently accused of indifference and passivity, turned into a passionate, turbulent, clamorous multitude, affirming in unprecedented fashion that they were part of the Jewish people and that Israel's survival was their survival. The Arabs had pledged Israel's destruction . . . . For the second time in a quarter of a century the Jewish people was facing annihilation. But this time, somehow, things would be different. There would be no passivity, no timidity. That was the mood of American Jews. [34]

With unprecedented identification with Israel and Zionism came unprecedented political action, donations, and volunteering for the IDF. Reading the Jewish press from these weeks reveals that grass roots campaigning raised previously unimaginable sums in the days *before* the United Israel Appeal launched its Emergency Fund. After 100 million dollars was raised in the month preceding the end of the war, 432 million was raised in its aftermath—this compared to 140 million in the entirety of 1966. [35]

Furthermore, statements by donors and community leaders indicate a more active meaning was attached to the donations than merely philanthropic ones. Thus when Rabbi Ralph Simon spoke extensively about the Holocaust at a "Rally for Israel" in Washington, DC, on May 30, he concluded: "We have an opportunity now which was not afforded us 25 years ago . . . . While our Israeli brethren prepare to shed their 'damim' blood, we shall give them transfusions of our 'damim' – funds . . . . No one can destroy us – because we can sing Hatikva." [36] The AJC Yearbook explained that, along with radically increased meeting and synagogue attendance and an "epidemic" of insatiable desire for news, "Jews kept asking what they could do, always with a frightening sense of impotence, fearful of the fate of a collective Auschwitz for the Jews in Israel." In a matter of days around 5,200 academics, many of whom had professed no Jewish identity previously, signed a petition to be printed in the *New York Times* that read, "As responsible members of the academic community, we must no stand by in silence in the face of Arab threats, illegal blockades and massive mobilization aimed at the destruction of the people and State of Israel . . . . Our generation has witnessed the monstrous result of silence." [37] Alongside rallies, lobbying, media and other means, American Jews completely overwhelmed the capacities of organizations offering volunteer programs in Israel with over 10,000 Americans volunteering for the IDF. [38]

Take the "Solidarity with Israel" rally, cited at the start of this chapter, held in Washington, DC, just before the outbreak of the war. Interestingly, we see the old assimilationist preoccupation of American Jewry alongside the new focus on Israel and the victims of the Holocaust. Hadassah (the major Jewish women's group) President Charlotte Jacobson delivered an approved "Proclamation" for the Conference of Presidents of Major American Jewish Organizations. Here is a longer excerpt from that proclamation:

> We are a people, one people. Gathered today in the Capital of the nation in which we rejoice as free and equal citizens, we proclaim our one-ness with our brethren in Israel. With them we suffer the wounds they have borne in their brave struggle to live in their own land, in peace and freedom. With them we vow that the victories won on the fields of battle shall not be lost at the tables of diplomacy. We pronounce this commitment conscious of what the reestablishment of a Jewish state in our own time means to us and to the history of our people. Out of the depths of grief for the loss of our six million in the ovens of Europe came the unutterable joy of Israel reborn. As we honor the memories of our martyrs, so do we cherish the faces of our children – the new generation in Israel. As we hold precious the freedom we enjoy as Americans, so do we honor the ties that bind us in love to our brethren in Israel. [39]

The proclamation makes a point of embracing the freedoms enjoyed by Jewish citizens of the United States. Still, it is clear that organized American Jewry had turned a page in their relationship to Israel and the Holocaust. Both had moved to the very heart of American-Jewish identity.

Finally, American media coverage of the 1967 crisis suggests American political discourse was moved to see Israel's situation in the context of the history of Jewish suffering. One notable example in the *New York Times* saw the influential James Reston write, "[Israel is] a very small country . . . [that] had to fight to save the existence of their country. This is true from any objective analysis . . . . But fighting and winning is only one more chapter in a long and tragic story."[40] A review of the American-Jewish press (see below) during and immediately after the crisis indicates an even stronger tendency to view Israel's war through the lens of a Jewish history dominated by victimization and the Holocaust, though we will see that this was most likely an Israeli export.

But how did this new Holocaust-laden narrative of victimhood catch on in the United States? It is clear that the proximate cause was the intra-Labor Party campaign to oust Prime Minister Eshkol and then the widespread, paradoxical perception of military superiority and existential anxiety that arose in Israel. By 1967, there were numerous pathways by which this new sentiment could find its way to the United States, and especially to American Jews. Remarkably, the American Jewish Press Association were holding their annual conference in Israel for the first time at precisely the moment this anxiety set in. This mechanism of cultural diffusion saw the recently returned editor of Pittsburgh's *Jewish Chronicle* aver, in a June 9 piece titled "Survival Now!":

Nasser's bent on nothing less than genocide. For years he's been employing former Nazis in a variety of anti-Semitic propaganda and covert activities. The World did not stop Hitler before Munich . . . . It must not be allowed to happen again . . . now only support from decent nations, in action, fact, not mere words, can avert another Hitler era in the Middle East. Israel has no choice but to defend her very existence.[41]

Furthermore, newspapers printing reports from Israel were, in the very same issues, running stories questioning the organizational and cultural viability of Jewish life in the United States and illustrating Jews' remarkable success in achieving mainstream acceptance in the United States. For example, in the June 2 edition of the same paper, one could read about the situation in Israel, the Supreme Court granting dual citizenship for the first time to an American-Israeli, an important AJC report on how "American Jews are encountering growing problems, both internal and external, in preserving their Jewishness," the sharp decline of anti-Semitism in the United States, Palestinian support for Hitler thirty years earlier, the repression of Soviet Jewry and the astonishing fund-raising drives undertaken by local, national and international Jewry.[42] In short, American Jews had plenty of reasons to rethink their Jewish identity in the summer of 1967, and the news from Israel brought everything into a new focus.

In sum, factors from the seemingly coincidental to long-term trends in American-Jewish communal life combined with propaganda from Israel to produce actions and attitudes among American Jewry that no one could have predicted, and apparently no one of note was agitating for just weeks earlier. American Jews were moved during the crisis of 1967 to see their fate as bound to that of "the Jewish People"—primarily in Israel, but also in the Middle East and Soviet Union—whose history and present was dominated by the specter of victimization and destruction. Amid changing socio-cultural conditions, and with their own security less precarious than ever, the new narrative of axiomatic victimhood saw American Jews embrace Zionism and Israel as never before.

CEMENTING THE NEW NARRATIVE AFTER 1967

The new narrative of Jewish victimhood was consolidated and mobilized in both countries in the months and years following Israel's decisive victory and territorial gains in the war of June 1967.

In Israel, the new chairman of the board of Yad Vashem, Gideon Hausner, spoke of committing Israeli Holocaust commemoration to "'trying to restore a balance' between the former notion that the Jews of Europe went 'as sheep to the slaughter' and the image of almost total resistance created in more recent years." At the same press conference he announced that Yad

Vashem would be publishing material on the "total parallelism" between Arab propaganda and Nazi ideology. As Hausner argued, "there is no reason for us to see their declarations as mere propaganda. We must expose it and condemn it for what it is. We must not allow the Arabs to brainwash the world into accepting another attempt at genocide of the Jewish People."[43] Indeed Hausner is an important actor in the transformation of Jewish identity, having served as chief prosecutor of Eichmann, attorney general, MK and chairman of Yad Vashem during the crucial post-1967 years. Consider the contrast between the press conference quoted above and what Hausner said as chief prosecutor during the Eichmann trial when he loudly interrupted Judge Moshe Beisky, who was giving testimony on the hangings at Płaszów concentration camp. Hausner incredulously asked: "15,000 people stood there, facing a few dozen or even hundreds of [Nazi] police. Why didn't you lash out, why didn't you rebel?"[44]

Perhaps even more strikingly, the first Holocaust commemoration day ceremony after the war saw Deputy Prime Minister Yigal Allon deriding the tendency to "condemn the millions of our brothers who were led to the slaughter" before continuing:

> The Passover Hagaddah tells us that in every generation our foes seek to destroy us. Where is there another people over whose head the danger of destruction hangs like the swinging sword of history? In one respect, at least, no change has occurred in Jewish uniqueness . . . the only state that is threatened not merely with war but by a war whose purpose is extermination, is Israel; and the world remains silent.[45]

In short, Israeli state memory of the Holocaust in the post-1967 period put much more emphasis on Jewish victimhood. It also represented the threat facing Jews as both unique and endemic, not something that could be cured by Zionism and its project of national rebirth.[46]

A newfound sense of Jewish identity that took stock of the outpouring of material and moral support from the Diaspora also seemed to be emerging in the aftermath of the war.[47] Segev outlines the keen awareness in Israel of increased solidarity from the Diaspora, particularly the United States, as when a Knesset member said, "Not only the State of Israel, but the People of Israel has been reborn . . . . We are moved by the awakening of the Diaspora: we did not see the like even during the War of Independence."[48] This shift can be seen sociologically as the partial unification of Israeli and Diaspora Jewish identity around a narrative that grants the Holocaust and the history of Jewish persecution a position of unrivalled centrality. In a striking piece, published in the *Jerusalem Post* on July 14, 1967, Jacob Hessing, an Israeli student, wrote of:

the sudden realization of the fact that has always been there – the Jewishness of the Israeli . . . . This was a Jewish battle, not just an Israeli – ours is the only modern nation in the world to face an enemy who declared destruction as his program. And history has taught us more than any other people to recognize the writing on the wall . . . . Not only the Jewish nation but world Jewry as a whole was suddenly endangered . . . the image of the "Eternal Jew" is there again. It is painful as usual – but it also is infinitely proud. The torch of eternity has passed over us, leaving everything it passed a-tremble.[49]

The perception of the war as a "Jewish battle, not just an Israeli" one was widespread among both American and Israeli Jews,[50] and it was clearly predicated on a narrative in which victimhood and the Holocaust had moved to center stage.

In the United States, Jewish identity and Holocaust memory were also indelibly transformed after 1967. Zionist politicians were quick to exploit and cement the burgeoning new narrative. Israel quickly dispatched soon-to-be Prime Minister Golda Meir and Foreign Affairs Minister Abba Eban to undertake speaking tours and lobbying in the United States to argue against a return to pre-war lines. Both Meir and Eban made frequent recourse to the Holocaust in their speeches to mostly Jewish audiences throughout the country, and Eban would famously denounce American proposals to withdraw to the pre-1967 armistice lines as a return to "Auschwitz Borders" in 1969. More broadly, as Israel sought to retain their recently conquered territories and France receded as a Western backer, American support became perhaps their key diplomatic objective—and one pursued with great success. From then on, the Labor leadership, the nascent settler Greater Israel Movement, the Israeli opposition Herut and American pro-Israel organizations all made frequent recourse to the Holocaust in pursuit of their political objectives.

Meanwhile, political and material support for Israel skyrocketed and Jewish-American organizations began to engage in projects of pro-Israel advocacy that would have been hard to imagine before the war. There were also dramatic increases in tourism and Americans making *Aliyah* (emigrating to Israel). Having risen fairly steadily from 9,520 American tourists visiting Israel per year in 1951 to 95,800 in 1966 (never rising more than 14,000 in a single year), 153,500 Americans visited Israel in 1968 after a modest drop in 1967 itself. That total was to rise to over a quarter of million with the end of the War of Attrition in 1971. American "aliyah" or emigration to Israel rose from 1,006 in 1964 (the record until that point) and 924, 749, 665 and 932 in 1965–1968 respectively to 5,739, 6,424, 7,364 and 5,515 in 1969–1972 respectively—levels which have not since been approached.[51] That is, once the dust settled from the 1967 war the flow of American tourists and immigrants to Israel skyrocketed.

Just as in Israel, Holocaust commemoration in the United States became more widespread, intense, and focused on Jewish victims of Nazi genocide as well. In the weeks immediately following the war, the Jewish American press had plenty else to keep the Nazi Holocaust on their readers' minds. There was extensive coverage of the bitter accusations and counter-accusations between Soviet Premier Kosygin and Israel regarding "nazi-like" behavior. A report from the Jewish Telegraphic Agency from Tel Aviv titled "Egyptian Gas Labs Found" saw the Israeli authorities claim that Egypt had deployed mobile gas chambers with airtight doors during the war.[52] One could continue citing such examples. In the years immediately following 1967, Palestinian terror attacks, the strengthening alliance with the United States and, above all, the surprise attack from Egypt and Syria in the Yom Kippur of in 1973 were all interpreted in ways that contributed to the new narrative's consolidation in both Israel and the United States.

American Jews' new commitments to Israel and to the victims of the Holocaust were seen as deeply related at the time. Take the remarks of Morris Laub, director of the Joint Commission on Social Action of the Conservative movement at an October 30, 1967, inter-religious discussion of "What Lies Behind the American Jewish Reaction to the Israel-Arab War of June 1967." The first of his "factors [that] entered into this expression of Jewish peoplehood" was "the holocaust and the threat of genocide. The holocaust is the profoundest experience which the contemporary Jew has undergone. It is probably the profoundest experience in the history of the Jewish people, leaving theological developments aside." He continues by discussing the trauma represented by Hitler and evoked by Nasser experienced by all Jews, from "Israeli sabra" to Jewish college student: "Anyone who reminds them of him will automatically cause the explosion of emotions only superficially hidden. *I use explosion advisedly and not hysteria because the latter has an aura of pathology, while the explosion is legitimate, healthy, and to be expected*" (my emphasis).[53]

Passages such as this one indicate that the shift of 1967 was experienced as a cathartic reengagement with a trauma that had long been repressed. Indeed, it is important to recognize that the Holocaust was a major collective trauma for Jewish communities that had to be marginalized for a time before its horrific enormity could be confronted and embraced. The idea of collective trauma, however, should be see seen as more than just a social-psychological explanation. It should also be understood as an element of the narrative itself, and one that helps actors to link the old to the new and understand the transition between them.[54] By tying the old and new narratives together, and by making sense of the years of silence and othering directed against the victims of the Holocaust, the idea of the Holocaust as collective trauma stands as an essential element of the new narrative of victimhood. Recognizing the Holocaust as a collective trauma therefore provides a framework to explain and experience the dramatic shift of 1967 as a kind of cathartic reawakening. It also helps us understand how that new narrative could be embraced so rapidly, despite its seeming contradiction with what came before and the situations facing Israeli and American Jews on the ground. The collective trauma of the Holocaust allowed Jews in Israel and the United States to suddenly rethink the implications of Jewish history and remake their group identities. What it meant to be Jewish, and the relations between the Israeli and Diaspora communities, would never be the same again after 1967.

If anything, the new narrative of Jewish victimhood came to play an even more prominent role in discussion and contention regarding Israel/Palestine as time passed. It is not hard to see why. Once it was in place, the new narrative undoubtedly helped to obfuscate at least four major post-1967 developments that led many to consider the role of Israel as *victimizer*: 1) In 1982 the IDF carried out perhaps its most blatant act of aggression to date with the invasion of Lebanon; 2) Israel's "revisionist historians" comprehensively undermined the founding myths of 1948: that of an "immaculate conception," a "purity of arms" and a "land without a people for a people without a land"[55]; 3) The first Palestinian intifada—largely unarmed and brutally repressed as it was—made the reality of Israel's role as victimizer all-too-apparent as the Palestinians sought to bring their status as a subjugated people to the attention of the world[56]; and 4) the ongoing Israeli occupation and settlement programs in the Palestinian territories and human rights abuses therein. Indeed Resnik notes the escalation of Jewish victimhood and Holocaust discourse during the Likud-dominated 1980s while Segev and others have noted that Menachem Begin was especially inclined to employ such rhetoric during his key six-year tenure as prime minister.[57] As the *prima facie* reality of Israel's oppression of the Palestinians became increasingly difficult to ignore, political moves to portray Jews as axiomatic victims intensified.

DISCUSSION

The June 1967 war precipitated a rapid process of identity change that bound the American and Israeli Jewish communities together around a new narrative centered on the Holocaust, victimhood and the State of Israel. Ever since 1967, the Zionist community has been exhorted to view Israel's situation through the distorting prism of the Holocaust. It is ironic (though surely no coincidence) that Uri Avnery—perhaps the first to employ the term 'Sabra' in popular Israeli discourse—went on to become one of the leading challengers to the idea of the Jew as axiomatic victim. Avnery caricaturizes the Israeli narrative like this:

> Palestinians kill Jews, and there is no difference between them . . . and the [Nazis]. We are, have always been and will always be the victims. . . . Zionism

was supposed to put an end to all this. It was supposed to turn us from a passive into an active people, from a helpless, suffering people into a nation that has taken its destiny into its own hands . . . . On the face of it, we have succeeded. We have set up a strong state, we have immense military power, but reality has not changed our consciousness. It has remained the conscious-ness of a helpless, suffering people. . . . This is a perception that is being inculcated in children in Israel by hundreds of different methods, from the national holidays to visits to Auschwitz.[58]

Zionism is no longer about putting an end to Jewish persecution through a program of national rebirth but about forestalling Jewish victimhood in a highly militarized bunker state. Despite all evidence to contrary, the idea of the Palestinians as victims becomes unintelligible—their enmity rendered akin to that of Cossacks and Nazis.

The new narrative of axiomatic victimhood has held sway in both Israel and the United States. Israel and the Holocaust now reside at the very core of American Jewish identity, as evidenced in countless commemorations, politi-cal representations, donations and so on. The days when the American Jew-ish Committee forced Ben-Gurion to renounce claims that American Jews owed loyalty to Israel (above) are long gone. In 2008, the AJC's executive director, David A. Harris, went as far as to brag in a fundraising email that "a senior Israeli official commented: 'If Israel had to privatize its foreign policy, AJC would be the first choice.'"[59]

In Israel, *Yom HaShoah* has achieved a status as a national holiday along-side Independence and Memorial Days, evidenced most powerfully by the blanket coverage and obligatory speeches by both the prime minister and president. Meanwhile, Holocaust commemoration has moved even further toward an identification with Jewish victimhood. Instead of the almost total focus on the Jewish resistance during WWII seen prior to 1967, records show how the annual *Yom HaShoah* themes are now almost always dedicated to Holocaust victims and survivors (decennials of the Warsaw uprising being the only exception). Furthermore, in an analysis focusing on physical monu-ments in Israel, Mooli Brog summarizes his findings: "the image of the ghetto fighters and partisans has been diminished as the primary representa-tion of Holocaust commemoration . . . the memory of the victims and survi-vors of the Holocaust have emerged as the more appropriate representa-tion."[60] As Prime Minister Olmert put it at the 2006 *Yom HaShoah* opening ceremony at Yad Vashem, "The State of Israel carries the memory of the burning . . . . It knows what the hatred of Jews generated in the past, it watches with open eyes the carnival of enmity taking place around it, and it has learned the lesson." At the same event, President Katsav said, "We must ensure that each generation sees itself as the one that emerged from the inferno of the Holocaust." Finally, President Shimon Peres concluded his speech at the 2011 ceremony by saying "Israel is the historical commemoration to the victims of the Holocaust"[61]

But how did this new narrative of axiomatic victimhood—which seemed to scholars of the time to be merely a transient instance of wartime hysteria[62]—take hold and become an enduring feature of Jewish identity in Israel and the United States?

It does not seem as though this shift was intentionally brought about or even sought by political actors. As we saw, Israeli Labor politicians did invoke the Holocaust in the runup to the war, but only in the hopes of making gains against rivals in their own ruling party. However, there is no evidence than any political actors of note ever sought to bring about a new narrative of Jewish victimhood, at least until it had already burst onto the scene and helped to mobilize action. To be sure, Zionist politicians and activists from both communities have worked hard to consolidate and exploit the narrative about Jewish victimhood. The new narrative that emerged so startlingly in 1967 has since been used to cement associations between the American and Israeli Jewish communities, justify Israeli policy and make sense of some otherwise disquieting realities. The political utility of this new narrative may therefore go a long way in explaining its consolidation and durability. And yet, one cannot convincingly argue that any sort of concerted identity building project caused the 1967 transformation of Jewish identity for the simple reason that no such project existed. Political claims making alone cannot possibly explain either how the new narrative came so rapidly to the fore in 1967 or the precise form that it took. Instead, the cultural ground for identity politics shifted quite unexpectedly in 1967. If anything, political actors responded to the emergence of this new narrative terrain as much as they helped to create it. Furthermore, this new narrative-identity proved durable *despite* its prima facie contradiction with American Jews' increasing social integration and Israel's demonstration of regional military superiority. Contrary to leading sociological discussions of collective identity change then,[63] the work of "political entrepreneurs" and sociopolitical conditions on the ground can at best only partly explain the transformation of 1967.

The Holocaust-laden propaganda deployed by opponents of Prime Minister Eshkol during the 1967 crisis may have had extremely limited aims, but it quickly combined with long-term trends to create a powerful, durable narrative that united American and Israeli Jewry. Once the narrative of victimhood emerged in May/June 1967, new Jewish identities came to the fore and facilitated unprecedented levels of solidarity and exchange on the part of the world's two largest Jewish communities. Some of the reasons for the surprising transformation of 1967 are quite clear from the history recounted above. Jews in Israel and the United States were confronting the memory of the Holocaust in increasingly public and intense ways, particularly with the capture and trial of Adolf Eichmann in the early 1960s. Jews in the United States had done almost too good a job of convincing their co-nationals and above all themselves that they were Americans through and through. This left American Jewish identity at something a crossroads, especially with the broader rise of identity politics in the United States. Meanwhile, Israel was in the process of establishing an unrivaled military advantage in the Middle East. The conquest of East Jerusalem, the West Bank and other territories in June of 1967 aroused new ideas about Jewish history but also began to raise further questions about Israeli oppression of Palestinian Arabs. Once the floodgates of memory were opened, Jews in both countries were ready to commemorate and embrace the victims of the Holocaust as never before—a rapid embrace of a neglected past that was experienced and understood as a kind of collective trauma. So, once the Holocaust was deployed as a propaganda weapon at the beginning of the 1967 crisis, it is not entirely surprising that it sparked intense new feelings and collective representations about Jewish history and victimhood.

But something else happened in 1967: Zionism itself changed in a profound way. Jews in Israel and the United States did not just reengage with the Holocaust and Jewish history—they did so in a way that allowed them unite around a new collective identity and a shared political project. After 1967, Zionism was no longer a movement designed to fundamentally change Jews and bring an end to their persecution through national rebirth. Instead, the Jewish state came to be seen as a bulwark against victimization rather than a means to put an end to it once and for all. Meanwhile, American Jews could consider themselves Zionists even if they had no intention of leaving the lives, security and communities they had built in the United States. This is the broader meaning of popular tropes about a "reawakening" of the Diaspora and the 1967 war being a Jewish battle, not just an Israeli one. Jews in the United States embraced something resembling a national loyalty to the Jewish state, while Jews in Israel embraced the Diaspora both past and present.

As a form of nationalism, Zionism was perhaps uniquely positioned to radically reimagine what it meant to be a member of the nation and welcome a new and far-flung constituency into its fold. From the very beginning, Zionist claims making was striking in scope. After all, what other nationalist movement began by claiming a group of people who were scattered throughout the world and a national homeland where less than one in every hundred members of the would-be nation could be found? Yet by reinterpreting Jewish culture and scripture through the lens of modern European nationalism, this is precisely what Zionism has done ever since its emergence around the turn of the twentieth century.[64] Zionism is actually so unusual in this regard that major theorists of modern nationalism have struggled to know what to make of it.[65] Zionism is truly "a national*ism* like no other" in the way it lays claim to a national community.[66]

To make sense of Zionist claims making, consider Benedict Anderson's influential approach to nationalism: "Communities are to be distinguished, not by their falsity/genuineness, but by the style in which they are imagined."[67] From this perspective, quite different Zionist nations obtained in the pre and post-1967 periods. On the one hand, Zionism changed so as to include Diaspora Jews in its national community, at least as partial members, even if they had no intention of making Aliyah. In this way, we can see what happened in 1967 as a radical expansion of the Zionist nation as a community imagined by its members to exist and to share a commonality, a past and a future. One can even argue that Zionism expanded its imagined community once before when Mizrahi Jews were welcomed as members (albeit unequal ones).[68] On the other hand, the dominant Zionist narrative about Jewish history and the role of a Jewish state changed dramatically in 1967: it embraced the idea that Jewish victimhood is endemic—something to be warded off by the Israeli state rather than resolved through national rebirth. Thus the scope and the very purpose of Zionism changed in 1967 when it began to embrace Diaspora Jews and a narrative of Jewish victimhood.

In sum, the way Jewish narratives in Israel and the United States were transformed in 1967 was remarkably rapid, radical, and unexpected. It depended on everything from a fleeting and propagandistic use of the Holocaust by ambitious rivals to the Israeli prime minister of the day through to the very structure of Zionism itself. There is surely more work to be done before we can fully understand how this dramatic moment of identity change came to pass or the form that it took. However, this chapter showed that a key part of any explanation is the way the new narrative united the world's two largest Jewish communities around a shared history of victimhood—a unification that was experienced as a sort of reawakening a generation after the collective trauma of the Holocaust. Once it came to the fore in 1967, the narrative of axiomatic victimhood bound the Israeli and American Jewish communities together as never before.

The long-term durability of the new narrative, I have argued, is somewhat easier to understand. The narrative of Jewish victimhood has enabled policy with respect to the ongoing conflict over Israel/Palestine which would have otherwise been more difficult to defend in the American, Israeli, and international arenas.[69] As Charles Tilly argued, answers to identity questions are "always assertions, always contingent, always negotiable, but also always consequential."[70] A recent survey-based study by Halperin et al. of Israeli collective memory, experience, hope and fear in the context of the Israeli-Arab conflict found:

> Individuals who tend to remember the very negative experiences of the Jewish people tend also to experience fear about the future of the Jewish collective. This finding is of special importance because it shows that remembering trau-

matic Jewish experiences that took place in the distant past affects collective fear related to the Israeli-Arab conflict. It confirms longstanding observations by a number of social scientists and historians who suggest that remembrance of the distant Jewish past, and especially the Holocaust experience as actively propagated and fostered in Israel, feeds into Israeli citizens' fear of Arabs.[71]

It would be surprising if similar results did not hold for American Jews as well.

The specter of catastrophe is so central to Zionist identity that Yossi Beilin, representing the left of the Zionist political spectrum, could write "[T]he most acute of all questions will surely be this: will Israeli society have a purpose when the problem of survival is no longer so high on our list of priorities?"[72] A fractured polity ethnically, religiously, politically, and economically, the narrative-identity of axiomatic victimhood can be interpreted as something of a societal glue for the Zionist nation; when we further consider the stake of Diaspora Jewry in this already cacophonous community, we see how vital this unifying narrative is for Zionist identity as we know it today. Of course, there are profound dissonances between these groups and their take on contemporary Israel—dissonances that are arguably becoming more acute.[73] Still, it is a near-certainty that Zionist politicians and activists will do everything in their power to forestall any serious challenge to the prevailing narrative of Jewish victimhood, the Nazi Holocaust, and Israel that emerged so suddenly and unexpectedly in 1967.

The conflict over Israel/Palestine is fundamentally about land and the political status of the people who live on it. That said, it is plain to see how a narrative of Jewish history centered on victimhood and the Holocaust has profoundly shaped the contours of the debate in both Israel and the United States, obfuscating the status of millions of Palestinians as victims in the process. Looking back to the startling transformation of Jewish identities that occurred in 1967 therefore presents an important opportunity for reflection. Perhaps, half a century since the start of the Israeli occupation, there are better and more thoughtful ways honor the long history of Jewish oppression at the hands of the powerful.

NOTES

1. A longer version of this paper was originally published as: Daniel Navon, "'We Are a People, One People': How 1967 Transformed Holocaust Memory and Jewish Identity in Israel and the US," *Journal of Historical Sociology* 28, no.3 (2015): 342–73. © 2014 John Wiley & Sons Ltd. I am grateful for invaluable feedback from Peter Bearman, John Chalcraft, Yinon Cohen, Claire Edington, James Kennedy, Laleh Khalili, Shamus Khan, Uri Shwed and especially Gil Eyal and Charles Tilly.

2. The first Intifada or uprising—literally a "throwing off" of the occupation—was, unlike its successor, a largely unarmed, grassroots affair whose suppression did much to establish the Palestinians as victims of Israeli policy in the American press and elsewhere. See Annemarie

A. Daniel, "U.S. Media Coverage of the *Intifada* and American Public Opinion," in *The US Media and the Middle East: Image and Perception,* ed. Y. R. Kamalipour (Westport, CT: Praeger, 1997), 62-72.

3. Yizhak Shamir, "Address by Prime Minister Yizhak Shamir, Opening Ceremony of the Holocaust Martyrs and Heroes Remembrance Day," (archival document) *Yad Vashem: The Martyrs' and Heroes' Remembrance Authority*, Jerusalem Israel.

4. "Anti semitism and the holocaust documents and communiques," accessed April 26th, 2011,http://www.mfa.gov.il/MFA/Anti-Semitism+and+the+Holocaust/Documents+and+communiques/ See below for further examples.

5. Simha Flapan, cited in Avi Shlaim, "The Debate about 1948," *International Journal of Middle East Studies*, 27, no. 3 (1995), 287–304: 229. For analyses that address the role of the Zionist narrative of Jewish victimhood in contemporary Israeli society and its impact on the prospects for peace, see: Eran Halperin, Daniel Bar-Tal, Rafi Nets-Zehngut, Erga Drori, "Emotions in Conflict: Correlates of Fear and Hope in the Israeli Jewish Society," *Peace and Conflict* 14, no. 3 (July 2008): 233–58; Daniel Bar-Tal, Eran Halperin and Neta Oren, "Socio–Psychological Barriers to Peace Making: The Case of the Israeli Jewish Society," *Social Issues and Policy Review* 4, no. 1 (December 2010): 63–109.

6. From Halbwachs's groundbreaking work on, a rich sociological body of work analyses, as Halbwachs puts it, how "collective frameworks" are used to "reconstruct an image of the past which is in accord, in each epoch, with the predominant thoughts the society." (Maurice Halbwachs, *On Collective Memory* (Chicago, IL: University of Chicago, 1992 [1925]), 40.; for a review, see: Jeffrey K. Olick & Joyce Robbins, "Social Memory Studies: From 'Collective Memory' to the Historical Sociology of Mnemonic Practices," *Annual Review of Sociology* 24 (1998). In this vein, Yael Zerubavel has masterfully sketched the foundational structure and moments of Zionist collective memory, showing how representations of the defense of *Tel Hai* during the *Yishuv* period, the *Masada* massacre and the *Bar Kochba* revolt were mobilized to bind early Zionist identity and the image of the *Sabra* to an ancient and heroic Hebrew past (Yael Zerubavel, *Recovered Roots: Collective Memory and the Making of Israeli National Tradition* (Chicago: University of Chicago, 1995)). This paper, however, aims to simultaneously adopt collective memory and identity in a study of what I call "narrative-identity" change. For a full theoretical discussion see Daniel Navon, "'We Are a People, One People': How 1967 Transformed Holocaust Memory and Jewish Identity in Israel and the US," *Journal of Historical Sociology* 28, no. 3 (2015): 342–73.

7. Benedict Anderson, *Imagined Communities* (London: Verso, 1983).

8. On the role of the Holocaust and its victims in Israel prior to the mid-1960s see Tom Segev, *The Seventh Million: The Israelis and the Holocaust* (New York, NY: Metropolitan, 1991); Dalia Ofer, "The Strength of Remembrance: Commemoration of the Holocaust during the First Decade of Israel," *Jewish Social Studies: History, Culture, and Society* 6, no.2 (2000): 24–55. For parallel analyses of the American situation, see Peter Novick, *The Holocaust in American Life* (New York, NY: Houghton Mifflin, 2000); Jeffrey C. Alexander, "On the Social Construction of Moral Universals," *European Journal of Social Theory* 5, no. 1 (2002): 5–85. Though see Hasia R. Diner, *We Remember with Reverence and Love: American Jews and the Myth of Silence after the Holocaust, 1945–1962* (New York: New York University Press, 2009) for a partial correction to the historiographical consensus that American Jews were personally and organizationally completely silent on the issue of the Holocaust.

9. On the American preoccupation with integration into mainstream American society, see Eric L. Goldstein, *The Price of Whiteness: Jews, Race and American Identity* (Princeton, NJ: Princeton University Press, 2006); Deborah E. Lipstadt, "America and the Memory of the Holocaust, 1950–1965," *Modern Judaism* 16, no. 3 (1996): 195–214; Michael L. Morgan, *Beyond Auschwitz: Post-Holocaust Jewish Thought in America* (Oxford: OUP, 2001). On the Israeli rejection of Jewish victimhood see Yael Zerubavel, *Recovered Roots*; Oz Almog, *The Sabra: The Creation of the New Jew,* trans. Waltzman (Berkeley, CA: University of California Press, 2000).

10. See Goldstein, *The Price of Whiteness*, on the unease with which assimilation was greeted by many in the American Jewish community.

11. On pre-1967 Holocaust commemoration ceremonies in the United States, see Arthur Herzberg, *A Jew in America: My Life and a People's Struggle for Identity* (New York, NY: Harper Collins, 2002). On the 'de-Judaization' of the Anne Frank story see Alexander, "On the Construction of Moral Universals." *Remembering the Holocaust: A Debate* (2009): 3–102

12. Diner, *We Remember with Reverence and Love.*

13. For the text of original 1950 "Blaustein-Ben Gurion aggreement," see: "AJC press release on the Blaustein-Ben-Gurion Agreement" (Sep. 10, 1950). Archival Document, *American Jewish* Accessed, 24 April 2011, http://www.ajcarchives.org/AJC_DATA/Files/508. PDF. For its 1961 reaffirmation, see: "AJC press release on the official reaffirmation of the Blaustein-Ben-Gurion Agreement" (1 May 1961). Archival Document. *American Jewish Committee,* Accessed 24 April 2011, http://www.ajcarchives.org/AJC_DATA/Files/513.PDF.

14. See Segev, *The Seventh Million.*

15. Almog, *The Sabra,* 76. On the relationship between early Zionist representation and Diaspora Jewry, see also Zerubavel, *Recovered Roots.*

16. Although Yiddish was widely spoken by European Jewry—supporting a transcontinental publishing network—it was Hebrew, one of the languages of the ancient Hebrew kingdoms, which was adopted by the Zionist leaders.

17. See Theodore Herzl, "A Solution of the Jewish Question," in *The Jewish Chronicle* (London) (January 1896), reprinted in P. Mendes & J. Reinharz (Eds.) *The Jew in the Modern World: A Documentary History* (Oxford: OUP, 1980): 533–38.

18. Almog, *The Sabra,* 6.

19. See Zerubavel, *Recovered Roots* and Yael Zerubavel, "The 'Mythological Sabra' and Jewish Past: Trauma, Memory and Contested Identities," *Israel Studies* 7, no. 2 (2002): 115–44.

20. But for a clash with Pesach, *Yom HaShoah* would have fallen on the anniversary of the Warsaw Uprising—the initial preference of Israeli legislators (see James E. Young, "When a Day Remembers: a Performative History of Yom hashoah," *History and Memory*, 2, Winter (1990): 54–75). Instead, they chose the 27th of Nissan, moving it into a remarkable organization of time. Beginning at sundown six days before Yom Hazikaron and seven days before Yom Ha'Atzmaut (Israel's "Day of Remembrance" for its fallen soldiers and Independence Day respectively), *Yom HaShoah* creates an ordering of time with deep parallels to the Pesach festival and story that finishes days earlier in the Hebrew Calendar.

21. Jerusalem Post Staff, "Remembrance and Redemption," *The Jerusalem Post*, May 7, 1967, 1. On *Yom HaShoah's* lack of attention in its first years, see Jerusalem Post Staff, "Holocaust Victims' Memory Honoured," *The Jerusalem Post*, April 24, 1960, 1. For excerpts of Ben-Gurion's 1963 address at Yad Vashem, see *Jerusalem Post Reporter*, "10,000 at Har Hazikaron Honour Memory of Martyrs," *The Jerusalem Post*, April 22, 1963, 1 (my emphasis).

22. As the Jerusalem Post put it on the following *Yom HaShoah* (Jerusalem Post Leader, "Lessons of Remembrance" *The Jerusalem Post*, April 30, 1962, 1), "the 'holocaust consciousness' of everyone of us [has been] immeasurably deepened and meaningfully widened."

23. Mooli Brog, "Victims and Victors: Holocaust and Military Commemoration in Israel Collective Memory," *Israel Studies* 8, no. 3 (Fall 2003): 65–99. See also Ofer, "The Strength of Remembrance."

24. Lipstadt, "America and the Memory of the Holocaust," 206–7. In a manner broadly parallel to the analysis of Israeli Holocaust commemoration above, Lipstadt argues (p. 208) that though "Eichamnn's capture and his subsequent trial did not . . . serve to open up the floodgates of memory . . . [they] may, however, have been responsible, at least in part, for laying the groundwork for what would become an intense interest in the Holocaust just a few years hence." On this point, see also Lucy S. Dawidowicz, "American Public Opinion" *American Jewish Year Book* 69 (1968): 198–232, 203–4.

25. See Lipstadt, "America and the Memory of the Holocaust," 195; Herzberg, "A Jew in America," 403.

26. See Philip Gleason, "Identifying Identity: A Semantic History," *The Journal of American History* 69, no. 4 (1983): 910–31.

27. See Lawrence Grossman, "Transformation Through Crisis: The American Jewish Committee and the Six-Day War," *American Jewish History* 86, no. 1 (1998): 27–54; Simon N.

Herman, *Jewish Identity: A Social Psychological Perspective* (New Brunswick, NJ: Transaction, 1989); Arad, G. N. Israel and the Shoah: A Tale of Multifarious Taboos. *New German Critique*, 90 (2003): 5–26; Gulie Ne'eman Arad, "Israel and the Shoah: A Tale of Multifarious Taboos," *New German Critique* 90 (2003): 5–26; Idith Zertal, *Israel's Holocaust and the Politics of Nationhood*, (Cambridge: Cambridge University Press, 2005); Eyal Zandberg, "Critical laughter: humor, popular culture and Israeli Holocaust commemoration," *Media Culture and Society* 28, no. 4 (2006): 561-579; Segev, *The Seventh Million*; Joshua Michael Zeitz, "'If I am not for myself . . .': The American Jewish Establishment in the Aftermath of the Six Day War," *American Jewish History* 88, no. 2 (2000): 253–86.

28. Tom Segev, *1967: Israel, the War, and the Year That Transformed the Middle East* (New York, NY: Metropolitan, 2007); Zertal, *Israel's Holocaust*, 117.

29. On the crushing blow the 1967 war dealt to Arab nationalism, see Adeed Dawisha, "Requiem for Arab Nationalism," *Middle East Quarterly* 10, no. 1 (2003): 25–41.

30. On the intra-Labour campaign and its introduction of a Holocaust-centered discourse, see Zertal, *Israel's Holocaust*. On the contradictory mood of confidence and fear of a second Holocaust, see Segev, *1967*. Both describe the general mood in Israel around the 1967 crisis, on which see also Segev, *The Seventh Million*.

31. For the classic account, see Novick, *The Holocaust in American Life*. See also Zandberg, "Critical Laughter," and Grossman "Transformation Through Crisis," for more sustained discussions. For a complementary discussion of the situation among French Jews, see Joan B. Wolf, "'Anne Frank is dead, long live Anne Frank': The Six-Day War and the Holocaust in French Public Discourse," *History & Memory* 11, no. 1 (Spring/Summer 1999): 104–40.

32. Dawidowicz, "American Public Opinion," 211.

33. Lipstadt, "America and the Memory of the Holocaust," 208.

34. Dawidowicz, "American Public Opinion," 198, 203–4.

35. Figures are from Morgan, *Beyond Auschwitz*, 80. Similarly, the AJC Yearbook notes that philanthropic agencies reported $101.2 million available for overseas use in 1965, $102.6 million in 1966, and around $275 million after the 1967 crisis, with the proportion available for expenditure in Israel also rising from 80 percent to 90 percent and that sales of Israel Bonds in the United States increased from 76,656,000 and 76,176,000 in 1965 and 1966 respectively to 189,976,000 in 1967 (S. P. Goldberg, "Jewish Communal Services: Programs and Finances," *American Jewish Year Book* 69 (1968): 291–343, 303, 329).

36. Ralph Simon, "Speech at Rally for Israel, Washington, DC, May 30th 1967," (archival document), American Jewish Historical Society, Near East Crisis Collection, AJHS, I-18 Box 5.

37. Dawidowicz, "American Public Opinion," 205, 217.

38. Dawidowicz, "American Public Opinion," 206–213; Joe Stork and Sharon Rose, "Zionism and American Jewry," *Journal of Palestine Studies* 3, no. 3 (1974): 39–57.

39. Charlotte Jacobson, "A Proclamation Issued at Rally of Solidarity With Israel, Conference of Presidents of Major American Jewish Organizations, Lafayette Park, Washington, DC, June 8 1967," (archival document) American Jewish Historical Society, Near East Crisis Collection, AJHS, I-18 Box 3.

40. James Reston, "The Irony of Israel's Success," *New York Times*, June 7th, 1967, 4.

41. Jewish Chronicle, "Survival Now!" *The Jewish Chronicle* (Pittsburgh), June 9th, 1967, 4.

42. Jewish Telegraphic Agency, "Identity, Assimilation Tear At US Jewry," *The Jewish Chronicle* (Pittsburgh), June 2nd 1967, 30; Jewish Chronicle, "Chronicles of the Past: Thirty Years Ago This Week," *The Jewish Chronicle* (Pittsburgh), June 2nd 1967, 20.

43. Jerusalem Post Reporter, "Yad Vashem to warn of Arab propaganda peril," *The Jerusalem Post*, April 1, 1969, 7.

44. Hanna Yablonka, *The State of Israel vs. Adolf Eichmann* (New York, NY: Schocken Books, 2004): 223–4.

45. Yigal Allon, "Address by Deputy Prime Minister Yigal Allon, Opening Ceremony of the Holocaust Martyrs and Heroes Remembrance Day," (archival document from 1968) *Yad Vashem: The Martyrs' and Heroes' Remembrance Authority*, Jerusalem Israel, obtained by post from archivist. Current Prime Minister Netanyahu also invoked the "In every generation . . ."

theme at the 2010 ceremony, going on to say, "And here we are today again witnesses to the fire of the new-old hatred, the hatred of the Jews, that is expressed by organizations and regimes associated with radical Islam, headed by Iran and its proxies. . . . The required firm protest is not heard—not a sharp condemnation, not a cry of warning. The world continues on as usual and there are even those who direct their criticism at us, against Israel." See Benjamin Netanyahu, "PM Netanyahu's Speech at the Holocaust Martyrs' and Heroes' Remembrance Day Ceremony," (April 4th, 2010), available at: http://www.pmo.gov.il/PMOEng/Archive/Speeches/2010/04/speechshoa1104010.htm

46. See Dan A. Porat, "From the Scandal to the Holocaust in Israeli Education," *Journal of Contemporary History* 39, no. 4(2004): 619–36; Julia Resnik, "'Sites of Memory' of the Holocaust: Shaping National Memory in the Education System in Israel," *Nations and Nationalism,* 9, no. 2 (2003): 297–315; Brog, "Victims and Victors."

47. Simon N. Herman, *Israelis and the Jews: The Continuity of an Identity* (New York, NY: Random House, 1970), 210-6.

48. See Segev, *1967*, 557–60; quote is from p. 558.

49. Jacob Hessing, "Something Has Changed in Us," *The Jerusalem Post Week-End Magazine*, July 14th, 1967, 19.

50. On the prevalence of the "Jewish battle, not just an Israeli" trope, see Herman, *Israelis and the Jews*.

51. Uzi Rebhun and Chaim I. Waxman, "The 'Americanization' of Israel: A Demographic, Cultural and Political Evaluation," *Israel Studies* 5, no. 1 (2000): 65–91. See pp. 67–69 for Aliyah statistics and 78–79 on tourism statistics.

52. Jewish Telegraphic Agency, "Egyptian Gas Labs Found," *The Jewish Chronicle* (Pittsburgh), June 30th, 1967, 7.

53. Morris Laub, "What Lies Behind the American Jewish Reaction to the Israel-Arab War of June 1967," *Seminar of Ad Hoc Interreligious Committee on International Affairs*, October 30, 1967, (archival document) American Jewish Historical Society, Near East Crisis Collection, AJHS, I-18 Box 5.

54. See Gil Eyal's discussion of the role of trauma as an element of Czech collective memory: Gil Eyal, "Identity and Trauma: Two Forms of the Will to Memory," *History and Memory* 16, no.1 (Spring/Summer 2004): 5–36; see also Jeffrey C. Alexander, Ron Eyerman, Bernhard Giesen, Neil J. Smelser, and Piotr Sztompka, Cultural Trauma and Collective Identity, (Berkeley, CA: University of California Press, 2004). For a thoughtful social psychological explanation, see Yael Zerubavel, "The "Mythological Sabra" and Jewish Past: Trauma, Memory and Contested Identities," *Israel Studies* 7, no. 2 (2002): 115–44.

55. For the best overview of the traditional Zionist narrative about 1948, see Avi Shlaim, "The Debate about 1948," *International Journal of Middle East Studies* 27, no. 3 (1995):287–304.

56. See Laleh Khalili, *Heroes and Martyrs of Palestine: The Politics of National Commemoration* (Cambridge: Cambridge University Press, 2007).

57. On the role of the Greater Israel Movement see Idith Zertal and Akiva Eldar, *Lords of the Land: The War for Israel's Settlements in the Occupied Territories, 1967–2007* (New York, NY: Nation, 2007). Herut's leader and, from 1977–1983, Likud prime minister Menachem Begin was particularly inclined to indulge in similar rhetoric—a significant factor in the establishment of the Holocaust at the center of the Zionist narrative. On this point, see: Arye Naor, "Lessons of the Holocaust Versus Territories For Peace, 1967–2001," *Israel Studies* 8, no. 1, 2003: 130–52; Segev, *The Seventh Million*. Conversely, this new narrative should be added to the list of factors undermining the hegemony of Labor Zionism in Israeli politics.

58. Uri Avnery, "Mourning Becomes Israel," *Uri Avnery Archive*, February 1st, 2004, available at: http://www.strike-the-root.com/4/avnery/avnery1.html. Accessed 7 December 2006.

59. David A. Harris, "Why AJC?" *American Jewish Committee*, fundraising email, December 23rd 2008.

60. Brog, "Victims and Victors," 65.

61. Katsav went on to say: "Antisemitism has not disappeared. It is still seething in Europe, which is steeped in the blood of our brethren. But anti-semitism rages principally around us, in the Middle East. It keeps reappearing in expressions of hatred towards the State of Israel. . . .

Once again we are hearing things we heard in the 1930s, and once again we are witness to restrained reactions, hesitation and scepticism. Do not underestimate the threat." Recent speeches from *Yom HaShoah* ceremonies at Yad Vahsem can be found at: http://www.mfa.gov. il/mfa/anti-semitism%20and%20the%20holocaust/documents%20and%20communiques/ (accessed April 26, 2011). For the Peres speech, see: http://www.mfa.gov.il/MFA/Anti-Semitism+ and+the+Holocaust/Documents+and+communiques/Opening_ceremony_Holocaust_ Remembrance_Day__1-May-2011 (accessed June 4th, 2011).

    62. For example see Stork and Rose, "Zionism and American Jewry," 51: "[T]here is one fact about the victory of 1967 which is essential . . . as far as future impact on American Jewry is concerned, the Israelis will never be able to duplicate their feat of 1967. They will never again be able to convince the American Jewish community that they are weak and helpless."

    63. See especially Doug McAdam, Sidney Tarrow, and Charles Tilly, *Dynamics of Contention* (Cambridge: CUP, 2001), esp. p. 56 and pp. 142–48; Jennifer Todd, "Social Transformation, Collective Categories, and Identity Change," *Theory and Society* 34, no. 4 (2005): 429–63.

    64. As Eric Hobsbawn put it, "It is entirely illegitimate to identify the Jewish links with the ancestral land of Israel . . . with a desire to gather all Jews into a modern territorial state situated on the ancient Holy Land." Eric J. Hobsbawm, *Nations and Nationalism* (Wiltshire, UK: Redwood, 1990): 47–48. On the idea of an ancient Jewish kingdom in making sense of a settler colony lacking a metropolis, see Yehouda Shenhav, "Modernity and Hybridization of Nationalism and Religion: Zionism and the Jews of the Middle East as a Heuristic Case," *Theory and Society* 36, no. 1 (2007), 1–30.

    65. Some have even tried to argue that there has been a Jewish nation since the days of Ancient Israel. To be sure, Jewish religious differentiation and a putative biblical link to the Levant were longstanding and constituted a powerful basis for nationalist narrative. However, the ascription of nationalism to them prior to Zionism's rise as a form of modern European nationalism is clearly a non sequitur: it was only modern Zionism that posited as a basis for a national program. Nevertheless, this non sequitur fills such a troublesome analytic gap that even Ernst Gellner—perhaps the preeminent modernist theorist of nationalism—was willing to take the plunge. Indeed in *Nationalism* (London: Weidenfeld & Nicolson, 1997, p. 23) Gellner tells us that Ancient Israel was perhaps the very first nation. Echoing Adrian Hastings' religious primordialism (see "Holy lands and their political consequences," *Nations and Nationalism* 9, no. 1 (2003): 29–54), whereby the Zionist movement always issued from the metropolis of the ancient Kingdom of Israel, Gellner writes, "It is possible to seek the origins of nationalism in ancient Israel, where an inherently unique and potentially universal deity had, at least for the time being, a culturally distinct and exclusive clientele."

    66. Neither the "modernizing" nationalisms in Europe, the anti, post-colonial and settler nationalisms throughout the world, nor the disintegrating nationalisms of more recent times will serve to capture the conditions that gave rise to Zionist aspirations. Indeed while Zionism undoubtedly *became* a form of settler nationalism, the community subject Zionist national claims was evidently not coextensive with a population borne of colonial enterprise.

    67. Anderson, *Imagined Communities*, 6. From this perspective, Zionism just had to compel its would-be adherents to imagine the Jews as a nation. An answer to the "Jewish question" whereby (at least according to anti-Semitic accounts) "Jews, the seed of Abraham, [were] forever Jews, no matter what passports they carried or what languages they speak and read" can qualify as a form of nationalism (Anderson, ibid: 149).

    68. See Yehouda Shenhav, "How did the Mizrahim 'Become' Religious and Zionist? Zionism, Colonialism and the Religionization of the Arab-Jew," *Israel Studies Forum: An Interdisciplinary Journal* 19, no. 1 (2003): 73–87.

    69. See especially Ilan Pappe, Fear, Victimhood, Self and Other. *MIT Electronic Journal of Middle Eastern Studies* 1 (2004): 1–14; Bar-Tal et al., "Socio-Psychological Barriers to Peace Making"; Halperin et al., "Emotions in Conflict"; Naor, "Lessons of the Holocaust Versus Territories For Peace."

    70. Tilly, *Identities, Boundaries and Social Ties*, 209.

    71. Halperin et al., "Emotions in Conflict," 251.

72. Yossi Beilin, *Touching Peace: From the Oslo Accord to a Final Agreement* (London: Weidenfeld & Nicolson, 1999): 4. Until 2006, Beilin led Meretz-Yachad—the most left-wing Jewish party in the Knesset—and he can perhaps claim primary responsibility on the Israeli side for the Oslo I Accords, the Beilin-Abu Mazen understanding and the Geneva Initiative.

73. On the American Jewry's growing disillusionment with Israel and the Israel-Palestine conflict, see Steven T. Rosenthal, *Irreconcilable Differences? The Waning of the American Jewish Love Affair with Israel* (Hanover, MA: Brandeis, 2001). Also see *J Street* for "Pro-Israel, Pro-Peace" Jewish American activism (http://jstreet.org/) and *Jewish Voice for Peace* for radical Jewish American activism in opposition to Israeli occupation (https://jewishvoiceforpeace.org/).

BIBLIOGRAPHY

Alexander, Jeffrey C., Ron Eyerman, Bernhard Giesen, Neil J. Smelser, and Piotr Sztompka. *Cultural Trauma and Collective Identity.* Berkeley, CA: University of California Press, 2004.

Alexander, Jeffrey C. "The Social Construction of Moral Universals." *Remembering the Holocaust Debate* , 2009, 3–102. doi:10.1093/acprof:oso/9780195326222.003.0001.

Alexander, Jeffrey C. "On the Social Construction of Moral Universals." *European Journal of Social Theory* 5, no. 1 (2002): 5–85.

Almog, Oz. *The Sabra: The Creation of the New Jew.* Berkeley: Univ. of California Press, 2009.

American Jewish Committee. "AJC press release on the Blaustein-Ben-Gurion Agreement" (Sep.10, 1950). Archival Document. Accessed, 24 April 2011. http://www.ajcarchives.org/AJC_DATA/Files/508.PDF .

American Jewish Committee. "AJC press release on the official reaffirmation of the Blaustein-Ben-Gurion Agreement." (1 May 1961). Archival Document. Accessed 24 April 2011. http://www.ajcarchives.org/AJC_DATA/Files/513.PDF.

Anderson, Benedict. *Imagined Communities.* London: Verso, 1983.

Arad, Gulie Ne'eman. "Israel and the Shoah: A Tale of Multifarious Taboos." *New German Critique* 90 (2003): 5–26.

Bar-Tal, Daniel, Eran Halperin, and Neta Oren. "Socio-Psychological Barriers to Peace Making: The Case of the Israeli Jewish Society." *Social Issues and Policy Review* 4, no. 1 (2010):63–109. doi:10.1111/j.1751-2409.2010.01018.x.

Beilin, Yossi, *Touching Peace: From the Oslo Accord to a Final Agreement.* London: Weidenfeld & Nicolson, 1999.

Brog, Mooli. "Victims and Victors: Holocaust and Military Commemoration in Israel Collective Memory." *Israel Studies* 8, no. 3 (2003): 65–99.

Charlotte Jacobson, "A Proclamation Issued at Rally of Solidarity with Israel, Conference of Presidents of Major American Jewish Organizations, Lafayette Park, Washington, DC, June 8, 1967," (archival document) American Jewish Historical Society, Near East Crisis Collection, AJHS, I-18 Box 3.

Daniel, Annemarie A. "U.S. Media Coverage of the *Intifada* and American Public Opinion." In *The US Media and the Middle East: Image and Perception,* edited by Y. R. Kamalipour, 62–72. Westport, CT: Praeger, 1997.

Dawidowicz, Lucy S. "American Public Opinion" *American Jewish Year Book* 69 (1968): 198–232, 203–4.

Dawisha, Adeed "Requiem for Arab Nationalism," *Middle East Quarterly* 10, no. 1 (2003):25–41.

Diner, Hasia R. *We Remember with Reverence and Love: American Jews and the Myth of Silence after the Holocaust, 1945–1962.* New York: New York University Press, 2009.

Ernst Gellner. *Nationalism.* London: Weidenfeld & Nicolson, 1997.

Eyal, Gil "Identity and Trauma: Two Forms of the Will to Memory." *History and Memory* 16, no.1 (2004): 5–36. doi:10.1353/ham.2004.0002.

Gleason, Philip. "Identifying Identity: A Semantic History." *The Journal of American History* 69, no. 4 (1983): 910–31.

Goldberg, S. P. "Jewish Communal Services: Programs and Finances." *American Jewish Year Book* 69 (1968): 291–343, 303, 329.

Goldstein, Eric L. *The Price of Whiteness: Jews, Race and American Identity.* Princeton, NJ: Princeton University Press, 2006.

Grossman, Lawrence. "Transformation through Crisis: The American Jewish Committee and the Six-Day War." *American Jewish History* 86, no. 1 (1998): 27–54.

Halbwachs, Maurice. *On Collective Memory.* Chicago, IL: University of Chicago, 1992.

Halperin, Eran. *Emotions in conflict: inhibitors and facilitators of peace making.* London: Routledge, 2016.

Hastings, Adrian. "Holy lands and their political consequences." *Nations and Nationalism* 9, no.1 (2003): 29–54.

Herman, Simon N. *Israelis and Jews: the continuity of an identity* . Philadelphia: The Jewish Publ. Soc. of America, 1971.

Herman, Simon N. *Israelis and the Jews: The Continuity of an Identity.* New York, NY: Random House, 1970.

Herman, Simon N. *Jewish Identity: A Social Psychological Perspective.* New Brunswick, NJ: Transaction, 1989.

Herzberg, Arthur. *A Jew in America: My Life and a People's Struggle for Identity.* New York, NY: Harper Collins, 2002.

Herzl, Theodore. "A Solution of the Jewish Question." *The Jewish Chronicle,* January 1896.

Hessing, Jacob. "Something has changed in us." *The Jerusalem Post Week-End Magazine* , July 14th 1967, 19.

Hobsbawm, Eric John, *Nations and Nationalism since 1780.* Wiltshire, UK: Redwood, 1990. http://www.pmo.gov.il/PMOEng/Archive/Speeches/2010/04/speechshoa1104010.htm

Jerusalem Post Leader. "Lessons of Remembrance." *The Jerusalem Post* , April 30, 1962, 1.

Jerusalem Post Reporter. "10,000 at Har Hazikaron Honour Memory of Martyrs." *The Jerusalem Post* , April 22, 1963, 1

Jerusalem Post Reporter. "Yad Vashem to warn of Arab propaganda peril." *The Jerusalem Post* , April 1, 1969, 7.

Jerusalem Post Staff. "Holocaust Victims' Memory Honoured." *The Jerusalem Post* , April 24, 1960, 1.

Jerusalem Post Staff. "Remembrance and Redemption." *The Jerusalem Post* , May 7, 1967, 1.

Jewish Chronicle. "Chronicles of the Past: Thirty Years Ago This Week." *The Jewish Chronicle* (Pittsburgh), June 2nd 1967, 20.

Jewish Chronicle. "Survival Now!" *The Jewish Chronicle.* June 9th 1967, 4.

Jewish Telegraphic Agency. "Identity, Assimilation Tear at US Jewry." *The Jewish Chronicle* , June 2nd 1967, 30;

Khalili, Laleh. *Heroes and Martyrs of Palestine: The Politics of National Commemoration.* Cambridge: Cambridge University Press, 2007.

Lipstadt, Deborah E. "America and the Memory of the Holocaust, 1950–1965." *Modern Judaism* 16, no. 3 (1996): 195–214.

McAdam, Doug, Sidney Tarrow, and Charles Tilly. *Dynamics of contention* . Cambridge: Cambridge Univ. Press, 2001.

Mendes-Flohr, Paul R. *The Jew in the modern world: a documentary history.* Oxford: Oxford University Press, 1980.

MFA Israel. "Anti semitism and the holocaust documents and communiques." Accessed April 26th, 2011.

http://www.mfa.gov.il/MFA/Anti-Semitism+and+the+Holocaust/Documents+and+communiques/

Morgan, Michael L. *Beyond Auschwitz: Post-Holocaust Jewish Thought in America.* Oxford: OUP, 2001.

Naor, Arye. "Lessons of the Holocaust versus Territories For Peace, 1967–2001." *Israel Studies* 8, no. 1, (2003): 130–52.

Navon, Daniel. "'We are a people, one people': How 1967 Transformed Holocaust Memory and Jewish Identity in Israel and the US." *Journal of Historical Sociology* 28, no. 3 (2014): 342–73. doi:10.1111/johs.12075.

Netanyahu, Benjamin. "PM Netanyahu's Speech at the Holocaust Martyrs' and Heroes' Remembrance Day Ceremony" (April 4th, 2010).

Novick, Peter. *The Holocaust in American Life.* New York, NY: Houghton Mifflin, 2000.

Ofer, Dalia. "The Strength of Remembrance: Commemoration of the Holocaust during the First Decade of Israel." Jewish Social Studies: History, Culture, and Society 6, no.2 (2000): 24–55.

Olick, Jeffrey K., and Joyce Robbins. "Social Memory Studies: From 'Collective Memory' to the Historical Sociology of Mnemonic Practices." Annual Review of Sociology 24 (1998).

Pappe, Ilan. "Fear, Victimhood, Self and Other." *MIT Electronic Journal of Middle Eastern Studies* 1 (2004): 1–14.

Porat, Dan A. "From the Scandal to the Holocaust in Israeli Education." *Journal of Contemporary History* 39, no. 4(2004): 619–36

Rebhun, Uzi, and Chaim I. Waxman. "The 'Americanization' of Israel: A Demographic, Cultural and Political Evaluation." *Israel Studies* 5, no. 1 (2000): 65–91. doi:10.2979/isr.2000.5.1.65.

Resnik, Julia. "'Sites of memory' of the Holocaust: shaping national memory in the education system in Israel." *Nations and Nationalism,* 9, no. 2 (2003): 297–315;

Reston, James. "The Irony of Israel's Success." *New York Times,* June 7th 1967, 4.

Segev, Tom, and Haim Watzman. *The seventh million: the Israelis and the Holocaust.* New York: Henry Holt and Company, 2005.

Segev, Tom. *1967: Israel, the War, and the Year that Transformed the Middle East.* New York, NY: Metropolitan, 2007.

Shenhav, Yehouda. "How did the Mizrahim 'Become' Religious and Zionist? Zionism, Colonialism and the Religionization of the Arab-Jew." *Israel Studies Forum: An Interdisciplinary Journal* 19, no. 1 (2003): 73–87.

Shenhav, Yehouda. "Modernity and hybridization of nationalism and religion: Zionism and the Jews of the Middle East as a heuristic." *Theory and Society* 36, no. 1 (2007): 1–30.

Shlaim, Avi. "The Debate about 1948." *International Journal of Middle East Studies* 27, no. 3 (1995):287–304. doi:10.1017/s0020743800062097

Simon, Ralph. "Speech at Rally for Israel, Washington DC, May 30th 1967," (archival document), American Jewish Historical Society, Near East Crisis Collection, AJHS, I-18 Box 5.

Stork, Joe, and Sharon Rose. "Zionism and American Jewry." *Journal of Palestine Studies* 3, no.3 (1974): 39–57. doi:10.1525/jps.1974.3.3.00p0197x

Tilly, Charles. *Identities, boundaries, and social ties.* Boulder, Colo.: Paradigm Publ., 2009.

Todd, Jennifer. "Social transformation, collective categories, and identity change." *Theory and Society* 34, no. 4 (2005): 429–63.

Wolf, Joan B. "'Anne Frank is dead, long live Anne Frank': The Six-Day War and the Holocaust in French Public Discourse." *History & Memory* 11, no. 1 (1999): 104–40.

Yablonka, Hanna, *The State of Israel vs. Adolf Eichmann.* New York, NY: Schocken Books, 2004: 223–24.

Young, James E., "When a Day Remembers: a Performative History of Yom hashoah," *History and Memory,* 2 (1990): 54–75.

Zandberg, Eyal. "Critical laughter: humor, popular culture and Israeli Holocaust commemoration." *Media Culture and Society* 28, no. 4 (2006): 561–79.

Zeitz, Joshua Michael. "'If I am not for myself . . .': The American Jewish Establishment in the Aftermath of the Six Day War." *American Jewish History* 88, no. 2 (2000): 253–86.

Zertal, Idith. *Israel's Holocaust and the Politics of Nationhood.* Cambridge: Cambridge University Press, 2005.

Zertal, Idith and Akiva Eldar. *Lords of the Land: The War for Israel's Settlements in the Occupied Territories, 1967–2007.* New York, NY: Nation, 2007.

Zerubavel, Yael. *Recovered Roots: Collective Memory and the Making of Israeli National Tradition.* Chicago: University of Chicago, 1995.

Zerubavel, Yael. "The 'Mythological Sabra' and Jewish Past: Trauma, Memory and Contested Identities." *Israel Studies* 7, no. 2 (2002): 115–44.

Chapter Five

Historical Victimhood and the Israeli Collective Consciousness

Incongruous Legacies

Yechiel Klar[1]

In memory of Yonat Klar, my beloved spouse and life-long partner in an endeavor to understand the presence of the Holocaust in our lives.

Victimhood is indubitably a focal part of the Jewish historical legacy.[2] The notion that Jews have been destined for perpetual victimhood is ingrained, for example, in the extremely chilling verse from the Passover *Haggadah*, which is recited (in fact, sung) annually during the Passover festival (the *Seder*) in almost all Jewish homes throughout the world. It says: "*For not just one alone has risen against us to destroy us but in every generation, they rise against us to destroy us.*" The actuality of this verse, which is thought to have been composed around the fifth century, seems to be everlasting. It suggests both an unnerving summation of Jewish history and an equally unsettling prophetic vision of the Jewish future for generations to come. In this chapter I argue that this sense of historical victimhood carries with it several often contradictory legacies. The chapter travels through Jewish history, starting with the formative epopée of the enslavement and exodus from Egypt and the three victimhood and liberation legacies that emanated from these events and their effects on Jewish life throughout the generations. It discusses the Holocaust, being the most defining event in modern Jewish history, and it shows how the Holocaust evolved from what was considered a negation of Israeliness into one of the corner stones of the Israeli identity. The chapter then delineates the four existential and moral obligations that the Holocaust has imparted on Israeli reality and examines the relations between these post-

Holocaust obligations and the traditional Jewish legacies of victimhood. It then presents several empirical studies in the field of social psychology that have examined the relationship between two differing psychological orientations to historical victimhood (i.e., *perpetual ingroup victimhood* [PIVO], and *fear of victimizing* [FOV]) and two recent highly debated issues related to the treatment of the other that have divided Israeli opinion: policies toward the African asylum seekers and Israel's dealings with the Palestinians.

VICTIMIZATION AND THE EXODUS FROM EGYPT: THREE DIFFERENT LEGACIES AND THEIR REFLECTIONS IN JEWISH HISTORY

The Biblical story about the ancient Israelites' enslavement and oppression in Egypt and their flight (exodus) to the Sinai desert en route to the Land of Israel forms the core of Jewish (and later Israeli) collective memory and identity. It has also become an almost universal paradigm for any group (e.g., national, ethnic, religious, and social) seeking liberation from victimization; oppression, and exploitation.[3]

This is the story, in brief. After a severe famine in Canaan, the family of Jacob, one of the founding fathers of the Israelite nation, emigrates to Egypt, where unbeknownst to them, Joseph, Jacob's long-lost son, is the de-facto ruler (as the deputy to Pharaoh, the Egyptian king). Initially they are greeted very well, invited to settle in "the best of the land of Egypt" (Genesis, 45:18) but years later (as would often happen in Jewish history), a new Pharaoh "who did not know Joseph" (Exodus, 1:8) comes to power. The Israelites are then placed in oppressive slavery, and Pharaoh even decrees that all newborn Israelite boys should be murdered, which would completely annihilate the Israelite people. Moses and Aaron are sent by God to liberate the Israelites by leading them across the sea into the desert after the ten plagues are inflicted on the Egyptians and their armies are swallowed up by the waves. In the desert, God gives them the Torah (i.e., the Hebrew scriptures) and for forty years they wander until a new generation that had not been corrupted by slavery emerges while the older generation, the desert generation, perishes. Then, they are instructed by God to conquer the Canaanite tribes in the Land of Israel.

It might be argued that the choice of this enslavement narrative as the account of the birth of a nation is quite unusual. Yet this story of victimhood and redemption can be construed in three different ways, each of which have different and even contradictory lessons and obligations for future generations. In fact, these three incongruous construals are found in the Biblical text itself.

The Perpetual Victimhood Legacy: The Biblical Roots of the Perpetual Victimhood Legacy

One (rather pessimistic) legacy emanating from the victimization in Egypt and the Exodus story is to view it as simply the first chapter in a litany of Jewish oppression and persecution. Although Pharaoh and his army were drowned in the sea, an endless line of fearsome enemies were already prowling, ready to pounce. The first of these were the Amalekites, a nomadic tribe which viciously attacked the Israelites when they were in the desert. In response, God issued a commandment, effective not only for the contemporaneous Israelites but also for generations to come: "Remember what Amalek did to you along the way when you came out from Egypt, how he met you along the way and attacked among you all the stragglers at your rear when you were faint and weary; and he did not fear God" (Deut, 5:18). "Therefore it shall come about when the Lord your God has given you rest from all your surrounding enemies, in the land which the Lord your God gives you as an inheritance to possess, you shall blot out the memory of Amalek from under heaven; you must not forget" (Deut, 25:19). In Jewish lore, Amalek became the incarnation of all the future enemies of the Jewish people throughout the generations. Annually, for more than two thousand years on the Sabbath before the festival of Purim, in which the Jewish victory over their enemy Haman in ancient Persia is celebrated (Haman is considered to be a descendent of the Amalekites), Jews are commanded to recite these blotting out the memory of Amalek verses in public and that particular Sabbath is known as the Sabbath of remembrance (*Shabbat Zechor*). Thus, the overriding concern reflected in this reading is protecting the safety of the ingroup against its existential (and eternal) enemies. Thus, Pharaoh simply became one figure in a long line of historical enemies.

Perpetual Victimhood Legacy: Its Impact on Jewish History

For most of their existence, Jews could only envisage freedom as a future utopia. During the festival of Passover that commemorates the Exodus, they recite hopefully every year: "This year we are slaves; next year we will be free people." However, the real hope for freedom and redemption, as rooted in the traditional Jewish framework, concerns a future Messianic era when Jewish misery (diaspora life and subjugation) will come to an end. Tragically, Jewish history with its short-lived stretches of independence or relatively unbothered community life can be portrayed as a series of calamities with some brief moments of independence and autonomy. These catastrophes include the destruction of the first Jewish temple in Jerusalem by the Babylonians and the exile to Babylonia (in 586 BCE) which was preceded by the captivity, exile and disappearance from history of the ten Israelites tribe in

Assyria. Later, in the aftermath of the destruction of the second temple in Jerusalem by the Romans (70 CE), roughly one million Jews revolted in Judea which further thinned the Jewish holdings in their land. Countless Jews perished, and tens of thousands went to exile. The Jews who were now dispersed in the diaspora experienced various forms of persecution throughout the centuries, including expulsions, forced conversions, religious discrimination, offensive and restrictive decrees and accusations (e.g., blood libels), harassment, and the destruction of entire communities. The massacres and other attacks on Jews in Germany and France during the Crusades, the expulsion of the entire Jewish community from Spain in 1492 and later from Portugal as well as the pogroms in nineteenth- and twentieth-century Russia, culminated in the Holocaust during WWII, when the Germans aimed to exterminate the entire Jewish people to the furthermost reaches of the Reich. In most Jewish eyes, Jewish existence has always been under constant major threat.

In depicting their survival strategy against these persistent adversities, Jews have traditionally adopted the ninth-century phrase that the Jewish people can be likened to "a solitary sheep surrounded by seventy wolves" (Midrash Tanhuma, 5, 10:11). This is because the Jewish predicament as a people among the gentile nations of the world is fragile and torn (and will always be until the coming of Messiah) and because the gentile nations' hatred of the Jews is ingrown and therefore permanent. This is simply because "Esau hates Jacob."[4] Thus, sitting around the Passover table, in the relative safety of their homes, Jews could only pray to God to take revenge upon the gentiles: "Pour out Your wrath upon those who do not know You and upon the governments which do not call upon Your Name. . . . Pour out Your fury upon them; let the fierceness of Your anger overtake them. . . . Pursue them in indignation and destroy them from under Your heavens." However, starting in the third century, the Jewish religious leadership developed a highly cautious and docile survival strategy that consisted of never antagonizing, rebelling or resisting the host gentile nations among whom they resided. This attitude was maintained by the Jewish Rabbinical leadership up to the twentieth century.[5] As late as 1978 in the independent State of Israel, Rabbi Eliezer Schach, the leading ultra-Orthodox figure of the time, wrote to then–Prime Minister Menachem Begin, warning him against taking overly hard-line positions in the peace negotiations with Egypt (under US auspices). Rabbi Schach wrote that the sages of the Talmud "thanks to divine inspiration, knew that the nations' hatred for the nation of Israel is an eternal, permanent hatred" and that the sages of the Talmud "forbade us to rebel against the nations of the world and storm the wall, because they sought the welfare of our people. [The gentiles] should not be provoked even if justice is on our side, because this will pile hatred on top of hatred."[6]

However, the belief in the perpetual hatred of the Jews by the gentile nations of the world should not in itself necessarily lead to such passive or docile strategy. The traditional Jewish response of never antagonizing or standing up to the gentile nations is reflected the assumption that Jews as a collective are weak and defenseless. However, in other situations, the belief in the overriding external hatred of the ingroup led to much more proactive and even militant reactions.

The Separateness Legacy: The Biblical Roots of the Separateness Legacy

While in the desert, preparing to enter Canaan (soon to be termed the *Land of Israel*), the Israelites were given a series of strict orders concerning the fate of the idolatrous seven Canaanite nations, the current inhabitants of the land: "and when the Lord your God has delivered them over to you and you have defeated them, then you must destroy them totally. Make no treaty with them, and show them no mercy" (Deut, 7:2). The reason for this harsh injunction differs considerably from the commandment to wage eternal war against the Amalekites. In fact, the Canaanites did nothing wrong to the Israelites to deserve such a stark fate. What motivates this injunction is the fear that the Israelites would be affected by their Canaanite neighbors and would imitate their idolatrous religious customs: "They shall not dwell in thy land, lest they make thee sin against me; for if thou serve their gods, it will surely be a snare unto thee" (Exodus, 23:33). To ensure the separateness of the Israelites and to keep their religious integrity uncorrupted by the current idolatrous inhabitants of the land, the most inhuman solution is prescribed; namely, "clearing" the land from the religiously inferior people. The book of Joshua provides a depiction of the swift campaign in which the Israelites (led by Joshua Bin Nun) conquered the land while exterminating the Canaanite nations.

Did the Israelites perpetrate the merciless genocide of the Canaanite tribes just forty years after their liberation from slavery and near-annihilation in Egypt? The historical validity of the "conquest of the land" story is highly questionable.[7] However, regardless of the historical reality of these stories, the harsh and merciless stipulations to totally destroy the Canaanites were part of the sanctified Torah commandments. Moreover, the Israelites were explicitly instructed to keep their distinction, and not to follow the gentile customs (e.g., "Do not follow the ways of Egypt where you once lived, nor of Canaan to where I am bringing you. Do not follow their customs"; Leviticus, 18:1–3). Thus, spiritual, social, and physical separation from the gentiles became major part of Jewish theology and practice.

The Separateness Legacy: Its Impact on Jewish History

For ordinary Jews living in the diaspora as powerless and persecuted minorities, and sometimes as aliens under the protection of local rulers, there was nothing more detached from their tangible reality than the hypothetical discussions of whether or not the Canaanites and idolatrous gentiles would be permitted to enter the Land of Israel after their own return to the land. This was mainly a matter of debate for Halachic scholars. For example, when relating to the passage from Exodus that "They shall not dwell in thy land," the Rambam (Maimonides, 1125–1204), one of the most influential Jewish figures in medieval Judaism, made a sharp distinction between present times "when Israel is exiled among the nations" and the future Messianic era when "Israel has the stronger hand." As for the present (or "normal") time, he instructed the Jews to show compassion and kindness to non-Jews living in in the Land of Israel, such as to let them collect the leftover crops from the field and even to greet them in peace (although not excessively so) on their holidays. However, in Messianic days idolatrous gentiles will not be allowed to reside or stay in the land, even temporarily, so not to religiously and morally corrupt the Jews.[8]

More broadly, however, being distinct and separate on almost all spiritual, social and physical dimensions from the gentiles became one of the tenets of Jewish life. A myriad of rules and practices governing daily life were devised for this purpose. For example, Jews were prohibited from eating bread baked by a non-Jew, food cooked by a non-Jew, or drinking wine made by a non-Jew and they were encouraged not to live in the same area as non-Jews. Apart from kosher concerns reflected in these prohibitions, the explicit goal of these injunctions was to minimize intermingling with non-Jews which could eventually lead to intermarriage.[9]

The notion of separateness from the gentiles (as an essential prerequisite for the survival of the Jewish faith and Jewish people) was extended by some Jewish schools of thoughts to mean inherent supremacist separateness. One of its prime exponents, the medieval Jewish poet and philosopher Rabbi Yehuda HaLevi, 1075–1141, argued in his book *The Kuzari* that the whole purpose of the creation of the world was to preserve and study the Torah. The Jewish people were inherently chosen to be the guardians and students of the Torah, and therefore are entitled to a preferential position in the world over all other peoples.[10] In the early twentieth century, the highly influential Rabbi Abraham Hakohen Kook wrote that:

> The difference between the Jewish soul, in all its independence, inner desires, longings, character and standing, and the soul of all the Gentiles, on all of their levels, is greater and deeper than the difference between the soul of a man and the soul of an animal, for the difference in the latter case is one of quantity, while the difference in the first case is one of essential quality.[11]

Given all the difficulties inherent to these uneasy distinctions, it is worth noting that most of them were put forward when the Jews in the Diaspora were routinely vilified, humiliated and victimized. Thus, this notion of "spiritual superiority" can be seen as a form of symbolic compensation for their victimization. The real issue in contemporary terms is what happens to these supremacist approaches when the protagonists themselves in positions of power and control over others.

The Caring for the Oppressed "Strangers" Legacy: The Biblical Roots of the Caring for the Oppressed "Strangers" Legacy

A quite different (and clearly more optimistic) reading of the Biblical story of Egyptian victimization and Exodus is to see it as a story of transition from slavery in "the house of bondage" to freedom, and from affliction and misery to affluence and happiness. In this spirit, Moses promises the newly liberated Israelites that they will prosper and be blessed in their new, promised land: "There also you and your households shall eat before the Lord your God, and rejoice in all your undertakings in which the Lord your God has blessed you" (Deut, 12:7). Redemption can be defined as a particularistic experience benefiting only the liberated slaves. However, the message for the newly liberated slaves does not end there. The wandering Israelites in the desert are ordered time and again to remember their past victimization: "You shall remember that you were a slave in the land of Egypt" (Deut, 15:5), and this commandment to *remember* is always provided with a specific purpose, which is to acknowledge that as liberated people they have a solemn obligation to care for less fortunate others, and mainly those who are *not* their brothers. That is, liberation from victimhood also entails some universalistic responsibilities. This is stated time and again: "You shall not wrong a stranger or oppress him, for you were strangers in the land of Egypt" (Exodus, 22:21); "You shall not oppress a stranger, since you yourselves know the feelings of a stranger, for you also were strangers in the land of Egypt" (Exodus, 23:9); "So show your love for the alien, for you were aliens in the land of Egypt" (Deut, 10:19); "The stranger who resides with you shall be to you as the native among you, and you shall love him as yourself, for you were aliens in the land of Egypt; I am the Lord your God" (Leviticus, 19:34). The ban against vindictive and hateful acts is even extended to the Israelites' past victimizers, the Egyptians: "you shall not detest an Egyptian, because you were an alien in his land" (Deut, 23:7). Thus, liberation from victimhood should bring with it, according to these Biblical stipulations, a special understanding of the pain and misery of the others, even those they have good reasons to resent. [12]

The Caring for the Oppressed "Stranger" Legacy: Its Impact on Jewish History

Throughout most of their diaspora existence, when Jews lived in segregated (and often despised, and frightened) communities, the primary value of Jewish life was caring for the welfare of other members of the Jewish community (and sometimes also for other Jewish communities), which was termed *ahavat Yisrael*.[13] However, when during the nineteenth and twentieth centuries, while some of this isolation had waned, many European (and later north American) Jews became actively involved in socialist movements, whose missions were universal solidarity and caring for the poor, the exploited and those deprived of their rights (e.g., the proletariat), regardless of their group affiliation. Traditional Jewish values, such as caring for the oppressed were a major underlying force in their mobilization.[14] Another late-nineteenth-century Jewish faction ideal was the Zionist movement,[15] which defined itself as a national liberation movement that aimed to distance itself from the traditional views of the Jewish fate as insular and entangled with perpetual victimhood. The Zionists redefined the Exodus as a transition from victimhood to liberation and normalization, "to be a free nation in our land" (as expressed in Hatikva, the national anthem) or to accomplish: "the natural right of the Jewish people to be masters of their own fate, like all other nations, in their own sovereign State" (from the Israeli Declaration of Independence). Many Zionists detested what they perceived as the victimhood-saturated diaspora mentality. For example, in a short but highly influential literary work by writer Haim Hazaz, titled "The Sermon" (Hadrasha) published in 1942, Yudke, the protagonist, attacks the Jewish tendency to passively and timidly accept calamities without adopting a more proactive approach. In fact, many of the first generations of Zionists viewed themselves as "new Jews," as the descendants of the heroic King David, and the heirs of the fearless Maccabees, rather than the sons and daughters of the Diaspora Jews, who were likened to the "desert generation" in Exodus.[16]

The yearning for national normalization was associated with the drive to view Jewish liberation in a broader, open, and more universalistic framework. Theodore Herzl, the founder of the Zionist movement, saw Zionism as part of a more progressive ideology that would not only provide a solution to the "Jewish problem," but also create a model for resolving social problems and improving the lot of other disadvantaged groups.[17] Similarly, the Socialist streams in the Zionist movement argued that the movement should be a part of the global struggle for liberation of the proletariat and other subjugated groups internationally and express its solidarity with other underprivileged, browbeaten, and suffering groups.[18]

For David Ben-Gurion, the leading Zionist statesman, Jewish national redemption should be accompanied by an equally important mission to become "a people of virtue" (*Am Segula*) or a "light unto the nations" (Isaiah, 42:6). In a letter written after the 1967 war to Charles de Gaulle in response to hostile remarks made by the French president, Ben-Gurion referred at length to the universalistic interpretation of the Exodus story: "We are of course proud of the fact that the 'Love thy neighbor as thyself' was said for the first time in our Bible, and that it is followed by the words: 'And if a stranger sojourn with thee in your land, ye shall not vex him. But the stranger that dwelleth with you shall be unto you as one born among you, and thou shalt love him as thyself; for ye were strangers in the land of Egypt; I am the Lord your God' (Leviticus, 19: 33–34). Such a law did not exist even in the Athens of Pericles, Socrates and Plato."[19]

Apart from the Zionist movement, in North American Jewry, mainly among reform and conservative, denominations *Tikkun Olam* ("restoration of the world") is a major value, which refers to bearing responsibility for the welfare of society as a whole, or even the world in general, for groups that are persecuted, wronged, discriminated against, or marginalized.[20]

The Three Legacies: Conclusion

Three different historical legacies can be said to have emerged from the Jewish narrative of their victimization in Egypt and their liberation from it. The first two legacies, perpetual victimhood and supremacist separateness, are group-centered (i.e., particularistic). They are focused on the protection of the group and its unique identity from non-Jewish "others." They entail two commitments for Jewish people. The first is to continuously be on the alert for lurking [gentile] enemies, and to always remain adamantly separate and distinct from the [sinful and morally inferior] gentiles. The third legacy, caring for oppressed strangers, is more universalistic and other-oriented. The commitment it entails is to be kind and empathic to others who are victims or currently suffering, even if they are not one's brethren. These legacies have been transmitted throughout the thousands of years of Jewish history, albeit in varying intensities in different Jewish schools of thought and at different historical periods. To weigh the influence of these three incompatible orientations on contemporary Jews and Israelis, we must first pause to ponder the Holocaust, which is the most defining event in modern Jewish history, and consider its effects on current Israelis and their awareness of victimhood. Has the Holocaust, which is unmatched in its scope and totality with any previous event in Jewish history, changed or instead reinforced the traditional conceptions and legacies of Jewish victimhood and liberation? Before turning to this issue, we need to briefly consider the evolution of the Holocaust consciousness in the Israeli collective mindset, from the antithesis of the Israeli essence to a major component of its core identity.

THE HOLOCAUST: FROM "WHAT ISRAELINESS IS NOT" TO "WHAT ISRAELINESS IS ALL ABOUT"

From the end of WWII until 1949, the first year of the new State, Israel absorbed about 350,000 Holocaust survivors. One out of every three Israelis was a Holocaust survivor at that time.[21] Nevertheless, over the course of this decade and a half, the role of the Holocaust in Israeli public consciousness was relatively marginal. The Holocaust at that time was not the defining feature of the Israeli collective identity. Veteran Israelis (those who had immigrated prior to WWII, or were born there) "knew and did not know about the Holocaust; ached and did not ache given the disaster."[22] This emotional divide existed despite the fact that most of these long term or native Israelis came from exactly the same countries and communities as the survivors, most of them had lost their families there, and many had relatives, friends and acquaintances among the survivors who managed to reach Israel.[23] Such unresponsiveness, or even what might be viewed as apathy toward the Holocaust and its survivors, was not unique to Israel, also characterized American Jewry[24] and in fact all the European countries where the Holocaust took place.[25]

Perhaps more striking was the condescending and even contemptuous attitude of long-term Israelis toward the survivors. The survivors were held accountable on three points: they had not been Zionist enough (or proactive enough) to move to Palestine when this was still possible; they (except for the scores of ghetto fighters and partisans) behaved like passive diaspora Jews; and thirdly, rather than facing their enemies with arms (which in fact they did not have), they went collectively to their death like "sheep to the slaughter". Had the Israelis, as the sons and daughters of the Maccabees, been in such situation, they surely would have fought the Germans.[26] An additional point, which was even more demeaning, and constituted an implicit sword of Damocles was "How/Why did you survive?" The hidden, ill-informed and erroneous assumption was that those who survived were selfish and unscrupulous or had even collaborated with the Nazis.[27]

However, this initial view that the Holocaust served mainly as the counterpoint to "real" Israeli-ness, gradually turned into a richer and more complex view, which embraced the Holocaust as an integral part of the Israeli identity. The Eichmann trial in 1961 is generally considered the major turning point.[28] For most of the Israeli public of the time, this was their first opportunity to be exposed in an emphatic and non-judgmental way to the personal stories of myriads of Holocaust survivors. More than one hundred appeared as witnesses during this trial, which became a form of "national group therapy" for the Israeli public.[29] Holocaust survivors in Israel have also taken an active role in preserving the memory of the Holocaust. They have been the impetus for museums, memorials, and active educational programs in Israel and abroad.[30] Survivors lecture frequently in schools in Israel and in other countries as the remaining "witnesses," whose own stories of the concentration camps are included in school curricula and during basic training.

The sons and daughters of the survivors, the "second generation" and their offspring (the "third generation") have become an important part of the Israeli social fabric. Many now transmit the Holocaust legacies and memories of their grandparents.[31] The impact of second- and third-generation authors, educators, and artists on public life is massive.[32] With their obvious native Israeli identity, they have contributed to the perception of the Holocaust as an integral part of Israeli life, as suggested by the title of the acclaimed Israeli novel *Our Holocaust.*[33]

The Six-Day War of 1967 and the Yom Kippur War in 1973 also transformed the Israeli view of the Holocaust.[34] The Six-Day War (which was a swift Israeli military triumph over its Arab neighbors) was preceded by weeks of mounting concerns, tensions, and anxiety in Israel, spurred by virulent Arab rhetoric to totally obliterate Israel, and intensified by doubts about Israeli leadership.[35] Anita Shapira noted "the sense of helplessness, of there being no way out, that had hitherto been identified only with the Holocaust and life in exile was seen now as being possible in the free Jewish state as well."[36]

Israel was unprepared for the Yom Kippur War, and initially the Israeli military supremacy appeared to waver, thus undermining the myth of the "invincible Israelis" and fueling the notion of the "feeble Jews of the Holocaust." Eighteen years later, in 1991, the Gulf War which opposed an international coalition led by the United States against Saddam Hussein's Iraq, in which Iraqi missiles were launched at Israeli cities, again prompted real concerns about Israel's vulnerable geopolitical predicament. Israelis were all equipped with gas masks and antidotes for nerve gas, which made the association with the Holocaust almost inescapable.[37] There were also reports that Iraq had purchased German military equipment, including deadly chemicals. Media depictions of Israelis fleeing Tel Aviv for the countryside and the comparison with the calm demeanor of Holocaust survivors faced with this new existential threat negated and further banished the previous images of fearful Holocaust Jews and brave new Israelis.[38]

More recently, the Iranian nuclear program, accompanied by routine threats by Iran's leadership to eliminate Israel, has prompted the ghastly term of the "second Holocaust", which now appears frequently in the media and in private conversations.[39] In 2006, Israeli prime minister to be Benjamin Netanyahu declared that "It's 1938 and Iran is Germany. And Iran is racing to arm itself with atomic bombs. . . . While the Iranian president denies the Holocaust, he is preparing another Holocaust for the Jewish state." Such statements connecting Iran and the Holocaust have often been repeated by the prime minister over the years.[40] In an off-hand remark, Prime Minister Netanyahu commented, during a 2017 closed Bible study session in his home that the Hasmonean kingdom [the last Jewish sovereign kingdom that lasted from 140 BCE to 63 BCE] survived for only around eighty years, and that he was working to make sure that modern Israel would surpass that point to reach the century mark.[41] As early as 1989, *New York Times* columnist Thomas Friedman, a shrewd observer of Israel, noted this aura of pessimism bordering on existential anxiety[42] and commented that Israel is becoming Yad Vashem with an air force.[43]

Thus, in the first decades of the Israeli State, the Holocaust was distanced and relegated to something that had happened "there" (in the Diaspora) to "them" (the Diaspora Jews), which has little relevance to "our (Israeli) reality", and can serve mainly as the direct opposite of the Israeli reality and essence.[44]

Gradually, however, the Holocaust has undergone a process of internalization (or perhaps "Israelification") and it has become an integral part of the Israeli core identity. It is possible, that the "second Holocaust" discourse that has grown stronger over time (paradoxically along with increased Israeli military and economic capacities) is part of this internalization process and can account for the greater role of the Holocaust in the public (and private) mindsets. However, it is noteworthy that the Holocaust is present not only when security and survival considerations are at stake. It is present in a wide range of issues facing Israeli society. It is manifested in conjunction with the three traditional victimhood and liberation legacies discussed earlier (i.e., perpetual victimhood, supremacist separateness, and care for oppressed strangers). These legacies have been translated into several moral and existential obligations, which just like the traditional legacies are mutually contradictory.

CONFLICTING MORAL OBLIGATIONS IN POST-HOLOCAUST ISRAEL

In his 2002 book *Rethinking the Holocaust*, historian Yehuda Bauer suggested that after the Holocaust, three commandments should be added to the original Ten Biblical commandments: *"Thou shalt not be a victim, thou shalt not be a perpetrator, but, above all, thou shalt not be a bystander."*[45] Inspired by this proposal, Klar, Schori-Eyal, and Yonat Klar (2013), and Klar (2016) defined four moral obligations that characterize members of historically victimized groups. They are: never be a passive victim; never forsake your brothers; never be a passive bystander; and never be a perpetrator. These moral directives, which range from exclusive concern for the security of the ingroup even at the expense of outgroups, to the protection and correct treatment of ingroup enemies even at the expense of the ingroup's security and well-being, are sometimes clearly at odds with each other. These four moral obligations are unequal in their prominence and prevalence. Klar (2016) suggested that they can be described as the four arms of a foldable fan (see Figure 1). This fan can be completely folded (i.e., only the first obligation to never be a passive victim is operative), or it can be spread open to include additional obligations. Thus, the four obligations are unequal in their dominance, prevalence and intensity, as will be discussed more fully later, and can be ordered from the most prevalent and dominant (the first obligation) to the least common and effective (the fourth obligation). The four moral obligations and the foldable fan image can be helpful in depicting some of the major concerns and dilemmas facing post-Holocaust Israeli society.

The First Obligation: Never Be a Passive Victim Again

For most Israelis, the Holocaust serves as the primary depiction of the existential predicament of Jews (and Israelis) in the world.[46] The Nazis and their accomplices were actively engaged in activities designed to entirely annihilate the Jews. Many other nations were apathetic bystanders and the Jews themselves were frail and defenseless during these dark times. The inevitable conclusion is that in order to survive, Israel must have enormous might and be ready to deploy it when needed. Prime Minister Benjamin Netanyahu is probably one of the most eloquent and persistent proponents of this orientation. For example, during his annual Holocaust Remembrance Day speech in 2017, Netanyahu told the audience that the Holocaust was the product of the terrible hatred for the Jewish people, the international indifference to the plight of the Jews while the horrors were taking place and "the terrible weakness of our people in the Diaspora." His conclusion was: "The strong survive, the weak are wiped out . . . our people learned this in the Holocaust. The lesson taught by this terrible time, is in front of our eyes at all times. The lesson is that we must be able to defend ourselves, by ourselves, against any threat, against any enemy."[47]

This lesson constituted one of the pillars of the Israeli national security policy as developed and implemented by David Ben-Gurion. The key assumption was that Israel should always be prepared for the worst and rely solely on itself.[48] This Holocaust-based lesson was behind Ben-Gurion's persistent determination to develop Israel's nuclear capabilities[49] and Prime Minister Menachem Begin's decision in 1980 to destroy the Iraqi nuclear reactor.[50] In sharing his thoughts with one of his closest aides, Begin cited the Holocaust as a major consideration:

To his cabinet secretary, Begin remarked, referring to traditional Jewish names given to children in the shtetls of his native Poland, that he had seen

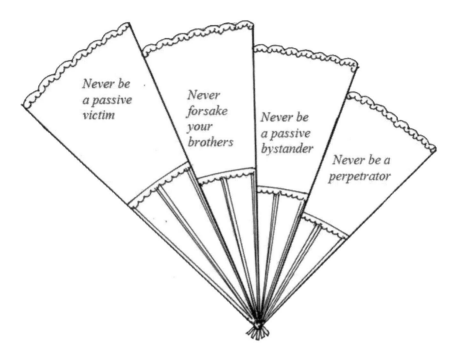

Figure 5.1.   The Klar (2016) model: The four moral obligations as a foldable fan Originally appeared in: Klar, Y. "Four Moral Obligations in the Aftermath of Historical Ingroup Victimization." *Current Opinion in Psychology* **58, 11 (2016): 54–58.**

some children playing and had said to himself, "We will never allow that contemptible villain to do to our Shloimelach [Solomon in Yiddish] and Surelach [Sarah in Yiddish] what was done to them then."[51]

Since 2001, the Israeli army (IDF) has sent thousands of army officers to visit the death camps in Poland as part of a program titled "Witnesses in Uniform." These trips (which also include Holocaust survivors and members of bereaved families from Israeli wars[52]) reflects a basic duality. On one hand, Israeli army personnel marching in their uniforms "above the death pits, beneath the flag"[53] are living proof of the sharp contrast between the anguish and humiliation of the silent victims whose ashes are buried there and the strength and pride of Israeli soldiers. On the other hand, the soldier-witnesses symbolically become one with the victims and are inculcated with the feeling that they are survivors themselves (several months after the trip, the participants are awarded the distinction of "ambassadors of the Holocaust victims"[54]). The overriding message is of continuity and justification for the actions of the State and the necessity of the army to act as a shield against another total extermination.

A related feature is the recurrent equation of Arab enemies with the Nazis. As noted by Zertal,[55] as early as 1947, David Ben-Gurion in a closed leadership meeting told his audience that in the approaching war they would be confronted by the "students and mentors of Hitler," and later in 1951 he declared that "we do not want to go back to the Ghetto . . . we do not want to be slaughtered by the Nazi-Arabs." More than thirty years later, Menachem Begin told the Israeli government that the alternative to the impending invasion of Lebanon was Treblinka and equated Yasser Arafat in Beirut to Hitler in his Berlin HQ bunker.[56] In 2005, More than thirty years later, Prime Minister Benjamin Netanyahu declared that "the Palestinian Mufti of Jerusalem, Haj Amin al-Husseini, was the one who instilled the idea of the extermination of the Jews in Europe in Adolf Hitler's mind, who otherwise had no intention of killing the Jews, but only to expel them." Thus, the Palestinian Mufti, according to this remark, was "one of the leading architects" of the "final solution" for the Jews.[57]

The Second Obligation: Never Forsake Your Brothers

For many Israelis, one of the haunting questions left unanswered after the Holocaust was whether or not they had done everything they could have done to save their brethren, or whether they were attentive enough to their fate when they were led to the gas chambers[58]: were they "my brother's keeper?" (Genesis 4:9). These questions continued to resonate as late as 1992, in the remarks of then chief of staff (later prime minister) Ehud Barak, when he headed an Israeli delegation to the Auschwitz death camp: "We, the soldiers of the Israeli Defense Forces, have come to this place fifty years later, perhaps fifty years too late." Eleven years later, in 2003, the Israel Air force conducted a ceremonial flyover of Auschwitz. The formation leader Brig.-Gen. Amir Eshel (later IAF Commander) read out the following radio message: "We, the pilots of the Air Force, flying in the skies above the camp of horrors, arose from the ashes of the millions of victims and shoulder their silent cries . . . promise to be the shield of the Jewish people and its nation Israel."[59]

These statements may reflect the belief (which is probably unfounded historically) that had the State of Israel existed with an army at the time of the Holocaust, it could have averted the Holocaust or stopped it. They also reflect a second consensual "never again" conviction and obligation that Israel is and must always be the protective shield for all the Jews in the world. The nascent state (with about 650,000 Jewish citizens) that was immediately mired in war and poverty took in almost 700,000 Jewish immigrants in its first three years. Indeed, this immigration was essential for its survival as a Jewish State, but this massive and accelerated effort was depicted as a rescue operation where entire communities were sometimes airlifted to Israel in military-like operations (e.g., from Yemen and Iran in the 1950s and from Ethiopia in the 1990s). The 1950 Israeli Law of Return, which states that "Every Jew has the right to come to this country as an *ole"* (i.e., Jew immigrating to Israel), provided the symbolic egis and unquestionable rationale. Every Jew and any Jewish community in jeopardy can rely on the State of Israel as a shelter and a home.

The "my brother's keeper" obligation is sometimes translated (mainly among Orthodox circles) into poignant lamentations and fervent condemnations of cultural assimilation and marriages to non-Jews mainly in Diaspora communities. This is repeatedly called "The Silent Holocaust" (referring to the ostensible decline in the population of the Jewish people due to such intermarriages), and this is frequently termed as something which is "worse than the Holocaust."[60] Some even connect "the quiet disappearance of tens of thousands of our people each year" of the young diaspora Jews to the distancing of the Holocaust "as a nucleus of their formative identity" among those young.[61]

The Third Moral Obligation: Never Be a Passive Bystander

One of the most powerful legacies of the Holocaust for Israelis is the moral outrage and contempt for bystander countries and nations who failed to help the Jews when they could or refused to provide them passage to avoid their fate.[62] A question that arises from this condemnation is how Israelis would have behaved if they had been in the shoes of these nations. From its inception, Israel has repeatedly tried to prove to others and to itself that it has higher humanitarian ideals than other countries.[63] In the 1960s, Israel prided itself on the aid and expertise it provided to dozens of new African and Asian countries. For example, Israeli International Squadron 120 was founded in 1964 as the long arm of Israel's foreign policy and excels in international humanitarian aid and rescue efforts mainly in Africa. As noted, many of its founders and crew members were Holocaust survivors.[64]

Israelis also feel great pride in the fact that whenever there is some natural disaster anywhere around the world (e.g., earthquakes, tsunamis typhoons, floods, massive fires), or other humanitarian catastrophes, airborne Israeli aid delegations, composed mainly of the Israeli military, are always among the first and the most efficient forces to provide help, which is often disproportional to Israel's size and economic resources. The lessons of the Holocaust are habitually referred to as the underlying impetus behind this rapid humanitarian mobilization. In June 1977, an Israeli merchant fleet saved from the sea sixty-six Vietnamese refugees whose boat sank off the coast of Vietnam. The first decision of the new Israeli PM, Menachem Begin, whose government had just been sworn in was to grant these refugees Israeli citizenship: "The people of Israel who knew persecution and knew, perhaps more than any other people, the meaning of the term refugee, could not see the suffering of these unfortunate people," PM Begin declared.[65]

However, such humanitarian commitments have become blurred, in particular recently, when the refugees and asylum seekers issue has become much more than merely an opportunity for a symbolic gesture.

Starting in 2006, tens of thousands of asylum seekers mainly from Eritrea and Sudan reached the border of Israel with Egypt. Both Eritrea and Sudan are infamous for their harsh military regimes and severe human rights violations. In Eritrea, men face compulsory military service that can last for forty years. In Sudan there has been famine and genocide in Darfur as well as fighting between Sudan and South Sudan. The UN Commission for Refugees (UNHCR) stated officially that refugees fleeing Eritrea and Sudan are in jeopardy and should not be sent back to their home countries. The route to Israel runs through Egypt and the Sinai, where many refugees are exposed to abuse, torture, robbery, rape and even murders by their smugglers. Until 2014, the border between the Sinai (i.e., Egypt) and Israel was porous, and refugees reaching Israeli soil were sent by bus after a brief inquiry to the Tel Aviv central bus station, where most of them found places to live in the poor neighborhoods of south Tel Aviv. In 2014, Israel completed the construction of a fence along the border with Sinai, which brought an end for all extents and purposes to the influx of African asylum seekers to Israel.

Those who had already come to Israel (about 39,000 of whom 26,000 are from Eritrea, 7,500 are from Sudan, and the roughly 5,000 children born to them in Israel) found themselves in a limbo. Israel, as a signatory to the 1951 UN Refugee Convention, complied with its obligation not to deport them back to their countries, but at the same time has neglected its duty to examine their right to refugee status. Out of the thousands who have applied for asylum, Israel has recognized only eleven Eritreans and one Sudanese (an acceptance rate of 0.056 percent). In the EU by comparison, 90 percent of the Eritrean applicants and 56 percent of the Sudanese have been granted refugee status. Instead, the State encourages African asylum seekers to go to a third African country (Uganda or Rwanda) or to return to their homelands. To pressure them to do so, the State has established a detention facility and a jail near the Sinai border, where several thousand the asylum seekers are detained.

Terms such as "refugees" or "asylum seekers" were rejected by the spokespersons of the State (and subsequently by some of the media), because they were so reminiscent of the fate of the Jews during the Holocaust. Instead, governmental spokespersons, who were subsequently followed by much of the media, began using the term "infiltrators" to describe these Africans.[66] In early 2017, the Knesset passed an amendment to the "Prevention of Infiltration Law" aimed at African asylum seekers. Prime Minister Netanyahu declared (in January 2018): "We are not taking action against refugees. We are taking action against illegal immigrants who come here for work purposes. Israel will continue to be a shelter for true refugees and will expel illegal infiltrators."[67]

In the aftermath of his televised September 2017 tour of south Tel Aviv, after conveying his disgust with the "filth and stench" he found there, Netanyahu declared: "We have the right to expel everyone who is here illegally." Subsequently, the governmental issued an expulsion plan. This time, strong-worded comparisons with measures taken against the Jews during the Holocaust appeared immediately in the Israeli press. Within several days a plethora of vehement petitions protesting the planned deportation overwhelmed the public arena. Each had hundreds (and in some cases also thousands) of signatories. These included academic staff, writers and artists, musicians, choreographers, psychologists, social workers, nurses, physicians (who also protested the fact that the head of the government office in charge of deportation is a physician), diplomats and former ambassadors, residents of Tel Aviv, school principals and students, and others. Particularly poignant was an open letter sent by dozens of Holocaust survivors (all over eighty) to the prime minister. They wrote: "As Jews, the world turned its back on us in our most difficult time, we have a special obligation not to remain indifferent and to prevent the expulsion of asylum seekers, the state must grant them a haven and not send them to their deaths in a foreign country."[68] Journalist Gideon Levi called on Israeli pilots to refuse to fly expelled asylum seekers. He drew a parallel with German pilots who refused to fly Afghan asylum-seekers back to their homeland.[69] Thousands of Israelis associated themselves with this call and subsequently dozens of airline crew members including pilots announced their refusal to forcibly fly asylum seekers out of the country. Other evocative initiatives, first spontaneously and later in a more coordinated fashion, were pledges by several thousand families around the country (including Holocaust survivors and their descendants) to host (and sometimes also to hide) African asylum seekers under threat of expulsion. One such concealment initiative which was announced by a group of rabbis working for human rights, was called "The Anne Frank Home Sanctuary Movement."[70] The association with the fate of the Jews during the holocaust could not be clearer.

These diverse and high-profile efforts all emerged almost simultaneously, and may give the impression that the entire Israeli public has rallied against the government's expulsion plans. But this picture is far from true: the protest, as described here, mainly reflected liberal circles in the Israeli public, and was greeted with indifference and sometimes hostility among other segments of the public. A poll conducted for a national TV channel in January 2018 (during the height of the protest activities) found that 56 percent of respondents supported the government's decision to deport African migrants, 32 percent opposed, and 12 percent had no opinion. Of those who favored deportation, 44 percent were even in favor of forcibly removing the migrants, while 46 percent opposed forced expulsion.[71]

The Fourth Moral Obligation: Never Be a Perpetrator

The fourth moral obligation deriving from the Holocaust is not to harm others, even rivals or enemies. Thus, victims must not "do unto others what they do not want others to do unto them."[72] This moral obligation takes on critical significance within the context of the Israeli-Palestinian conflict. Although many Israelis consider Israeli conflict-related actions to be a form of legitimate self-defense, others are more critical of Israel's role. Clearly, condemning one's own group or expressing guilt is difficult,[73] but this has been shown to be even more so when the group's past victimization history (such as the Holocaust) is made salient.[74] However, it is worth inquiring whether reminders of the Holocaust can make people less inclined to support Israeli transgressions. A letter written to the *Ha'aretz* newspaper on the seventieth anniversary of the 1938 Kristallnacht, the first orchestrated attacks against Jews in Germany and Austria, said in part: "I was born in Berlin and was three years old when the rioting occurred on Kristallnacht. . . . For me, stories about Kristallnacht necessarily evoke the actions of the Israeli occupation army in the occupied territories."[75] Such statements, it should be acknowledged, are always controversial. In Israel, comparisons of Israel conduct with Nazi Germany continue to spark heated condemnation from the public and governmental agencies.[76]

However, studies on women's protest and human rights movements in Israel ("Women in Black" and "Machsom Watch") found that second generation women and even Holocaust survivors in their eighties were overrepresented in these activities. These women often stated that they took part out of fear of becoming passive bystanders "like the Germans."[77] A typical comment was that although it is impossible to compare the Holocaust to the situation in the occupied territories, "we would desecrate the memory of the Holocaust if we did not compare the processes leading to it."[78]

This particular Holocaust influence is also evident in protest activities of younger Israelis. One example is "Breaking the Silence" (*Shovrim Shtika*), a grassroots group of veteran Israeli soldiers "working to raise awareness about the daily reality in the occupied territories." Breaking the Silence (BtS) collects testimonials from veteran Israeli soldiers and reservists who served in the occupied territories (i.e., the West Bank and Gaza) and disseminates them in both Israel and abroad. Yehuda Shaul, one of the founders of this NGO, told about the army experiences that led him to found the group:

When we entered Hebron, we realized the settlers could do whatever they wanted, and no one would stop them. . . . There is a huge ideological gap between me and a person who can walk up to an Arab's door and spray paint the Star of David or write "Arabs out." The historical memory is unnerving. We all know what symbols did to Jews' storefronts and whose symbols those were. We all know the writing when "Arabs" is replaced with "Jews." We know this history.[79]

Another BtS founder, Noam Chayut, described an encounter with a young Palestinian girl in the city of Hebron (in the West Bank), where he served as an IDF soldier, as the turning point that led him to protest activities. The title of his book is *The Girl Who Stole My Holocaust*[80]:

She took from me the belief that absolute evil exists in this world, and the belief that I was avenging it and fighting against it. For that girl, I embodied absolute evil. . . . Since then I have been left without my Holocaust, and since then everything in my life has assumed a new meaning: belongingness is blurred, pride is lacking, belief is faltering, contrition is heightening, forgiveness is being born.[81]

This small BtS group is highly controversial in the Israeli public. On one hand, it won Israeli human rights awards, and several leading figures in the Israeli defense and security establishment have publicly supported BtS, stating that it "helps strengthen the IDF and its morality by providing transparency for military," and helps Israel to "maintain the required vigilance about the most sensitive human issues."[82] On the other hand, governmental officials have manifested continued hostility to the NGO. For example, in April 2017, Prime Minister Netanyahu cancelled a meeting with Germany's foreign minister, Sigmar Gabriel, after being notified that he had met with BtS people. One of the major allegations is that the NGO disseminates negative soldiers' testimonials and other disparaging materials abroad and hence it is "part of an advocacy campaign intended to harm Israel's image overseas."[83] Journalist Ariel Schnabel wrote that NGO's such as BtS:

help the Germans move one step further in their attempt to feel normal again after the atrocities they committed just a moment ago. . . . A German who gets a report—and more than that from a Jew—about Jews who supposedly commit atrocities against other people, cannot help but feel a little more comfortable with his problematic past.[84]

The lesson that in present-day Israel any reference, even the most remote, to twentieth-century European history, in tandem with any critical remark, even the most subtle, about Israeli moral quandaries might be problematical for the speaker, should have been anticipated by Major General Yair Golan, then the Deputy IDF Chief of Staff, who delivered the annual Holocaust

Remembrance Day speech in May 2016. Golan's remarks were made in the aftermath of several troubling events involving IDF soldiers.[85] He said:

> On Holocaust Remembrance Day, it is worthwhile to ponder our capacity to uproot the first signs of intolerance, violence, and self-destruction among us that arise on the path to moral decline. For all intents and purposes, Holocaust Remembrance Day is an opportunity for soul-searching. If Yom Kippur (Day of Atonement) is the day of individual soul-searching, then it is imperative that Holocaust Remembrance Day be a day of national soul-searching, and this national soul-searching should include phenomena that are disruptive.

He also said:

> The Holocaust, in my view, must bring us to deep reflections about the nature of human beings, even when these human beings are ourselves. It must bring us to deep reflections about the responsibility of leadership, and about the quality of the society, and it must lead us to a thorough thinking, about how we – here and now – treat the stranger, the orphan and the widow and those who are like them. It should lead us to think about our public life, and more-over, it must lead all those who can – and not only those who want – to bear public responsibility. Because if there is something that frightens me in the memory of the Holocaust, it is the identification of horrifying processes that took place in Europe and particularly in Germany 70, 80, and 90 years ago, and finding remnants of that here among us in the year 2016.

Maj. General Golan's plea to consider Holocaust Remembrance Day as a day of soul-searching about moral transgressions in Israeli society (and the army) toward the "strangers" (which was couched in a well-known Biblical reference) was certainly unusual and departed from both official and standard discourse which tends to point the finger at other countries and nations, and demand that they do some soul-searching of their own, given their attitudes toward Jews (then) and Israel (today). However, the thorniest and most difficult part of the speech for most Israelis was the appeal to reflect on the "treatment of the stranger" in Israel 2016 in light of the "horrifying processes that took place in Europe and particularly in Germany 70, 80, and 90 years ago." Maj. General Golan was implying that these "processes" (i.e., of "intolerance, violence, and self-destruction") should serve as warning signals for Israeli society (and for any human society, for that matter). Apparently, however, any mention, even the slightest one, of the processes that led to the Holocaust, in concert with critical remarks about moral violations in Israeli society is met with hostility and anger in Israel. Following his speech, Major General Golan in fact experienced such rebukes.

THE FOUR POST-HOLOCAUST OBLIGATIONS AND THE THREE HISTORICAL VICTIMHOOD LEGACIES

As shown above, the Holocaust permeates Israeli life, and its effects on Israeli public agendas and discourse are varied, in fact, contradictory: The Holocaust hangs over any debate on perceived external threats or the country's survival and continued existence. It colors any discussion of its responsibility toward and relations to the Jews living outside of Israel. It looms over its actions or lacks thereof in humanitarian disasters affecting communities around the world, regardless of religion, and its (mis)treatment of those who are seeking asylum and protection within its borders. The Holocaust also impacts about any discussion of Israel's treatment of those who, are living under its control and domination, who sometimes resist or openly combat it, and it affects Israel's approach to its neighboring countries, with which it is in conflict (which is also embedded in several points of agreement and cooperation). In fact, the Holocaust also affects Israel's relations with the rest of the world.

The earlier-presented foldable fan model provides a convenient framework to rank the relative prevalence and potency of these post-Holocaust existential and moral obligations within Israeli society: The "Never be a passive victim again" and to a somewhat lesser extent the "never forsake your brothers" obligations appear to be highly consensual and dominant in Israeli society, whereas the "never be a passive bystander" (mainly when such humane assistance incurs great costs to the ingroup) and the "never be a perpetrator" obligations are, no doubt, much less prevailing and influential in present-day larger Israeli society, and they even elicit antagonism and counterattacks among segments of society, but they are still striking at the heart of some other segments of the Israeli society.

Clearly, the four post-Holocaust moral obligations are closely related to the three more traditional Jewish victimhood legacies. Therefore, the foregoing discussion can also shed some light on the relative weight of these three legacies in contemporary Israeli society, at the aftermath of the Holocaust, and given the Israeli geo-political predicament.

The Perpetual Victimhood Legacy

Patently, the perpetual victimhood legacy is deeply ingrained in the *never be a passive victim again* and *the never forsake your brothers* moral obligations: According to this traditional legacy, Jews are being killed or in fact murdered in Israel, but also in many other places in the world (e.g., by Palestinians, Arabs, Muslims, and other anti-Semites), just because they are Jews. The Holocaust, as a horrendously well-planned and well-executed scheme to entirely eradicate the "Jewish race" has rightly confirmed and toughened the "in every generation they rise against us to destroy us" verse and made it the predominant lesson of the Holocaust for Israelis and many other Jews around the world. The tough enduring conflict with the Palestinians, and the Arab world, which has been followed by repeated threats (e.g., Shukeiri, Saddam Hussein, Ahmadinejad) to annihilate Israel has further strengthened the grip of this legacy, while at the same time loosening the power of the obligations associated with concern and compassion toward those who are not members of a group (i.e., never be a passive bystander and never be a perpetrator). However, asserting that Jews are being killed or hurt as part of the Jewish-Arab conflict just because they are Jews obviously ignores the obvious fact that this is a violent intergroup conflict, like many other violent conflicts around the world and, more importantly, that in this conflict Israel is not merely a passive victim but rather an active participant inflicting and subject to violence.

The Separateness Legacy

The supremacist separateness legacy is firmly anchored in the *never forsake your brothers* obligation, and just like the perpetual victimhood legacy just discussed, it serves to dilute the "other oriented" obligations to never be a passive bystander and never be a perpetrator.

First, it should be reiterated that caring for Jewish communities and individuals around the world is part of the lesson of the Holocaust. However, most Jews outside Israel are not, presently, under physical threat, and as previously discussed, ensuring the survival of the Jewish people is perceived as combating spiritual and cultural assimilation, the weakening of the Jewish ties, but primarily the rising number of interfaith marriages. Large-scale projects such as Taglit-Birthright were designed "to foster the Jewish identity of a generation of young adults who it was feared would not feel a connection to the Jewish community and Israel"[86] via a ten-day intensive tour and educational program in Israel. One of the stated goals of this program is to increase intra-faith marriages, thus combatting the "silent Holocaust." As shown in the evaluation study[87] "the Taglit participants are 45 percent more likely than nonparticipants to get married to someone Jewish."

The separateness legacy can also explain why the Israeli government and much of the public so adamantly want to expel African asylum seekers. The 40,000 Eritreans and Sudanese constitute half a percent of the Israeli population. In comparison to many European countries that have also been affected by the global refugee crisis this percentage is quite low and the Africans have been swiftly and eagerly integrated into the Israeli economy, which desperately needs manual laborers. They do not, pose a security risk, and their presence does not increase the crime rate. Most of them simply wish to earn their living and they are basically grateful to their hosts. However, as PM

Netanyahu declared the: "phenomenon of infiltrators into Israel endangers the Jewish and democratic character of the state."[88] A right-wing site close to the prime minister explains this as follows:

> most of the country's citizens are interested in preserving the unique characteristics of the state as a Jewish state, while this type of migration can pose a demographic threat to the existence of the Jewish majority in Israel. Israeli citizens have the right to choose the nature of government in Israel and to define as they see fit to preserve their culture. To this end, they also have the moral right to limit external influences such as the uncontrolled migration of infiltrators from different cultures.[89]

In discussing how legacies of historical victimhood can turn into aggression toward opposing outgroups, I have mainly discussed so far the role of the perpetual victimhood legacy. This legacy legitimizes and even sanctifies the use of violence against enemies, motivated by the conviction that the ingroup is under constant threat and it will approve retaliatory and vengeful actions, and lead to "suffering begets suffering" outcomes.[90] However, the supremacist separation legacy can also become a source of intergroup aggression and moral violations. To elucidate this issue, we need to return to the Biblical command to ancient Israelites to expel and even destroy the Canaanite tribes, not because the Canaanites had harmed the Israelis, but rather because their presence in the land violated exclusive Israelite ownership over the land and because they could morally and religiously corrupt the Israelis. Thus, the Israelites' obligation to be distinct from the Canaanite idol worshippers, and their god-given ownership of the land sanctified their inhuman treatment of the Canaanites.

As discussed earlier in this chapter, the future of non-Jews living in the Land of Israel after the prayed-for return of the Jews to the land was merely a hypothetical theological question during the millennia of Jewish exile. However, mainly after the 1967 military conquest of the entire western part of the Land of Israel (in the Six-Day War), the presence of millions of Palestinians in this area and their growing opposition and sometimes violent resistance to the Jewish aspirations, became a prime obstacle to the dream of a "Greater Israel" that began to dominate the hearts of major groups within Jewish-Israeli society (mainly the religious Zionists and the Israeli right) in the aftermath of what they defined as the miraculous military victory in that war. The Palestinians then became the Canaanites, the Philistines, the heirs of the Amalekites, foreign nomads, or migrant workers who came to Israel following the Jewish return starting at the end of the nineteenth century.[91] Yehoshua Ben-Nun's mythical image began to emerge among some circles in the Jewish religious right as a model for ways to treat the Palestinians.[92]

The Legacy of Caring for the Oppressed Stranger

The legacy of caring for the oppressed stranger is the pillar guiding the moral obligations to *never be a passive bystander* and *never be a perpetrator*. This legacy rests on the premise that the memories of experienced suffering and pain remain vivid in both the former victim and their descendants, and that such memories, coupled with the operative moral attitude of *"what is hateful to yourself, do not to other(s)"* will make them more attentive and responsive to the suffering and pain of other sufferers. This logic is best illustrated in a comment made by Israeli author David Grossman at the end of a hearing at the High Court of Justice in March 2018, which dealt with appeals to postpone the deportation of the African asylum seekers. Grossman said:

> My grandmother knocked on the doors of this country, and everybody has a grandfather or great-grandfather who knocked on doors and nobody would open them. And now we're turning our backs, behaving brutally, even cruelly. Turning our backs actually says there was logic to the way our forefathers were treated. [93]

As demonstrated in this and other examples discussed in this chapter (e.g., the Berlin-born Israeli who is reminded of Kristallnacht; the soldiers who sees a frightened young Palestinian girl in Hebron and is unwillingly reminded of the Holocaust), the Holocaust, which is omnipresent in the minds of Israelis, can evoke unpleasant associations that can be transformed into moral obligations to "be kind" and "do no harm," at least in some Israelis.

However, the more universalistic legacy of caring for the oppressed stranger is often in conflict with the particularistic perpetual victimhood and supremacist separateness legacies, which are gaining increasing clout in contemporary Israeli society. Proponents of this legacy are very often forced to be on the defense and are frequently accused of being unpatriotic, loyal to non-group members (e.g., African migrants or refugees) or the group's enemies (e.g., the Palestinians) rather than to the ingroup. Insistence on these moral obligations (on what is seen as the group's greater good) may earn them such epithets as "bleeding hearts," which is not a popular role to play in Israeli society (and, in fact, in many other societies) today.

CONTRASTING LEGACIES OF HISTORICAL VICTIMIZATION: SOCIAL PSYCHOLOGICAL EXPLORATIONS

Social psychological studies can also contribute to a better understanding of the effects of different victimhood orientations on individuals and the collective attitudes, behavioral intentions and actions mainly toward "the others" ("outgroups" in the social psychological terminology), such as the ingroup's adversaries, and those who depend on the group. Below I describe several empirical studies which have recently been conducted at Tel Aviv University.[94] They focus on two historical-trauma-based orientations: the *perpetual ingroup victimhood orientation* (PIVO) and *fear of victimizing* (FOV). They represent the two ends of the foldable fan.

Perpetual Ingroup Victimhood Orientation (PIVO)

The perpetual ingroup victimhood orientation (PIVO) is the belief that the ingroup (e.g., the Jewish people) is a constant, eternal victim persecuted continually by different enemies. This orientation views victimhood as the ingroup's destiny given the persistent and unyielding hostility and malevolent intentions of many outgroups toward the ingroup.

PIVO, as described by Schori-Eyal et al.,[95] is a cluster of beliefs that the group is currently under threat (e.g., "Our existence as a group and as individuals is under constant threat") caused by outside hatred (e.g., "Many people hate us"), that these harassments are persistent over time ("As they have harmed us in the past, so will our enemies wish to harm us in the future") and by different enemies who are in fact an incarnation of one basic enemy (e.g., "Even under different guises, the hatred toward us is basically the same"; "All our enemies throughout history share a common denominator—their hatred toward us"; "All our enemies throughout history share a common denominator—the will to annihilate us"). The group's suffering is unparalleled to that of any other group ("The suffering we have been through cannot be compared to that of any other group"). The group's fate obligates suspicion toward other groups ("We must not rely on other countries and peoples"; "History teaches us that we must be suspicious of other groups' intentions toward us"; "At the end of the day, we can only trust ourselves"). Although such beliefs may be well rooted in groups with histories of victimization, their intensity, firmness and exclusivity can vary considerably among individual group members (and different subgroups within the ingroup).

Fear of Victimizing (FOV)

Schori-Eyal et al.[96] proposed that historical group victimization may also lead to a very different response (albeit a probably much less prevalent one). This is the view that the ingroup might harm enemies with little regard for moral considerations because past suffering may induce moral callousness and indifference to the anguish of others. FOV expresses the concern that the ingroup in its current conflict will switch from victim to victimizer. This may occur through moral contagion: the fear is that qualities, including evil, are transmitted when two objects come into contact,[97] and thus historically traumatized groups may sometimes become contaminated by the evil essence of their victimizers and become evil themselves.

According to Schori-Eyal et al.,[98] FOV may be expressed by adherence to statements such as "The severe harm we have suffered has made us impervious to other peoples' suffering"; "because we have a history of being persecuted, we are in danger of grievously harming other peoples"; "we are in danger of treating other peoples in the same way that we were treated by our worst enemies."

Reactions to the Ingroup's Treatment of the "Stranger": The Asylum Seekers and the Palestinians

PIVO and FOV, which stem from orientations to the group's history of victimization, are likely to affect the views and attitudes of group members toward others, whether "strangers" seeking refuge within the group's borders or those who are in national conflict with the ingroup.

The African migrants: In a study conducted on Jewish Israeli commuters (N=100), participants completed the PIVO and FOV scales, then determined the extent to which the terms *illegal infiltrators* or *asylum seekers* was descriptive of African migrants in Israel. As might be theoretically predicted, PIVO was positively related to the term illegal infiltrators and negatively to the term asylum seekers; FOV, in contrast was positively related to the term asylum seekers and negatively to the term illegal infiltrators. In a second study, Jewish Israeli participants (N=200) were presented with a short summary of a private bill, which was submitted to the Knesset (and rejected later) called "The Refugee Convention for the Regulation of the Status of Asylum Seekers and Refugees in Israel," which requires the state to grant refugee status to those persecuted in their country on political, religious or national grounds. Here too, FOV was positively (and PIVO negatively) related to this "pro-refugees" bill.[99]

Regarding the conflict with the Palestinians: Schori-Eyal et al.[100] tested how PIVO and FOV manifest with respect to two attitudes related to this conflict. The first is the sense of *group-based guilt*, namely, the sense of regret and shame that individual group members experience for the group's moral violations (e.g., Israelis) against outgroups (e.g., Palestinians), even if they were not personally involved in these immoral acts. Considerable social psychological research has demonstrated that group members vary considerably.[101] The second attitude is *tolerance of enemy collateral casualties* (TECC). During violent conflicts, uninvolved civilians (including children) from the enemy group are often killed or injured. In the military (somewhat euphemistically) this is called "collateral damage." Unintended civilian casualties can be the result of an unintended error, but at times a calculated decision to hit an important military target even though uninvolved people might be hurt as well. All this elicits ethical and moral dilemmas.[102] Schori-Eyal et al. reasoned that because PIVO entails a commitment to the security of the ingroup, and thus greater support for aggressive measures against enemy outgroups (i.e., greater tolerance of the outgroup's casualties, intended or unintended[103]), it also leads to less guilt over the harm engendered by these violent measures. FOV, in contrast, entails a commitment to refrain from harming enemy outgroup members, leading to opposite responses. This attitude may thus lead to reduced TECC and a greater sense of group-based guilt. Schori-Eyal et al.[104] found that both during relative calm in the conflict and also during an escalation in the conflict (i.e., a military operation in the Gaza Strip), PIVO was negatively related to group-based guilt and positively with TECC. FOV on the other hand, was positively associated with group-based guilt and negatively with TECC.

Another construct that was studied by Schori-Eyal et al. is *the sense of moral entitlement*, which is the belief that it is permissible for the ingroup to commit morally reprehensible acts against the enemy outgroup. The authors speculated that this sense of moral entitlement would be positively preceded by PIVO and negatively by FOV. Furthermore, the sense of moral entitlement was predicted to reduce group-based guilt and enhance TECC. In other words, the sense of moral entitlement can be conceived as mediating the relationship between PIVO and FOV and group-based guilt and TECC. This indeed was found in the Schori-Eyal et al. study.[105]

IN CONCLUSION

The concept of victimhood is deeply rooted in Jewish collective memory and consciousness. The enslavement and the Exodus from Egypt which constitute the formative epopée of the Jewish people has given rise to three different legacies: the first link in a chain of victimizations (i.e., "A new Pharaoh every generation"), the core of Jewish separateness, chosenness and supremacy, or the origin of the moral obligation to care for the oppressed stranger even when this is an adversary. These three legacies are entangled in Jewish consciousness, and have been experienced in different contexts, at different strengths at different periods and in different Jewish communities, and they have vastly affected the ways in which the Holocaust, the most defining event in modern Jewish history, is interpreted.

For Jewish Israelis, the Holocaust has become unavoidably entwined in the intractable Jewish-Arab conflict, the major feature of contemporary Israeli reality, initially as the antithesis of Israeli identity, and gradually as an integral part of its essence. The Holocaust is experienced as a presence in almost all key issues in Israeli society: Israel's survival and resilience, its relations with the Jewish Diaspora, its treatment of those who seek refuge at its gates, and even more protractedly, its dealings with the Palestinians under its control and beyond its borders. In terms of these and other issues, the Holocaust evokes four moral obligations (*never be a passive victim, never forsake your brothers, never be a passive bystander*, and *never be a perpetrator*), which can be easily attributed to the three traditional Jewish victimhood legacies, and which are at times conflicting in their effects, but are also unequal in their prominence and prevalence in Israeli society today. Many of the dramas and upheavals in Israel public life can be characterized as a function of the interplay between these conflicting obligations.

In 1988 an Israeli philosopher, Professor Yehuda Elkana (who as a ten-year-old was deported to Auschwitz and survived), published an article titled *The Need to Forget* in *Ha'aretz* that triggered a heated debate in which he called on Israeli society to "forget" the Holocaust and turn toward the present and the future. He wrote:

> [I] wish to assert normatively that any philosophy of life nurtured solely or mostly by the Holocaust leads to disastrous consequences. Without ignoring the historic importance of collective memory, a climate in which an entire people determines its attitude to the present and shapes its future by emphasizing the lessons of the past, is fraught with peril for the future of that society, if it wants to live in relative tranquility and relative security, like all other peoples.

And more particularly:

> I see no greater threat to the future of the State of Israel than the fact that the Holocaust has systematically and forcefully penetrated the consciousness of the Israeli public, even that large segment that did not experience the Holocaust, as well as the generation that was born and grew up here. [106]

Beyond the question of whether the Holocaust indeed needs to be forgotten to create a tranquil and relatively secure Israeli future, there is the question of whether this is at all humanly and societally possible to 'forget' such an event. A more realistic conclusion might be that the future of the Israeli society is likely to be determined, to a great extent, not by its ability to forget, but rather by its ability to deal intelligently and ethically with the often contradictory legacies of the Jewish history and the Holocaust in particular.

NOTES

1. I am greatly indebted to Dana Zohar for her constructive comments on this chapter.
2. See Hareven, "Victimization: Some Comments by an Israeli," 1983: 145–55; Novick, *The Holocaust in American Life,* 1999; Zertal, *Israel's Holocaust and the Politics of Nationhood,* 2005; Zertal, "The Holocaust in the Israeli Discourse," 2007: 307–8; Zerubavel, *Recov-*

ered Roots: Collective Memory and the Making of Israeli National Tradition, 1995; Yerushalmi, *Zakhor: Jewish History and Jewish Memory,* 1996.

3. See Walzer, *Exodus and Revolution*,1985.

4. From *Midrash Sifrei Bemidbar*. Esau, Jacob's twin brother is regarded the forefather of all gentile nations.

5. These Talmudic stipulations are called the "Three Oaths." For a scholarly account of their nature and influence on Jewish history see Ravitzki, *Messianism, Zionism, and Jewish Religious Radicalism*, 1996. For an abridged description see also Klar, "From 'Do Not Arouse or Awaken Love Until It So Desires' through 'Return to Zion' to 'Conquest of the Land': Paradigm Shifts and Sanctified Reenactments in Building the Jewish State," 2014: 87–99.

6. Rabinowitz Aaron, "When a Leading Ultra-Orthodox Rabbi Urged Begin to Trade Land for Peace," *Ha'aretz*, August 9, 2017, http://www.haaretz.com/israel-news/.premium-1. 805900.

7. Historically, the Israelite process of settling in the land was probably a slow and gradual process, in which they did not have the power to drive out or exterminate their Canaanites neighbors (despite the many intergroup clashes). The Bible is filled with stories about these intergroup interactions and the religious influences of the Canaanite culture and customs. Some examples of the lack of separation between the early Israelites and their neighbors are the facts that King David, the founder of the Judaic kingdom was the grandson of Ruth the Moabite. Bathsheba, the mother of David's son King Solomon was married to Uriah the Hittite, one of David's generals (the Hittites were one of the Canaanite nations). King Solomon himself (who was the builder of the First Jewish temple in Jerusalem) was known for his love for women: "Now King Solomon loved many foreign women along with the daughter of Pharaoh: Moabite, Ammonite, Edomite, Sidonian, and Hittite women" (1 Kings, 1:11). The vast Canaanite influence on the daily lives and religious practices of the early Jews in the kingdom of Judea around 700 BC (more than half a millennium after the presumed "conquest of the land") may have motivated these extreme injunctions (e.g., "you must destroy them totally. make no treaty with them and show them no mercy") in the Book of Deuteronomy. This may also have prompted the retrospective account of the alleged genocidal "conquest of the land", described in the Book of Joshua (for detailed analyses, see Na'aman, "The 'Conquest of Canaan' in the Book of Joshua and in History," 1995: 218–81; Rowlett, *Joshua and the Rhetoric of Violence: A New Historicist Analysis*, 1996).

8. See Klar, "From 'Do Not Arouse or Awaken Love Until It So Desires' through 'Return to Zion' to 'Conquest of the Land': Paradigm Shifts and Sanctified Reenactments in Building the Jewish State," 2014: 87–99.

9. See Steinfeld, "On the Prohibition of Dining with a Gentile," 1989: 131–48.

10. For the concept of "chosen-ness" and its relations to nationalism see Smith, *Chosen Peoples: Sacred Sources of National Identity,* 2003.

11. In *Orot*, chap. 5, article 10: 156.

12. The Jewish sage, Hillel the Elder (110 BCE–10 CE) formalized this in the statement "*What is hateful to yourself, do not to other(s)*" (similar observations were made by the Greek philosophers, Socrates and Epictetus, and Chinese thinker Confucius). It is true that this moral obligation is applicable to all human beings. However, the Biblical insight is that liberated victims, given their acute awareness of their own past suffering, should be more capable of grasping the pain and suffering of others than those who have never been victims.

13. Love of Israel, see Lamm, "Some Comments on Centrist Orthodoxy," 1986: 1–12.

14. See Frankel, *Prophecy and Politics: Socialism, Nationalism, and the Russian Jews,* 1984: 1862–1917.

15. Avinery, *The Making of Modern Zionism: The Intellectual Origins of the Jewish State*, 2017.

16. Shapira, *New Jews, Old Jews*, 1997.

17. Vagner and Raz, *Herzl: His Struggles at Home and Abroad*, 2017.

18. See Sternhell, *The Founding Myths of Israel: Nationalism, Socialism, and the Making of the Jewish State*, 2009.

19. "David Ben-Gurion: Letter to French General Charles de Gaulle," December 6, 1967, http://www.jewishvirtuallibrary.org/ben-gurion-letter-to-french-general-charles-de-gaulle-de-cember-1967.

20. See Shatz, Waxman, and Diament, *Tikkun Olam: Social Responsibility in Jewish Thought and Law (The Orthodox Forum Series)*, 1997.

21. See Segev, *The Seventh Million: Israelis and the Holocaust*, 2000.

22. Shapira, *Walking on the Horizon*, 1989: 325.

23. For detailed accounts see Liebman and Don-Yihya, *Civil Religion in Israel: Tradition-al Judaism and Political Culture in the Jewish State*, 1983; Klar, Schori-Eyal, and Klar, "The "Never Again" State of Israel: The Emergence of the Holocaust as a Core Feature of Israeli Identity and its Four Incongruent Voices," 2013: 125–43; Ofer, "Israel," 1996: 839–923; "The Past that does not Pass: Israelis and Holocaust Memory," 2009: 1–35; Segev, *The Seventh Million: Israelis and the Holocaust*, 2000; Shapira, "The Holocaust: Private Memories, Public Memory," 1998: 40–58; Yablonka, *Survivors of the Holocaust: Israel after the War*, 1999; Zertal, *Israel's Holocaust and the Politics of Nationhood*, 2005.

24. See Novick, *The Holocaust in American life,* 1989.

25. See Wyman, and Rosenzveig, *The World Reacts to the Holocaust*, 1996.

26. Both these two counts ignore the fact that if Rommel's German armies had not been stopped by the British army at El Alamein, Palestine would have been swiftly conquered by the Germans and the fate of the Jewish Yeshuv (community) there would have not be much different than that of the other Jewish communities in Europe.

27. Segev, *The Seventh Million: Israelis and the Holocaust*, 2000.

28. See Segev, *The Seventh Million: Israelis and the Holocaust*, 2000; Shapira, "The Holo-caust: Private Memories, Public Memory," 1998: 40–58; Yablonka, *The State of Israel vs. Adolf Eichmann*, 2004.

29. Segev, *The Seventh Million: Israelis and the Holocaust*, 2000: 351.

30. See Ofer, "The Past that does not Pass: Israelis and Holocaust Memory," 2009: 1–35.

31. See Milner, *Kiray Avar: Biografia, Zahut Vezikaron Basiporet Hador Hasheni [Past-Present: Biography, Identity and Memory in Second-Generation Literature]*, 2003; Vardi, *Me-morial Candles: Children of the Holocaust (The International Library of Group Psychotherapy and Group Process)*, 1992.

32. E.g., Milner, *Kiray Avar: Biografia, Zahut Vezikaron Basiporet Hador Hasheni [Past-Present: Biography, Identity and Memory in Second Generation Literature], 2003*.

33. Gutfreund, *Our Holocaust, 2007*.

34. Shapira, "The Holocaust: Private Memories, Public Memory," 1998: 40–58; see also Brog, "Victims and Victors: Holocaust and Military Commemoration in Israel Collective Memory," 2003: 65–99; Navon, in this volume.

35. See Oren, *Six Days of War, 2002*.

36. Shapira, "The Holocaust: Private Memories, Public Memory," 1998: 41.

37. Zuckerman, *Shoah in the Sealed Room, 1993*.

38. Porat, *Israeli Society, the Holocaust and Its Survivors, 2008*.

39. E.g., Benny Morris, "The Second Holocaust," *The New York Sun*, January 22, 2007, https://www.nysun.com/opinion/second-holocaust/47111/.

40. Peter Herschberg, "Netanyahu: It's 1938 and Iran Is Germany; Ahmadinejad Is Prepar-ing Another Holocaust," *Ha'aretz*, October 18, 2018, https://www.haaretz.com/news/netanyahu-it-s-1938-and-iran-is-germany-ahmadinejad-is-preparing-another-holocaust-1.205137. For some examples see Jonathan Lis, "Netanyahu: World Must Stop Iran from Con-ducting Second Holocaust," *Ha'aretz*, October 18, 2018, https://www.haaretz.com/netanyahu-world-must-stop-iran-from-conducting-second-holocaust-1.409063; Ari Rabinovitch, "Netan-yahu Defends Comparison of Iran, Nazi Holocaust," *Reuters*, April 19, 2012, https://www.reuters.com/article/us-israel-iran-netanyahu/netanyahu-defends-comparison-of-iran-nazi-holocaust-idUSBRE83H1EF20120418; Paul Bedard, "Netanyahu Warns of Second Holocaust from Iran," *Washington Examiner,* April 15, 2015, http://www.washingtonexaminer.com/netanyahu-warns-of-second-holocaust-from-iran/article/2563105; Toi Staff, "Iran 'Preparing Another Holocaust,' Netanyahu Charges," *The Times of Israel*, May 15, 2016, https://www.timesofisrael.com/iran-preparing-another-holocaust-netanyahu-charges/.

41. Editorial, "Netanyahu the Hasmonaen," *Ha'aretz*, October 11, 2017, https://www.haaretz.com/opinion/editorial/netanyahu-the-hasmonean-1.5457024.

42. E.g., Yair, "Israeli Existential Anxiety: Cultural Trauma and the Constitution of National Character," 2014: 346–62.

43. Friedman, *From Beirut to Jerusalem,* 1989.

44. Two "grand dichotomies" governed public stances about the Holocaust during the 1950's and 1960's in Israel. The first was *Shoah and Gvura* ("Holocaust and Heroism"), see Klar et al., "The "Never Again" State of Israel: The Emergence of the Holocaust as a Core Feature of Israeli Identity and Its Four Incongruent Voices," 2013: 125–43; Ofer, "The Past that Does Not Pass: Israelis and Holocaust Memory," 2009: 1–35; Stauber, *The Holocaust in Israeli Public Debate in the 1950s: Ideology and Memory,* 2007; Zertal, *Israel's Holocaust and the Politics of Nationhood,* 2005, which differentiated between the vast majority of ostensibly passive Holocaust victims and the small number of Ghetto fighters and Jewish partisans who actively fought the Nazis (the latter embodying the "proper Israeli response"). The second was *Shoah and Tkumah* ("Holocaust and Rebirth") referring to the building of the State of Israel out of the ashes of the Holocaust.

45. Bauer, *Rethinking the Holocaust,* 2002: 67.

46. See Bar-Tal & Antebi, "Siege Mentality in Israel," 1992: 251–75; Elon, *The Israelis: Founders and Sons*, 1971; Hareven, "Victimization: Some Comments by an Israeli," 1983: 145–55; Yair, "Israeli Existential Anxiety: Cultural Trauma and the Constitution of National Character," 2014: 346–62.

47. Ilse Posselt, "Never Again: Israel Marks Holocaust Remembrance Day 2017," *Bridges for Peace*, April 24, 2017, https://www.bridgesforpeace.com/2017/04/never-israel-marks-holocaust-remembrance-day-2017/.

48. Aronson, "Israel's Security and the Holocaust: Lessons Learned, but Existential Fears Continue," 2009: 65–93; Freilich, "National Security Decision-Making in Israel: Processes, Pathologies, and Strengths," 2006: 635–63.

49. Cohen, *Israel and the Bomb,* 1998; Hersh, *The Samson Option: Israel, America and the Bomb,* 1991.

50. Twenty-seven years later, in 2007, Israel also destroyed a military Syrian nuclear reactor.

51. Nili, "The Nuclear (and the) Holocaust: Israel, Iran, and the Shadows of Auschwitz," 2011: 51.

52. As noted by Ben-Amos, and Hoffman, "We Came to Liberate Majdanek," 2011: 331–54.

53. Feldman, *Above the Death Pits, Beneath the Flag: Youth Voyages to Poland and the Performance of Israeli National Identity*, 2008

54. Ben-Amos, and Hoffman, "We Came to Liberate Majdanek," 2011: 331–54.

55. 2007, "The Holocaust in the Israeli Discourse," 2007: 307–8.

56. Zertal, "The Holocaust in the Israeli Discourse," 2007: 307–8.

57. Adiv Sterman, and Raphael Ahren, "Netanyahu Blames Jerusalem Mufti for Holocaust, Is Accused of 'Absolving Hitler,'" *The Times of Israel,* October 21, 2015, https://www.timesofisrael.com/netanyahu-accused-of-absolving-hitler-for-holocaust/.

58. See Porat, *The Blue and the Yellow Star of David: The Zionist Leadership in Palestine and the Holocaust, 1939–1945,* 1990; Segev, *The Seventh Million: Israelis and the Holocaust,* 2000.

59. Arieh O'Sullivan, "IAF Jets Fly over Auschwitz: Commemorate Holocaust Victims", *The Jerusalem Post,* September 4, 2003, http://www.jr.co.il/pictures/israel/history/f15-jets-over-auschwitz.htm.

60. For some examples see "Top Rabbi: Jews' Assimilation in Europe 'Worse Than Holocaust,'" *Jewish News*, March 31, 2014, http://jewishnews.timesofisrael.com/top-rabbi-jews-assimilation-europe-worse-holocaust/.

61. Dror Idar, "We Are Here: The Cry of American Jewry," *Israel Ha'yom*, March 6, 2018, http://www.israelhayom.co.il/article/540461.

62. E.g., Firer, *Sokhnim shel ha-Lekakh* [Agents of Holocaust lesson], 1989.

63. E.g., Elon, *The Israelis: Founders and Sons*, 1971.

64. See Orkaby, "Israel's International Squadron and the 'Never Again' Mentality," 2015: 83–101.

65. See Segev, *The Seventh Million: Israelis and the Holocaust*, 2000: 398. However, this humanitarian gesture has been contrasted with the behavior of other nations toward Jews attempting to flee from the Nazis. PM Begin continued: "We all remember the ships with Jewish refugees in the 1930s that wandered the surface of the seven seas, asking to enter a specific country, or any number of countries, only to encounter rejection. Today, there exists the state of the Jews. We have not forgotten. We will behave with humanity. We will bring these unfortunate people, refugees saved by our ship from drowning in the depths of the sea, to our country. We will provide them shelter and refuge," See Murray Teitel, "Lessons from Begin: Is Rescue No Longer a Jewish Imperative?," *The Canadian Jewish News*, June 23, 2017, http://www.cjnews.com/perspectives/rescue-no-longer-jewish-imperative.

66. It is worthwhile to note that in Israeli collective memory, "infiltrators" are the Palestinians who in the 1950s surreptitiously crossed the border and committed sabotage and harm, see Morris, *Israel's Border Wars, 1949–1956: Arab Infiltration, Israeli Retaliation, and the Countdown to the Suez War*, 1997.

67. Melanie Lindman, "10 Key Questions about Israel's African Asylum Seeker Controversy," *The Times of Israel*, February 2, 2018, https://www.timesofisrael.com/in-israels-new-plan-to-deport-africans-details-abound/.

68. Toi Staff, "Holocaust Survivors Urge Netanyahu Not to Deport African Asylum Seekers," *The Times of Israel,* January 25, 2018, https://www.timesofisrael.com/holocaust-survivors-urge-netanyahu-not-to-deport-african-asylum-seekers/.

69. Gideon Levy, "Israeli Pilots Must Refuse to Fly Expelled Asylum Seekers toward Their Deaths," *Ha'aretz*, December 14, 2017, https://www.haaretz.com/opinion/.premium-israeli-pilots-must-refuse-to-fly-expelled-asylum-seekers-to-their-deaths-1.5628618.

70. Ruth McCambridge, "Anne Frank Home Sanctuary Movement Takes Off in Israel," *Non Profit News*, January 18, 2018, https://nonprofitquarterly.org/2018/01/18/anne-frank-home-sanctuary-movement-takes-off-israel/.

71. Melanie Lindman, "Holocaust Survivors Urge Netanyahu Not to Deport African Asylum Seekers," *The Times of Israel*, February 2, 2018, https://www.timesofisrael.com/in-israels-new-plan-to-deport-africans-details-abound/.

72. See Terry, *Golden Rules and Silver Rules of Humanity: Universal Wisdom of Civilization*, 2004.

73. Roccas, Klar, and Livitan, "The Paradox of Group-Based Guilt: Modes of National Identification, Conflict Vehemence, and Reactions to the In-Group's Moral Violations," 2006: 698–711; Wohl, Branscombe, and Klar, "Collective Guilt: Emotional Reactions When One's Group has Done Wrong or Been Wronged," 2006: 1–37.

74. Schori-Eyal, Klar, Roccas, and McNeill, 2017a; Wohl, and Branscombe, "Remembering Historical Victimization: Collective Guilt for Current Ingroup Transgressions," 2008: 988–1006.

75. Gideon Spiro, "Similar Situations [Letter to the Editor]," *Ha'aretz*, 2008, http://www.haaretz.co.il/hasite/spages/1037100.html.

76. As a consequence, critiques of Israeli policies toward Palestinians tend to use euphemisms such as "it is reminiscent of dark periods in history" see for example, Daniel Blatman, "1932 is Already Here", *Ha'aretz*, December 26, 2010, http://www.haaretz.com/print-edition/opinion/1932-is-already-here-1.332974.

77. Benski, and Katz, "Women's Peace Activism and the Holocaust: Reversing the Hegemonic Holocaust Discourse in Israel," 2016: 93–113.

78. See Sa'ar Tsafy, "They Will Not Stand Idly by Like the Germans," *Ha'aretz*, May 1, 2008, https://www.haaretz.co.il/gallery/1.3370485.

79. Justvision, Interview with Yehuda Shaul, 2008, http://www.justvision.org/he/ portrait/76159/highlights, See also Klar et al., "The "Never Again" State of Israel: The Emergence of the Holocaust as a Core Feature of Israeli Identity and Its Four Incongruent Voices," 2013: 125–43.

80. Chayut, *The Girl Who Stole My Holocaust: A Memoir*, 2013.

81. Noam Chayut, *The Girl Who Stole My Holocaust: A Memoir*, 2013, https://www.versobooks.com/books/1424-the-girl-who-stole-my-holocaust.

82. For example, Major General Amiram Levin. See Isabel Kershner "Israeli Veterans' Criticism of West Bank Occupation Incites Furor," *The New York Times*, December 23, 2015, https://www.nytimes.com/2015/12/24/world/middleeast/israeli-veterans-criticism-of-west-bank-occupation-incites-furor.html, and retired Israel Police Major General Alik Ron and Shin Bet security services chief Major General Ami Ayalon and Yuval Diskin, former head of the *Shin Bet*. See "Two New Defense Brass Join in Support for Breaking the Silence," *Ha'aretz*, Dec 22, 2015, https://www.haaretz.com/israel-news/.premium-two-new-defense-brass-join-support-for-breaking-the-silence-1.5380575.

83. Toi Staff, "Breaking the Silence Director Announces Her Resignation," *The Times of Israel*, February 14, 2017, https://www.timesofisrael.com/breaking-the-silence-director-announces-her-resignation.

84. Toi Staff, "Stormy Debate Erupts over Bill to Ban Breaking the Silence from Schools," *The Times of Israel*, December 28, 2016, https://www.timesofisrael.com/stormy-debate-erupts-over-bill-to-ban-breaking-the-silence-from-schools.

85. One such event that sparked widespread public debate in Israel was a shooting incident (on March 24, 2016) when a Palestinian assailant who stabbed an Israeli soldier was later shot in the head by an IDF soldier, as he lay wounded and "neutralized" on the ground.

86. Saxe, et al., *Jewish Futures Project. The Impact of Taglit-Birthright Israel: 2012 Update*, 2012: 1.

87. Saxe, et al., *Jewish Futures Project. The Impact of Taglit-Birthright Israel: 2012 Update*, 2012.

88. More recently, in March 2018, PM Netanyahu defined the influx of African migrants as more dangerous than terrorism, Almog Ben Zachary, "Netanyahu: If It Were Not for the Fence, There Would be Terrorism from Sinai, and, Worse, Infiltrators," *Ha'aretz*, March 20, 2018, https://www.haaretz.co.il/news/politics/1.5930609.

89. Refael Minnes, "Expelling Illegal Infiltrators from Israel – Legal and Moral," *Mida*, January 30, 2018, https://en.mida.org.il/2018/01/30/expelling-illegal-infiltrators-israel-legal-moral/.

90. Noor, Shnabel, Halabi, and Nadler, "When Suffering Begets Suffering: The Psychology of Competitive Victimhood Between Adversarial Groups in Violent Conflicts," 2012: 351–74.

91. See Klar, "From 'Do not Arouse or Awaken Love Until it so Desires' through 'Return to Zion' to 'Conquest of the Land': Paradigm Shifts and Sanctified Reenactments in Building the Jewish State," 2014: 87–99; Klar, and Naor, "You Should Understand Who Is Temporary Here and to Whom This Country Belongs To: The New Religious Zionism and the Palestinians," 2017.

92. For example, the late Hanan Porat, one of the ideological leaders of the religious-nationalist right, raised a story that originated in the Jerusalem Talmud regarding the choices given by Joshua Ben-Nun to the Canaanites. Porat said that the Palestinians should be offered to fight the Jews (and then their fate would be like the fate of the ancient Canaanites), to go far to another country and thus to free themselves from the rule of the Jews, or to surrender to the Jews, acknowledge the Jewish exclusive eight to the land, and willingly be subjugated to them (Hanan Porat in Makor Rishon 29.8.2014). Similar proposals were made also by other political and religious leaders. For example, in response to the publication of statistical estimates in March 2018, that the number of Palestinians in western Land of Israel is already greater than the number of Jews, Knesset Member Bezalel Smotrich said in a radio interview: "This means that one of the sides has to get up and leave, of course we will not do it, that means the other side will have to go" (in Kaan, Reshet B, 27.3.2018). Several weeks earlier, in early February 2018, Rabbi David Dudkevitch, a religious leader one of the west-bank settlements, said at a funeral to a fellow settler who had been murdered by a Palestinian: "We are not the guests here . . . an entire nation has risen up against us . . . we are the owners here. It is not one Mohammed, it is a nation that lives on its sword against a nation that increases the good in the world. They are not partners to this land, they are completely strangers. We have returned home in justice and in mercy. It would be proper for us to cut off this murderous nation", Nir Hasson, "Hundreds Attend Funeral for Israeli Slain in Stabbing Attack as Manhunt Widens," *Ha'aretz*,

February 6, 2018, https://www.haaretz.com/israel-news/hundreds-attend-funeral-for-rabbi-slain-in-stabbing-attack-1.5791428.

93. Nir Hasson, "We Israelis Are Turning Our Backs on African Refugees," *Ha'aretz*, March 20, 2018, https://www.haaretz.com/opinion/.premium-we-israelis-are-turning-our-backs-on-african-refugees-1.5918136.

94. Schori-Eyal, Klar, and Ben-Ami, "Perpetual Ingroup Victimhood as a Distorted Lens: Effects on Attribution and Categorization," 2017a: 180–94; Schori-Eyal, Klar, Roccas, and McNeill, "The Shadows of the Past: Effects of Historical Group Trauma on Current Intergroup Conflicts," 2017b: 538–54

95. Schori-Eyal, Klar, and Ben-Ami, "Perpetual Ingroup Victimhood as a Distorted Lens: Effects on Attribution and Categorization," 2017a: 180–94, Schori-Eyal, Klar, Roccas, and McNeill, "The Shadows of the Past: Effects of Historical Group Trauma on Current Intergroup Conflicts," 2017b: 538–54.

96. Schori-Eyal, Klar, Roccas, and McNeill, "The Shadows of the Past: Effects of Historical Group Trauma on Current Intergroup Conflicts," 2017b: 538–54; see also Klar, et al., "The 'Never Again' State of Israel: The Emergence of the Holocaust as a Core Feature of Israeli Identity and its Four Incongruent Voices," 2013: 125–43; Klar, "Four Moral Obligations in the Aftermath of Historical Ingroup Victimization," 2016: 54–58.

97. Rozin, Haidt, and McCauley, "Disgust," 2008: 757–76.

98. Schori-Eyal, et al., "The Shadows of the Past: Effects of Historical Group Trauma on Current Intergroup Conflicts," 2017b: 538–54.

99. Klar, Yom Tov, Unpublished Data.

100. Schori-Eyal, et al., "The Shadows of the Past: Effects of Historical Group Trauma on Current Intergroup Conflicts," 2017b: 538–54.

101. E.g., Doosje, Branscombe, Spears, and Manstead, "Guilty by Association: When One's Group Has a Negative History," 1998: 872–86; Roccas, Klar, and Liviatan, "The Paradox of Group-Based Guilt: Modes of National Identification, Conflict Vehemence, and Reactions to the In-Group's Moral Violations," 2006: 698–711; Zimmermann, Abrams, Doosje, & Manstead, "Causal and Moral Responsibility: Antecedents and Consequences of Group-Based Guilt," 2011: 825–39.

102. E.g., Roblyer, "Beyond Precision: Morality, Decision Making, and Collateral Casualties," 2005: 17–39; Wolfe, and Darley, "Protracted Asymmetrical Conflict Erodes Standards for Avoiding Civilian Casualties," 2005: 55–61.

103. To test TECC, participants in the Schori-Eyal et al. study, "The Shadows of the Past: Effects of Historical Group Trauma on Current Intergroup Conflicts," 2017b: 538–54, were presented with a vignette depicting a hypothetical dilemma facing the IDF during the military conflict in Gaza to assassinate a Hamas militant leader by firing rockets from an attack helicopter. However, this military goal was associated with the risk of also killing civilians in the vicinity. Participants were presented with a table showing the trade-off between the number of likely collateral casualties and the probability of a successful assassination of the target and were asked to decide on the magnitude of the missile based on the resulting expectancy of success/collateral casualties. The response scale ranged from 1 (40 percent chance of success, no civilian casualties) to 5 (100 percent chance of success, up to twenty civilian casualties).

104. Schori-Eyal et al., Schori-Eyal, Klar, Roccas, and McNeill, "The Shadows of the Past: Effects of Historical Group Trauma on Current Intergroup Conflicts," 2017b: 538–54.

105. Schori-Eyal, Klar, Roccas, and McNeill, "The Shadows of the Past: Effects of Historical Group Trauma on Current Intergroup Conflicts," 2017b: 538–54.

106. Yehuda Elkana, "The Need to Forget," *Ha'aretz*, March 2, 1988, http://web.ceu.hu/yehuda_the_need_to_forget.pdf.

BIBLIOGRAPHY

Aronson, Shlomo. "Israel's Security and the Holocaust: Lessons Learned, but Existential Fears Continue." *Israel Studies 14,* no. 1 (2009): 65–93.

Avineri, Shlomo. *The Making of Modern Zionism: The Intellectual Origins of the Jewish State*. UK: Hachette, 2017.

Bar-Tal, Daniel, and Antebi Dikla. "Siege Mentality in Israel." *International Journal of Intercultural Relations 16*, (1992): 251–75.

Barton, Keith C., and McCully Alan. "History Teaching and the Perpetuation of Memories: The Northern Ireland Experience." In *The Role of Memory in Ethnic Conflict*, edited by Ed Cairns, Michael D. Roe, 107–24. London: Palgrave Macmillan, 2003.

Bauer, Yehuda. *Rethinking the Holocaust*. New Haven, CT: Yale University Press, 2002.

Ben-Amos, Avner, and Hoffman Tamar. "We Came to Liberate Majdanek." *Israeli Sociology 12*, no. 2 (2011): 331–54.

Benski, Tova, and Katz Ruth. "Women's Peace Activism and the Holocaust: Reversing the Hegemonic Holocaust Discourse in Israel." In *The Holocaust as Active Memory: The Past in the Present*, edited by Marie Louise Seeberg, Irene Levin, and Claudia Lenz, 93–113. Farnham, England: Ashgate Press, 2016.

Brog, Mooli. "Victims and Victors: Holocaust and Military Commemoration in Israel Collective Memory." *Israel Studies 8*, no. 3 (2003): 65–99.

Chayut, Noam. *The Girl Who Stole My Holocaust: A Memoir*. London UK: Verso, 2013.

Cohen, Avner. *Israel and the Bomb*. New York: Columbia University Press, 1998.

Doosje, Bertjan, Branscombe Nyla R., Spears Russell, and Manstead Antony S. R. "Guilty by Association: When One's Group Has a Negative History." *Journal of Personality and Social Psychology 75*, no. 4 (1998): 872–86.

Elon, Amos. *The Israelis: Founders and Sons*. London, U.K: Weidenfeld & Nicolson, 1971.

Feldman, Jackie. *Above the Death Pits, Beneath the Flag: Youth Voyages to Poland and the Performance of Israeli National Identity*. New York, NY: Berghahn, 2008.

Firer, Ruth. *Sokhnim shel ha-Lekakh* [Agents of Holocaust lesson]. Tel Aviv, Israel: Hakibbutz Hameuchad, 1989.

Frankel, Jonathan. *Prophecy and Politics: Socialism, Nationalism, and the Russian Jews, 1862–1917*. Cambridge: Cambridge University Press, 1984.

Freilich, Chuck D. "National Security Decision-Making in Israel: Processes, Pathologies, and Strengths." *The Middle East Journal 60*, no. 4 (2006), 635–63.

Friedman, Thomas L. *From Beirut to Jerusalem*. New York: Doubleday, 1989.

Gutfreund, Amir. *Our Holocaust*. New Milford, CT: Toby Press, 2007.

Hareven, Alouph. "Victimization: Some Comments by an Israeli." *Political Psychology 4*, no. 1 (1983): 145–55.

Hazaz, Hayyim. *The Sermon*. Foundation for Cultural Projects, 1956.

Hersh, Seymour Myron. *The Samson Option: Israel, America and the Bomb*. London, England: Faber & Faber, 1991.

Klar, Yechiel. "From 'Do not Arouse or Awaken Love Until it so Desires' through 'Return to Zion' to 'Conquest of the Land': Paradigm Shifts and Sanctified Reenactments in Building the Jewish State." *International Journal of Intercultural Relations 43* (2014): 87–99.

Klar, Yechiel. "Four Moral Obligations in the Aftermath of Historical Ingroup Victimization." *Current Opinion in Psychology 58*, no. 11 (2016): 54–58.

Klar, Yechiel, and Naor Amit. "You Should Understand Who Is Temporary Here and to Whom This Country Belongs To: The New Religious Zionism and the Palestinians." In *Stop –no Border in Front of You! About Borders and the Lack of Them in Israel*, edited by Henny Zubaida and Raanan Lifshitz, Rishon Lezion, Israel: Yedioth Books Press, 2017.

Klar, Yechiel, Schori-Eyal Noa, and Klar Yonat. "The 'Never Again' State of Israel: The Emergence of the Holocaust as a Core Feature of Israeli Identity and Its Four Incongruent Voices." *Journal of Social Issues 69*, no. 1, (2013): 125–43.

Lamm, Norman. "Some Comments on Centrist Orthodoxy." *Tradition: A Journal of Orthodox Jewish Thought 22, no.3* (1986): 1–12.

Liebman, Charles S., and Don-Yehiya Eliezer. *Civil Religion in Israel: Traditional Judaism and Political Culture in the Jewish State*. Berkeley, CA: University of California Press, 1983.

Milner, Iris. *Kiray Avar: Biografia, Zahut Vezikaron Basiporet Hador Hasheni [Past-Present: Biography, Identity and Memory in Second-Generation Literature]*. Tel-Aviv, Israel: Am Oved, 2003.

Morris, Benny. *Israel's Border Wars, 1949–1956: Arab Infiltration, Israeli Retaliation, and the Countdown to the Suez War*. Oxford University Press, 1997.

Na'Aman, Nadav. "The 'Conquest of Canaan' in the Book of Joshua and in History," In *From Nomadism to Monarchy: Archaeological and Historical Aspects of Early Israel*, edited by Israel Finkelstein, and Nadav Na'aman, 218–81. Jerusalem, Israel: Yad Izhak Ben-Zvi: Israel Exploration Society; Washington: Biblical Archaeology Society, 1994.

Nili, Shmuel. "The Nuclear (and the) Holocaust: Israel, Iran, and the Shadows of Auschwitz." *Journal of Strategic Security 4*, no. 1 (2011): 37–56.

Noor, Masi, Shnabel Nurit, Halabi Samer, and Nadler Arie. "When Suffering Begets Suffering: The Psychology of Competitive Victimhood between Adversarial Groups in Violent Conflicts." *Personality and Social Psychology Review 16*, no. 4 (2012): 351–74.

Novick, Peter. *The Holocaust in American life*. Boston, MA: Houghton Mifflin, 1999.

Ofer, Dalia. "Israel." In *The World Reacts to the Holocaust*, edited by David S. Wyman, 839–923. Baltimore, MD: Johns Hopkins University Press, 1996.

Ofer, Dalia. "The Past That Does Not Pass: Israelis and Holocaust Memory." *Israel Studies 14*, no. 1 (2009): 1–35.

Ofer, Dalia. "Victims, Fighters, Survivors: Quietism and Activism in Israeli Historical Consciousness." *Common Knowledge 16*, no. 3 (2010): 493–517.

Oren, Michael B. *Six Days of War*. Oxford University Press, 2002.

Orkaby, Asher. "Israel's International Squadron and the 'Never Again' Mentality." *The Journal of the Middle East and Africa 6*, no. 2 (2015): 83–101.

Porat, Dina. *The Blue and the Yellow Star of David: The Zionist Leadership in Palestine and the Holocaust, 1939–1945*. Cambridge, Mass: Harvard University Press, 1990.

Porat, Dina. *Israeli Society, the Holocaust and Its Survivors*. London, U.K.: Vallentine Mitchell, 2008.

Ravitzki, Aviezer. *Messianism, Zionism, and Jewish Religious Radicalism*. Chicago: University of Chicago Press, 1996.

Roblyer, Dwight A. "Beyond Precision: Morality, Decision Making, and Collateral Casualties." *Peace and Conflict: Journal of Peace Psychology 11*, no. 1 (2005): 17–39.

Roccas, Sonia, Klar Yechiel, and Liviatan Ido. "The Paradox of Group-Based Guilt: Modes of National Identification, Conflict Vehemence, and Reactions to the In-Group's Moral Violations." *Journal of Personality and Social Psychology 91*, no. 4 (2006): 698–711.

Rowlett, Lori L. *Joshua and the Rhetoric of Violence: A New Historicist Analysis*. Sheffield, England: Sheffield Academic Press, 1996.

Rozin, Paul, Haidt Jonathan, and McCauley Clark R. "Disgust." In *Handbook of Emotions*, edited by Michael Lewis, Jeannette M. Haviland-Jones, and Lisa Feldman Barrett, 757–76. New York, NY: Guilford Press, 2008.

Saxe, Leonard, Shain Michelle, Wright Graham, Hecht Shahar, Fishman Shira, and Sasson Theodore. *Jewish Futures Project. The Impact of Taglit-Birthright Israel: 2012 Update*, 2012.

Schori-Eyal, Noa, Klar Yechiel, and Ben-Ami Yarden. "Perpetual Ingroup Victimhood as a Distorted Lens: Effects on Attribution and Categorization." *European Journal of Social Psychology 47*, no. 2 (2017a): 180–94.

Schori-Eyal, Noa, Klar Yechiel, Roccas Sonia, and McNeill Andrew R. "The Shadows of the Past: Effects of Historical Group Trauma on Current Intergroup Conflicts." *Personality and Social Psychology Bulletin 43*, no. 4 (2017b): 538–54.

Segev, Tom. *The Seventh Million: Israelis and the Holocaust*. New York, NY: Holt, 2000.

Shapira, Anita. *Walking on the Horizon*. Tel Aviv: Am Oved (Hebrew), 1989.

Shapira, Anita. *New Jews, Old Jews*. Tel Aviv: Am Oved (Hebrew), 1997.

Shapira, Anita. "The Holocaust: Private Memories, Public Memory." *Jewish Social Studies 4*, no. 2 (1998): 40–58.

Shatz, David, Waxman Chaim I., and Diament Nathan J., ed. *Tikkun Olam: Social Responsibility in Jewish Thought and Law (The Orthodox Forum Series).* Lanham, Maryland: Jason Aronson, Inc., 1997.

Smith, Anthony D. *Chosen Peoples: Sacred Sources of National Identity.* Oxford University Press, 2003.

Staub, Ervin, and Vollhardt Johanna R. "Altruism Born of Suffering: The Roots of Caring and Helping after Victimization and Other Trauma." *American Journal of Orthopsychiatry 78,* no. 3 (2008): 267–80.

Stauber, Roni. *The Holocaust in Israeli Public Debate in the 1950s: Ideology and Memory.* London, UK: Vallentine Mitchell, 2007.

Steinfeld, Zvi A. "On the Prohibition of Dining with a Gentile." *Sidra: A Journal for the Study of Rabbinic Literature* 5 (1989): 131–48.

Sternhell, Zeev. *The Founding Myths of Israel: Nationalism, Socialism, and the Making of the Jewish State.* Princeton, NJ: Princeton University Press, 2009.

Spiro, Gideon. "Similar Situations [Letter to the Editor]", *Ha'aretz,* 2008, http://www.haaretz.co.il/hasite/spages/1037100.html.

Terry, Howard. *Golden Rules and Silver Rules of Humanity: Universal Wisdom of Civilization.* Bloomington, IN: Author House, 2004.

Vagner, Yigal, and Raz Adam. *Herzl: His Struggles at Home and Abroad.* Jerusalem, Israel: Carmel (Hebrew), 2017.

Vardi, Dina. *Memorial Candles: Children of the Holocaust (The International Library of Group Psychotherapy and Group Process).* London, U.K.: Routledge, 1992.

Vollhardt, Johanna R. "The Role of Victim Beliefs in the Israeli-Palestinian Conflict: Risk or Potential for Peace?" *Peace and Conflict: Journal of Peace Psychology 15,* no. 2 (2009): 135–59.

Walzer, Michael. *Exodus and Revolution.* New York, NY: Basic Books, 1985.

Wohl, Michael J. A., and Branscombe Nyla R. "Remembering Historical Victimization: Collective Guilt for Current Ingroup Transgressions." *Journal of Personality and Social Psychology 94,* no. 6 (2008): 988–1006.

Wohl, Michael J. A., Branscombe Nyla R., and Klar Yechiel. "Collective Guilt: Emotional Reactions when One's Group Has Done Wrong or Been Wronged." *European Review of Social Psychology 17,* no. 1 (2006): 1–37.

Wolfe, Rebecca J., and Darley, John M. "Protracted Asymmetrical Conflict Erodes Standards for Avoiding Civilian Casualties." *Peace and Conflict: Journal of Peace Psychology 11,* no. 1 (2005): 55–61.

Wyman, David S., and Rosenzveig Charles H. *The World Reacts to the Holocaust.* Baltimore, MD: Johns Hopkins University Press, 1996.

Yablonka, Hanna. *Survivors of the Holocaust: Israel after the War.* New York: New York University Press, 1999.

Yablonka, Hanna. *The State of Israel vs. Adolf Eichmann.* Tel-Aviv, Israel: Schocken Publishing House, 2004.

Yair, Gad. "Israeli Existential Anxiety: Cultural Trauma and the Constitution of National Character." *Social Identities 20,* no. 4–5 (2014): 346–62.

Yerushalmi, Yosef H. *Zakhor: Jewish History and Jewish Memory.* Seattle, Washington: University of Washington Press, 1996.

Zertal, Idith. *Israel's Holocaust and the Politics of Nationhood.* Cambridge, U.K.: Camridge University Press, 2005.

Zertal, Idith. "The Holocaust in the Israeli Discourse." In *New Jewish Time: Jewish Culture in a Secular Age: An Encyclopedic View,* edited by Shulamit Volkov, Yirmiyahu Yovel, Yair Tzaban, and Morton Weinfeld. Jerusalem: Keter (Hebrew), 2007.

Zerubavel, Yael. *Recovered Roots: Collective Memory and the Making of Israeli National Tradition.* Chicago and London: University of Chicago Press, 1995.

Zimmermann, Anja, Abrams Dominic, Doosje Bertjan, and Manstead Antony S. R. "Causal and Moral Responsibility: Antecedents and Consequences of Group-Based Guilt." *European Journal of Social Psychology 41,* no. 7 (2011): 825–39.

Zukerman, Moshe. *Shoah in a Sealed Room*, Tel-Aviv, Israel, 1993

Chapter Six

The Politics of Victimhood and the Palestinian Collective Identity

Ido Zelkovitz

The ongoing dialectics of the Israeli-Palestinian dispute between two antithetical national narratives, are characterized by conflicting views not only on the question of historical truth but also on the right to exist as a fundamental element of a political entity, with the two sides apparently locked into incessant conflict.[1]

This outlook was reinforced by the outcome of the 1948 war, in which almost every representative Palestinian political body was overthrown. The Palestinian political leadership entered a state of stagnation. The Palestinian tragedy is one of organizational-political-social destruction with the potential of leading to an identity crisis.

In retrospect, one can say that from a Palestinian viewpoint, one way of coping with the outcome of the 1948 war was to develop a discourse of victimhood. Thus, the difficulty in dealing with the disastrous consequences of the war engulfed in a discourse that embodied the plight of the refugees and the sense of injustice that ensued. This victimhood discourse did not constitute a cure for collective pain but helped the defeated side endure the harsh consequences of the 1948 war.

This article will consider the characteristics of victimhood discourse and its place within Palestinian collective memory. Despite the centrality of victimhood in Palestinian national discourse, today as historians, we are aware that this is social construction, based upon the emotional gap between the events as they occurred and their historical interpretation.

WAS EVERYONE A VICTIM?

When fighting broke out on November 30, 1948, the Arabs in Palestine could not have foreseen the future consequences, and while entire villages were abandoned and disappeared, not all of the Palestinian Arabs experienced the war as victims. The *Nakba* was not experienced physically in a same way throughout all parts of mandatory Palestine. There were whole areas such as parts of the West Bank territories and the Jordan Valley not experiencing the defeat in the same way as the Palestinian Arabs of the Galilee and the coastal plain. In this context one should remember that in the end of the 1948 war that not a single Jew remained in the Gosh Etzion or the Hebron era. In fact, none of the parties involved could have known the eventual outcome at the start of the war. Fawaz Turki described this well in his memoirs:

> In our refugee camp in Beirut, my father complains that the Lord's way has become wanton and absurd, but adds that every event in His creation has reason, meaning. If it had not meaning, then what has happened to us would not have happened. He could not explain the meaning of the events that led to our last day in Palestine. He just trusted that it was there, somewhere. The beginning of every act in His creation was simply the beginning of another.
>
> Maybe he was right. No one could say. I just know that for my own generation of Palestinians our last day in Palestine was the first day that we began to define our Palestinian was the first day that we began to define our Palestinian identity.[2]

The experience of exile, being refugees, was enwrapped within a sense of loss of sovereignty. Even those Palestinians who remained in their homes, both within the newly State of Israel and those in the West Bank or Gaza Strip, found themselves without control over their political fate and excluded from political decision making processes. Furthermore, the Palestinians, as a collective entity, had been disarmed, and lost their military organized capabilities. The Nakba created the moment in history when the Palestinians' world order changed dramatically.[3]

The victimhood discourse, which to begin with could have been interpreted as an attempt to avoid responsibility, or as part of a broader context of living in denial, paradoxically became instrumental in moving toward a new reality in which the sense of injustice and helplessness were replaced by political activism, which ultimately developed into the armed struggle.

It was this sense of helplessness of the masses, resulting from the collapse of the weak Palestinian political establishment which never recovered from the wounds inflicted during the Palestinian revolt of 1936–1939,[4] that became a center cornerstone in laying the foundations of Palestinian victimhood. With the second phase of fighting starting at the outbreak of the 1948 war, large sections of Palestinian society answered the call of the Arab armies to abandon their homes and villages. The leadership crisis and the absence of an elite who could take responsibility and offer direction in the moment of truth in the Israeli–Palestinian conflict, then left the outcast Palestinians seeking an explanation for what had just happened. This in turn created a longing for an alternative reality, the chimerical lost paradise of 1948 described in Palestinian literature, the paradise which had disappeared once the fighting ceased.[5]

The sense of victimhood serves as a central axis in the construction of Palestinian narrative following on from the Nakba, with the national body of knowledge which was accumulated through historical writing and literature, revering the experience of loss. In addition to the loss of the homeland, Palestinian society also suffered from the shattering of the traditional patriarchal family unit. Thus the victims were also those fathers and sons who exchanged roles or became distanced from one another and the whole society which changed unrecognizably.

One of the main arguments made by the Palestinians in their literature aimed at the international community has been the attempt to present themselves as victims of the victim. The Palestinians swathed their defeat in the war in a swaddling cloth of injustice, which they claimed was accepted or excused by the world because of Jewish history and memories of the Holocaust. The Palestinians attempted through their writing to forge a symmetry between their tragedy and the Jewish Holocaust. This attempt wasn't successful.

There are no similarities in the historical circumstances between of the holocaust and the Palestinian Nakba. In the Palestinian case, the living and dead victims were a result of a war between the national Palestinian movement and the armies of five Arab states who fought alongside them against the Zionist movement. In other words, the loss suffered by the Palestinians in the 1948 war was the defeat of the majority group who fought against a defensive minority.

Furthermore, any such comparison between the Holocaust and the Nakba may also be refuted by definition. The Palestinians were never faced during the 1948 war with the institutionalized genocide that the Jewish people experienced in Europe. Hence the discourse on "victims of the victim" was intended from the offset for propaganda purposes. This reflects well in the writing of al-Mutawakkil Taha, former chair of the of the Association of Palestinian Writers in the West Bank and the Gaza Strip, that wrote in his poem "Letter to Israeli Soldier":

> Years ago you bent under the whips of Dachau, Your father died in Warsaw.
> You wept for your sister broiled in the purgatory of Auschwitz
> Have you forgotten?[6]

After reminding the soldier of the historic past of his family, the author blames him directly in creating a new Auschwitz for the Palestinians.[7] The attempt to make use of comparative discourse including Holocaust memory damaged the legitimacy of the Palestinian struggle in the opinion of many groups in the Western world. After this political attempt to create empathy in the wake of comparative discourse, the Palestinians changed their approach to the Holocaust. Instead of attempting to create empathy by presenting themselves as victims, they created a new political discourse denying the Holocaust, with the intention of damaging the legitimacy of a Jewish nation-state serving as a refuge for the Jewish people. This narrative reflected well especially in the writing of Palestinian writers in a days of escalation between Israel and the Palestinians. For example, under the title "Marketing Ashes," the semi-official Palestinian Authority Daily *al-Hayat al-Jadida* published an article by the Palestinian columnist Khayri Mansur. This article was published during the hard days of the al-Aqsa intifada in March 2001, sheds a light on this discourse. In order to attack the legitimacy of the state of Israel as a Jewish state, the Khayri Mansur article raised recurring themes of Holocaust denial such as the claim of political and economic exploitation by Zionist propaganda, the deflated number of the exterminated Jews, and lack of scientific evidence on the use of gas and chemicals.[8]

Culturally, the Palestinians constructed their victimhood discourse mainly through literature, with many literary works emphasizing the Palestinian sense of victimhood. For example, the novella *The Return to Haifa* by Ghassan Kanafani attempts to create a parallel between an elderly couple, Holocaust survivors who have lost their family in Khaldun (the eternal) behind. The son, who was adopted by the Holocaust survivors, grew up as a Jew. A modern "trial of Solomon" develops between the adoptive mother, now a widow, and the biological parents, who recognize that aside from the empathy they share, their fate will be decided by war and not through reconciliation. This is the only novella by Kanafani, who was a poet, writer, and spokesperson for the Popular Front for the Liberation of Palestine, in which Israeli-Jewish characters appear.[9] It describes a classic case of victimhood which is expressed as a mirror image of the opponents' beliefs.

The attempts to compare the Nakba (literally: the calamity) of the Palestinians to the Holocaust became central to the Palestinian victimhood discourse. That's mainly due to the fact that, from the Israeli-Zionist perspective, the war of Independence which followed the Holocaust constitutes the start of redemption, symbolizing revival and growth, while the Palestinian narrative views the establishment of the State of Israel as the essence of its disaster as reflected in the title of the article by the Communist-Palestinian activist Emil Habibi "Your Holocaust—Our Catatrophe!"[10]

Even though Habibi maintains in his paper that the suffering of the Jews in Europe cannot be compared to that of the Palestinians, it is evident that he makes a direct connection between the two in the title, the purpose of which is not only to raise awareness about the suffering of the Palestinians but also drastically raise the perceived intensity of their suffering. This is the foundation of presenting the victimization by the victims, as Habibi elaborates:

> if not for your – and all of humanity's Holocaust – in World War II, the catastrophe that is still the lot of my people would not have been possible. [11]

Following this line of thought, Sari Nusseibeh, former Palestinian Authority Minister and the president of al-Quds University, wrote in his memories that the most common argument among the Palestinian notables that have rejected the partition plan of November 29, 1947, was: "Why should we pay for what the Europeans did to the Jews?" [12]

Women Symbolizing Victimhood in Palestinian Discourse

Another emerging theme in Palestinian literature and art is the personification of victimhood in the image of a woman, with Palestine itself often metaphorically presented as a woman. She is variously presented as a lover or as a mother endowing life, giving birth to her sons. The land as the woman is also a victim of war. In Palestinian literary and political discourse women are also frequently presented as rape victims. Furthermore, Palestinian histrionics and scholars such as Kana'na, Zaytawi and Khalidi mentioned that rumors about rapes in the Arab Rural areas encouraged the Palestinian villagers flee during the spring of 1948. [13]

Reading in Palestinian literature, we will find out that the violated land is usually compared to a woman who has been victimized by the Zionists. For example, the Palestinian writer Ibrahim al-Alam describes in his story "al-Dhib" (The Wolf) how a young girl who is raped by her Israeli employer recalls the ninth century Abbasid Caliph al-Mutasim, who sent his armies to revenge the rape of Muslim women by the Byzantines. In this way the fictional work blends the individual experience with that of the collective thus intensifying the sense of victimization by placing the defensive women at the heart of the story. [14] The analogy between the woman and the earth depicts a situation of perpetual conflict. Although she is under constant attack, and is highly traumatized, the land is portrayed as a woman struggling to survive, so she will be able to ensure her children have a place to return to.

The motif of the struggling woman has also been adopted by Palestinian armed organizations as part of their rebirth project, which represents a process of purification. Frantz Fanon wrote about purification as a cleansing act which would purge the colonized man and enable him to forget the damage of the past and create a new era. [15]

The Fatah movement, the pioneer of the Palestinian armed struggle, gave the image of women a central place in its early political discourse. The Palestinian woman, Alba de Fatah, is a woman who survived the hardships of the war in 1948, who takes part in shaping the fate of the Palestinian people, giving birth to a new generation of fighters.[16] The woman is the homeland, she is the land, which, even if it is not physically accessible, continues to exist with the very survival of the Palestinians in the diaspora. A good example of this is seen in the Fatah poster from its early years, which connects women, birth, and armed struggle through the connection to the land. This is a natural motif, since the majority of Palestinian society was a rural agricultural society before the 1948 war.

The image of the woman has been intensified in light of the Palestinian struggle. The ideological armed struggle also brought the Palestinian woman back into the literary discourse. The woman is no longer a passive factor, pushed to the margins of the patriarchal relationships which characterize Arab society, but rather participates in the struggle for self-liberation and national definition. During the first intifada, mainly after it enters into its second year, women's role in the struggle took a more prominent place in literature, mainly as a mother of a martyr, wounded, or the prisoner. Later on, the passive stance disappears, and they started to be more active and even to take sometimes man's role.[17] On the ground, those developments, provoked a political dispute between factions of the PLO and Hamas against the backdrop of the implications that the social changes that could be created through the women's struggle within the Palestinian public space.[18]

The way in which Palestinians related to themselves as victims was intended not only to elicit empathy among the political consciousness in the international arena but also to prepare for the armed struggle that became the ethos around which Palestinian nationalism was built in the 1960s after the establishment of the PLO and the burgeoning of armed groups.

The armed struggle was perceived as the Palestinian response to the image of the victimhood. In order to justify their aggression and attacks on civilian targets, the Palestinian organizations launched a propaganda campaign in the late 1960s centered on the idea of the Palestinians being victims of the Jewish people. This campaign was conducted on campuses and in European cities.

The discourse on victimhood was also accompanied by calls for political support that may become violent, including political gatherings and cultural events that were conducted in the local European languages.[19] This type of activity was particularly prominent in West Germany, where Marxist left-wing organizations together with the Palestinians promoted this discourse and expressed public support for the armed struggle waged by "the victims of the Zionist movement." It was not for nothing that victimhood was the central component of the Palestinian enlistment discourse in Germany, where various marginal elements of society wanted to remove or reject the sense of responsibility for the genocide of the Jewish people perpetrated by the Nazi extermination machine. [20]

This argument is well reflected in Palestinian discourse. Ghassan Abdallah, a poet and social activist, expressed this concept of victimhood following his visit to the Yad Vashem Museum in 2002:

> I went to the Yad Vashem Holocaust Memorial in Jerusalem with the usual convictions of a Palestinian Arab: We were never responsible for the pogroms and discrimination against Jews in Europe, neither in the past nor in the Nazi era. So why should Palestinians pay for the crimes of Europeans against Jews? [21]

While trying to understand to the Jewish suffer during the Holocaust Ghassan Abdallah pointed out the difficulties that he has as a Palestinian:

> But I cannot help looking with a Palestinian's eyes and heart. And my reactions could not be isolated from the recent history of our country, invaded and taken over by force, money, intrigue, and alliances with the powerful of the day. In short, as Palestinians put it, Palestine was stolen from its original inhabitants, who are the descendents of all the people who inhabited the land. Not only did 'Israel' take over and claim for itself the geography of Palestine but also its history, religion, language, mythology, culture – even the falafel and hommus. [22]

Although feeling empathy to the Jewish collective suffer, Ghassan Abdallah came back to the Palestinian traditional position of victimhood. In recent years, this approach of recognizing the Jewish suffering in the Holocaust has become more central to the Palestinian discourse. The change can be seen in the manner in which Palestinian Authority President Mahmoud Abbas (Abu Mazen) refers to the Holocaust. Abbas, whose doctoral dissertation at the University of Moscow was published as an Arabic book in 1983, created contempt for the Holocaust and challenged the number of Jews slaughtered by the Nazi killing machine. In 2011, Abbas began changing his approach to the Holocaust when he publicly said that he did not deny the Holocaust and accepted the number of six million killed. [23] In later public speeches not only did Abbas not deny the Holocaust but declared it an event that reflected ethnic discrimination which the Palestinian people reject and oppose. [24]

Abbas's statements were meant to reflect the beliefs of his adversaries and then use them against them, in this case using Jewish history in order to attack the actions of the State of Israel and the political legitimacy of the Zionist Movement. Later in the same speech at the United Nations General Assembly, Abbas called on the nations of the world to intervene in the West Bank and provide the Palestinian people with "international protection." The

Palestinians, according to Abbas, are victims of history. Within this context, Abbas also demanded that the British apologize for the Balfour Declaration at the General Assembly of the United Nations in 1917.[25] Once again, by doing so, President Abbas strengthened the sense of historical victimization, and ran away from taking responsibility for the current complicated political situation.

PALESTINIAN VICTIMHOOD AND THE ARAB STATES

The doctrine of the Palestinian victimhood, with the Nakba and its aftermath being its central axioms, also views the Arab states as oppressing forces responsible for the miserable fate of the Palestinians. The Arab states are accused not only of encouraging Palestinians to leave their homes during the 1948 war, so as not to disturb their military operations aimed at destroying the nascent State of Israel,[26] but also of turning their backs on the Palestinians after they failed to fulfill their side of the deal.[27]

Salah Khalaf (Abu Iyad), one of Fatah's founders, writes in his memoirs that:

> In retrospect, I believe that my people erred in trusting the Arab governments and allowing them freedom of action in their attempt to conquer the Jewish settlers. They should have stayed on the land, whatever the price would have been. The Zionists could not have destroyed each and every one of them. Furthermore, for many of us, exile was worse than death.[28]

The perception of victimhood in relation to the Arab states also takes a central place in Palestinian cultural space. The song "Where Are the Millions" (Wayn al-Malayyn) expresses the feelings of Palestinian victimhood, protesting the helplessness and indifference of the Arab states and the frustration and disappointment of their position, which turns the Palestinians into victims. this song was written by Ali Qilani, a Libyan poet, and composed by Mohamad Abdallah Mansour, also from Libya. The original video of this song is preformed three Arab singers Julia Boutros from Lebanon, Amal Arafa from Syria, and Sawsan Hammami, from Tunisia. In a paradoxical way, the three Arab singers send a clear message on the behalf of the Palestinians to the Arab Nation:

> Where are the millions? Where is the Arab people?
> Where is the Arab rage? Where is the Arab blood? Where is the Arab honor?[29]

Since the first intifada, the song "Where are the Millions" has become one of the most popular and prominent icons of Palestinian victimhood. This song is an anthem of rage, as spoken in its words:

Allah is with us. He is stronger and greater than the Sons of Zion. Even if they hang, kill and bury me, my land will not be humiliated. My red blood will water the green earth. [30]

The song "Where Are the Millions" become icon of Palestinian victimhood. This song is often played on Palestinian radio and television and been sung to audiences at every significant events, ceremonies, or memorials of Palestinian victimhood. [31] This popular song has dozens of versions and YouTube videos that use pictures of the dead, the wounded, and the acts of destruction of Palestinian houses by the the Israeli army, all of which make the Palestinians the direct victims of the conflict. [32] The song ends with an open question:

And we ask, where are our brothers?
Where are you, my brothers? [33]

The sense of abandonment in the song characterizes the sense of victimhood in the Pan Arabism sense, with Fatah having been the first to point an accusing figure at the Arab states immediately after its establishment. The sense of guilt threatened to ripen into rage, but because of their weakness the Palestinians understood that they had to keep their intervention in the internal affairs of the Arab states to a minimum, realizing that demonstrations of rage against the Arab governments would only harm the Palestinian people. The Palestinians learned to accept the absurd situation of seeking Arab support, even if the Arab countries pay only lip service to the Palestinian issue. Fatah made it clear that the Palestinian people, and not the Arab states, are the representatives of the Palestinian cause. [34]

As with all of the Palestinians who were forced to submit to heavy insults, Abu Iyad had his fair share of grievances. He recalls in his memoirs the night he spent in the airfield in Beirut when he was making his way with his family from Kuwait to Egypt. When he was arrested in at the airport, Abu Iyad relates, that he was placed in the kennel of a dog, which had been placed in quarantine as its owners did not have proper licenses from the Ministry of Health. Abu Iyad went on to relate that the dog was released from quarantine before he was, thanks to orders from above. This incident, which was indelibly etched into his memory, symbolized the sad fate of the Palestinian people for him. [35]

The feeling of humiliation and loneliness envelops the Palestinians in their self-representation as victims, with this perception embedded in the Palestinian collective memory. Fawaz Turki expresses this well:

I hated. I hated the world and the order of reality around me. I hated being dispossessed of a nation and an identity. I hated being the victim of social and political Darwinism. I hated not being part of a culture. I hated being a hybrid, an outcast, and a zero. A problem. Dwelling in a world that suspended me aloft, petrified my being and denied me a place among man until the problem resolved. A world where this problem and I become interchangeable. Where I, the problem, was ignored by some, rejected by others, and derided by the rest. [36]

The sense of rage had to be channeled toward action. Thus the Palestinian armed struggle was born, but its birth did not rescind victimhood discourse, but became the fuel that fanned the flames of the struggle and intensified its power.

Summary

Victimhood is a state of mind in which the individual perceives himself as a victim. The social beliefs of the victim's existence deal with the group's collective self-presentation as victims. These develop in the wake of difficult personal and collective experiences, especially following traumatic events caused by the adversary, and are etched into the collective memory of the victimized society and become formative events the effects of which are influential for many years. The Palestinian society has been saturated with such events throughout the history of the conflict, at the epicenter of which is the foremost traumatic event—the Nakba. The Palestinian feeling of victimhood stems from a series of events in which they feel betrayed, lonely, and helpless. Palestinian society sees itself as a passive object that has become a victim of a reality dictated by the "other." Like other societies that are in an uncontrolled conflict and feel that justice is on their side, the Palestinians divest themselves of all responsibility. That brought the Palestinian to create an alternative culture of denial, [37] casting it onto the "other" and it is almost impossible to find self-criticism for their part and their own contribution to being victims. [38]

Being enwrapped in the sense of victimization is at the center of the Palestinian political experience, and it occupies a prominent place in the central speeches memorial days and major events. It was this sense of victimhood which paved the way for the development of an armed struggle instigated by Fatah in the early 1960s, with the use of violence designed to change the state of consciousness that was reflected in the statement of an anonymous Palestinian refugee, as quoted by Rosemary Saiyeh:

> We are Othman's shirt. After the assassination of Caliph Othman, leaders claimed that "we act in the name of 'Othman" when they wanted to gain the public's trust, but they only used his name and waved his bloody shirt. This I the Palestinian's situation. We are Othman's shirt. [39]

After its inception in 1965 Fatah called on the Palestinians to shake off the sense of victimhood and to stop being the same bloodied shirt that they brandished as a symbol of injustice. The armed struggle for self-determination and liberation turned to the broad consciousness of the Palestinian public and encouraged them to take their own fate into their own hands. This concept, developed by Fatah, became a bridge between different approaches prevalent in Palestinian society.

The idea of armed struggle influenced by the writing of Frantz Fanon, a French Martinique–born, Afro-Caribbean psychiatrist who joined the Algerian National Liberation Front (FLN). Fanon was the ideologist of this movement, and his book *The Wretched of the Earth* dealt with the struggles of national liberation in the Third World.

Fanon sanctioned the use of unrestrained violence as a tool for liberation from colonialism. This violence described as a catharsis that stimulates the sense of freedom in man, with this feeling being achieved by sacrifice. According to Fanon, decolonization will always appear as a violent phenomenon. Its purpose is to replace one "variety" of man with another.[40] However in the Palestinian case it can be said that the struggle continues and the new variety of man has not been created, it may achieved when independent Palestinian state will be established. The sense of victimhood has not been erased and continues to play a pivotal role in directing political practice and the armed struggle has also remained an ethos.

These facts reinforce the perception of self-righteousness and create a selective process of receiving and processing information. The result of this process is the preservation and strengthening of the underlying dispute and the beliefs supporting the continuation of the Palestinian-Israeli conflict.

The theme of victimhood is reinforced by the prolonged Israeli-Palestinian conflict, characterized by periodicity and the recurrence of acts of violence, with the discourse of collective victimization having become central to Palestinian society and, as such, a barrier to reconciliation. As the weaker side in the conflict, the Palestinians rely on this sense of victimization and continue to live it as a collective on a daily basis; this can be find clearly in the refugee camps and in the Palestinian culture of memorialization.

The Palestinian victimhood, which mainly relay on the memories of 1948 creates a present experience that brings together the Palestinian communities living in the West Bank, the Gaza Strip, and the Diaspora. The Palestinians feel as if they are the victims of history and fate.[41]

This perception of reality has created an atmosphere of collective abrogation of all responsibility for the political destiny of the people by the Palestinian leadership. Palestinian victimhood is part of the collective memory and it is reinforced and legitimized by the Palestinian national ethos. Without sacrificing the image of the victim, it will be hard to the Palestinians to build vital and functioning state and it will not be possible to reach a political solution to the Israeli-Palestinian conflict.

NOTES

1. This article, the result of a long period of academic research, based on in-depth study of sources in Arabic and Hebrew, is directed not only toward the academic community but also to the wider community. For this reason I decided to make the information more accessible in a few places by compromising on the use of scientific transliteration of Arabic to English (and to the original Hebrew). Key terms and names of places and people, familiar to the public from the media, are written in their familiar forms. So for example, I have chosen to write Intifada instead of intifāḍ **ah**, Likewise I have adopted simplified spellings in the main text while in the endnotes I have chosen to maintain the original scientific transliterations. This has been to make the article more readable for the general public.

2. Fawaz Turki, *Soul in Exile – Lives of a Palestinian Revolutionary* (New York, 1988), 17–18.

3. Ahmad H. Sa 'di, "Catastrophe, Memory and Identity: Al-Nakbah as a Component of Palestinian identity," *Israel Studies* 7,2 (2002), 185.

4. Avraham Sela, "ManhHaravim Ha-Falastinim Be-MIlhemet 1948 [the Palestinians Arabs in 1948 War] in B.Z. Keida, Moshe Maoz (Eds) *Ha-Tnu'a ha-Leumit ha-Falastinit – me-'Imut le-Hashlama?* [The Palestinian National Movement: From Confrontation to Reconciliation?] (Tel-Aviv: Misrad ha-Bitahon, 1997), 190.

5. See, for example, Arif Al-Arif, Al -Nakba: Nakbat Bayt al -Muqaddas Wa al -Fardus al -Mafqud 1947–1952 [Al-Nakba: The Nakba of the sacred house and the lost of Paradise] (Beirut, 1956)

6. Al-Muatawakkil Taha, "Risala ila Jundi Israili [Letter to an Israeli Soldier], in Ami Buskila-Elad, *Modern Palestinian Literature and Culture* (London: Frank Cass 1999), 114–15.

7. Ibid

8. Meir Litvak and Esther Webman, *From Empathy to Denial: Arab Responses to the Holocaust* (London: Hurst and Company, 2009), 357.

9. Ghassan Kanafani *Returning to Haifa*, 1969

10. Emil Habibi, "Your Holocaust, Our Catastrophe," *Politica*, no.8 (June–July 1986) (Hebrew) pp. 26–27, discussed in Meir Litvak and Esther Webman, *From Empathy to Denial: Arab Responses to the Holocaust* (London: Hurst and Company, 2009), 315

11. Ibid

12. Sari Nusseibeh, *Once Upon a Country: A Palestinian Life* (London: Halban Publishers, 2007), 43.

13. Laleh Khalili, *Heroes and Martyrs of Palestine: The Politics of National Commemoration* (New York: Cambridge University Press, 2007), 43.

14. Ami Elad-Bouskila, *Modern Palestinian Literature and Culture*, 121.

15. Franz Fanon (Translated by Richard Philcoxs), *The Wretched of the Earth* (New York: Groove Press, 1961), 83–84.

16. See for example Fatah poster at the: https://www.palestineposterproject.org/poster/the-intilaqa

17. Ami Elad-Bouskila, *Modern Palestinian Literature and Culture*, 96–97.

18. Rema Hammai, "From Immodesty to Collaboration: Hamas, the Women's Movement and National Identity in the Intifada." in *Political Islam; Essays from Middle East Report.* Joel Beinin and Joe Stork eds. (University of California Press, 1997), 204–6.

19. Ido Zelkovtiz, *Students and Resistance in Palestine: Books, Guns, and Politics* (Routledge, 2015), 44–47.

20. Jeffrey Herf, *Undeclared Wars with Israel East Germany and the West German Far Left 1967–1989* (New York: Cambridge University Press, 2016), 61.

21. Ghassan Abdallah, "A Palestinian at Yad va-Shem," *Jerusalem Quarterly*, 15, 22 (2002), 42.

22. Ibid.

23. Jodi Rudoren, "Mahmoud Abba Shifts on Holocaust," *New York Times*, 26 April, 2014, https://www.nytimes.com/2014/04/27/world/middleeast/palestinian-leader-shifts-on-holocaust.html?mcubz=0.

24. Ibid

25. President Abbas to the United Nations General Assembly, 20 September, 2017, https://www.haaretz.com/middle-east-news/palestinians/1.813524.

26. Musa al-Almi, "The Lesson of Palestine", *The Middle East Journal*, 3, 4, (1949), p. 381.

27. Mahmoud Abbas, *al-Sahayuniyya- Bidaya wa-Nihaya* (Ramallah, 1977), p. 104

28. Abu Iyad, (Salah Khalaf*), Lelo Moledet: Sihot im Eric Rouleau* [with a homeland] (Jerusalem: Mifras, 1979), 34.

29. Julia Boutros, Amal Arafa, Sawsan Hammami, "Where Are the Millions," https://www.youtube.com/watch?v=0jK388GEWiE.

30. Ibid

31. Ronni Shaked, *The Eyes behind the Kaffyeh* [In Hebrew] (Rishon Letzion: LaMiskal, 2018), 178–79.

32. Ibid, see also: Julia Boutros, Amal Arafa, Sawsan Hammami, "Where are the Millions," https://www.youtube.com/watch?v=0jK388GEWiE

33. Shaked, *The Eyes Behind the Kaffyeh*, 179.

34. Naji Alush, Fikr Harakat al-Muqwama al-Filastiniyya – Nizara Amma (no place of publication, no date), 29.

35. Abu Iyad, Lelo Moledet, 73.

36. Fawaz Turki, *The Disinherited*: *Journal of a Palestinian Exile* (New York: New York: Monthly Review Press, 1972), 77

37. Yohanan Tzoref, Hasamim be-Yeshuv ha-Sihsuch Im Israel- Haprespectiva ha-Falastinit, in Yaacov Bar Siman Tov (Ed), *Hasamim le-Shalon ba-Sihsoch ha-Israeli-Falastini* (Jerusalem: the Jerusalem institute for Israel Studies, 2010), 91.

38. Shaked, *The Eyes behind the* Kaffyeh, 184.

39. Nels Johnson, *Islam and the Meaning in Palestinian Politics* (London, 1982), 60.

40. Fanon, *The Wretched of the Earth* (Grove Press New York, 1963), 21.44.

41. Shaked, *The Eyes behind the* Kaffyeh, 184–85.

BIBLIOGRAPHY

Abbas, Mahmoud (Abu Mazen) *al-Sahayuniyya- Bidaya wa-Nihaya*. Ramallah, 1977.

Abbas, Mahmoud (Abu Mazen), President Abbas to the United Nations General Assembly, 20 September, 2017, https://www.haaretz.com/middle-east-news/palestinians/1.813524

Abdallah, Ghassan. "A Palestinian at Yad va-Shem," *Jerusalem Quarterly*, 15,22 (2002), pp. 42–45.

Abu Iyad, (Salah Khalaf), *Lelo Moledet: Sihot im Eric Rouleau*. Jerusalem: Mifras, 1979.

al-Almi, Musa. "The Lesson of Palestine," *The Middle East Journal*, 3, 4, (1949), pp. 373–405.

Alush, Naji . *Fikr Harakat al-Muqwama al-Filastiniyya – Nizara Amma*, no place of publication, no date.

Elad-Bouskila, Ami. *Modern Palestinian Literature and Culture*. London: Frank Cass 1999.

Fanon, Frantz. *The Wretched of the Earth*, New York: Groove Press, 1963.

Habibi, Emil, "Your Holocaust, Our Catastrophe," *Politica*, no.8 (June–July 1986) (Hebrew) pp. 26–27.

Hammai, Rema. "From Immodesty to Collaboration: Hamas, the Women's Movement and National Identity in the Intifada." In Beinin, Joel, and Stork, Joe (Eds) *Political Islam; Essays from Middle East Report*. University of California Press, 1997.

Jeffrey Herf, *Undeclared Wars with Israel East Germany and the West German Far Left 1967–1989*. New York: Cambridge University Press, 2016.

Johnson, Nels. *Islam and the Meaning in Palestinian Politics*. London, 1982.

Kanafani, Ghassan. *Returning to Haifa,* 1969.

Khalili, Laleh *Heroes and Martyrs of Palestine: The Politics of National Commemoration*. New York: Cambridge University Press, 2007

Litvak, Meir. Webman, Esther. *From Empathy to Denial: Arab Responses to the Holocaust*. London: Hurst and Company, 2009.

Nusseibeh, Sari. *Once Upon a Country: A Palestinian Life* (London: Halban Publishers, 2007

Rudoren, Jodi. "Mahmoud Abba Shifts on Holocaust," *New York Times*, 26 April, 2014, https://www.nytimes.com/2014/04/27/world/middleeast/palestinian-leader-shifts-on-holocaust.html?mcubz=0.

Sa 'di, Ahmad H. "Catastrophe, memory and identity: Al-Nakbah as a component of Palestinian identity", *Israel Studies* 7,2 (2002) 175–98.

Shaked, Ronni. *The Eyes Behind the Kaffye*h (In Hebrew). Rishon Letzion: Lamiskal, 2018.

Turki, Fawaz. *The Disinherited.* New York: Monthly Review Press, 1972.

Turki, Fawaz. *Soul in Exile – Lives of a Palestinian Revolutionary.* New York: Monthly Review Press, 1988.

Tzoref, Yohanan. Hasamim be-Yeshuv ha-Sihsuch Im Israel- Haprespectiva ha-Falastinit, in Yaacov Bar Siman Tov (Ed), *Hasamim le-Shalon ba-Sihsoch ha-Israeli-Falastini*. Jerusalem: the Jerusalem institute for Israel Studies, 2010.

Zelkovtiz, Ido. *Students and Resistance in Palestine: Books, Guns, and Politics*. Routledge, 2015.

Chapter Seven

Transforming Victimhood

From Competitive Victimhood to Sharing Superordinate Identity

Irit Keynan[1]

I. COMPETITIVE VICTIMHOOD AND ITS DETRIMENTAL EFFECTS

Ethnic, national, or religious groups who have suffered severe traumas in their past share a "chosen trauma."[2] This concept characterizes an unconscious choice of such a traumatized group to add to its identity the catastrophic event whose shared psychological representation keeps passing from generation to generation, influencing the life of each current generation. The historic event that caused the group an extensive loss of people or land and a collective feeling of helplessness, fear, and humiliation becomes a major part of the group's collective memory, and it imposes on the following generations the societal tasks and goals of reversing the past helplessness, shame, and humiliation and turning the previous passivity into activity and assertion, in order never to allow such traumas to happen again.[3] Large groups with chosen trauma in their past share a sense of victimization, which determines to a large extent their attitude toward other groups, especially rival ones, with whom they are involved in intractable conflicts. The negative attitudes toward the victim's past perpetrator may develop to include present perceived aggressor in addition to the historic one, thus casting past traumas on present conflicts. Negative attitudes may also develop toward other groups that do not recognize the group's victim status, while positive feelings may arise toward those groups who support and recognize own group's victimization (i.e., through empathy or aid). Bar-tal, Chernyak-Hai, Schori, and Gundar[4] claim that these effects, in addition to the conviction to prevent future harm, lead to emotional tendencies of fear, anger, and self-pity and incite vengeful attitudes that are enshrined in the collective memory of the group. They label these beliefs, attitudes, emotions, and behavioral tendencies as a "syndrome of victimhood."

Once victimhood is adopted into society's self-schema, it begins to play a crucial role in society's collective perception of itself, the outside world, and the rival group.[5] This has detrimental consequences, the most salient of which, are constant fear and anxiety, a sense of entitlement, and moral superiority,[6] and they often drive traumatized groups to use excessive violence.[7] The chosen trauma has been shown to be a major cause for the impossibility to put an end to conflicts,[8] and it does not have to be of the same scale to determine how such groups cope with present conflicts or how much empathy they are able to feel toward each other when in conflict.

Despite its negative consequences, collective victimhood is closely associated with ingroup cohesion and unity.[9] At the same time, however, strong ingroup relations often comes at the expense of relations with the outgroup in intergroup conflict.[10] Leaders, Pittinsky and Simon found,[11] promote ingroup cohesion not necessarily for the sake of society, but as a tool to strengthen their own leadership, even at the price of exacerbating intergroup conflict. The two researchers use several theoretical and historical examples to show the cycle of ingroup cohesion and connectedness, exacerbation of intergroup conflict, and in return the rise of strong leadership within the ingroup. Cohesion is such a salient effect that it is a predictor of behavioral and attitudinal intergroup bias against the outgroup, developing an "us vs. them" mentality.[12] On this basis, leaders may use entitativity[13] of the outgroup to further the conflict and increase ingroup bias, creating fear and contempt toward the outgroup.

Once the victimhood identity takes hold, it becomes an easy tool to gain support and rally followers based on the elements of fear, entitlement, and moral superiority. Unscrupulous leaders therefore often use the powerful means of collective memory and the chosen trauma, implanting it as a part of the group's social identity, and continuously arousing fear and a sense of an ongoing collective threat, propagating it through education, media, speeches, etc., thus aggravating the conflict.[14]

The nature of intractable intergroup conflict seems to be universally correlated with a belief of each side that it is the *true* victim of the conflict. In such persistent conflicts, collective victimhood becomes more deeply engrained in the society's identity, and central in society's ethos and collective memory of the conflict itself.[15] As mentioned before, the scale of the chosen trauma does not have to be the same to determine its effects on each of the traumatized groups; in the case of the Israeli-Palestinian conflict, for Israelis it is undeniably the Holocaust; for the Palestinians, the Naqba. Moreover, the two parties of the conflict, when adopting collective victimhood as an element of their identity may choose to maintain it during intractable conflict due to social roles and benefits attributed to this position such as: justification of society's goals in the conflict, positive self-perception, and de-legitimization of the rival.[16]

In most conflicts the two sides suffer, hence reasonably one would argue that when looking into the future, suffering of one side "compensates" for that of the other and that they should "move on" and end the conflict. If, however, one side sees itself as the one who has suffered more than the other, then this side becomes the *true* victim, deserving more considerateness and concessions.[17] Often therefore a Competitive Victimhood (CV) emerges where both sides compete over recognition as the *real* victim.[18] This competition reflects groups' need for moral acceptance and for a sense of restored power and it has been shown to be a major impediment to the resolution of conflicts and an important factor in the conservation or intensification of conflicts.[19]

The phenomenon of CV is well known from around the world, but in this chapter, I use the Israeli experience to explore the possibility to control it. After a period of decline, the issue of victimhood in Israel has been on the rise since the assassination of Prime Minister Yitzhak Rabin. Ever since this period the use of CV and Collective Traumatic Memory have escalated and nurtured by politicians, and the one sided "no choice" conflict narrative,[20] based on "Israel's greater victimhood," has gained more support. This underscores the importance and urgency of overcoming or at least containing this phenomenon, and hence new research that explores ways to overcome CV is needed. This chapter follows this direction and proposes that overcoming CV is possible.

The chapter is constructed as follows: section II looks into the detrimental effects of the syndrome of victimhood in Israel. Section III presents the superordinate shared identity concept and explores the question of how it can overcome competitive victimhood and its detrimental effects. Section IV presents successful examples of Palestinian-Israelis groups that fit the superordinate shared identity concept. Discussion and concluding remarks are provided in the last section which also analyzes the potential viability and growth of these groups and the concept they represent.

II. ISRAEL—VICTIMHOOD AND THE "FEAR AND JUSTICE LOOP"

The emotional burden of the "syndrome of victimhood,"[21] coupled with a sense of entitlement and moral superiority that evolves from it,[22] often leads the collective to believe that it may bypass moral norms in order to ensure the safety of the group, whatever the cost may be. The perception of moral superiority provides such a collective with a conviction of its just nature and appropriateness of its moves, thus justifying actions that generally defy moral norms.[23] Moreover, this perception conveys a sense of a right to permanent sympathy by others, consideration, and protection from criticism.[24]

Israelis are driven by these motifs combined with a strong conviction of their nation's collective victimhood.[25] Moreover, as I have elsewhere defined, Israelis are trapped in a "loop of fear and justice,"[26] meaning that they are motivated by a profound fear for their existence, coupled with a deep desire—which they perceive as existential—to feel that their cause and their actions are not only justified, but also are just, thus maintaining their self-view of innocent victims even in cases when that feeling is deceptive. In this loop, anxiety leads to un-proportionate use of power against the Palestinians, which in turn threaten the nation's moral identity, which adds to the anxiety, and so on and so forth, in a vicious circle.

This "fear-and-justice loop" in which Israelis are caught, is itself an important factor in nurturing their sense of victimhood. Trapped in this loop, many Israelis tend to assess all security related events via a political prism, shaped by the need for moral reassurance, often dismissing information that may suggest a different view as false attempts to harm the reputation of the Israeli Defense Forces (IDF), rather than regrading them objectively; seeing any criticism of the IDF as based on illegitimate factors. This same overpowering philosophy lies behind Jewish Israelis' disregard of the suffering experienced by Palestinians, whether they are residents of Gaza and the West Bank or Israeli citizens. In other words, war trauma of the outgroup and the moral injuries of the ingroup are both rejected by the collective for the sake of maintaining a sense of justice and moral superiority,[27] the lack of which augments the group's overwhelming sense of threat. The "fear-and-justice loop" may also have negative consequences on the way the group treats its own members, such as the society's and military's negative view of war trauma casualties. Since combat trauma experienced by soldiers contains symptoms that may be translated as weakness, society is threatened by it, fearing for the ability of the soldiers to protect it, thus increasing fear of imminent danger and vulnerability.[28] It also blinds Israelis from recognizing and accepting cases of Israel's own soldiers' moral injuries.[29] Due to yearning to maintain a sense of moral superiority and a sense of being just, society will reject and refuse to recognize the moral injury suffered by the individual soldier.[30] The motivation of fear and the motivation of rightness are linked as variables in an equation that demands an unquestioned faith in the justice of Israel's cause, and in it being the *real* victim of the conflict in all situations. This equation has dominated Israeli discourse for many years and may partly explain the inner contradiction that characterizes large segments of Israeli society—a nation whose public life is so thoroughly permeated by an experience of shared suffering yet finds it so hard to feel empathy toward the suffering of the other side, and expresses suspicion and insusceptibility toward its own individuals who suffer from trauma of war and moral injury.[31]

III. WHAT IS SUPERORDINATE SHARED IDENTITY, AND HOW CAN IT OVERCOME COMPETITIVE VICTIMHOOD?

Intractable conflicts among traumatized groups who suffer from the syndrome of victimhood strengthen the ingroup's level of identification with own ethnic/religious group, as a mechanism to cope with the ongoing conflict.[32] This augmented identification with the ingroup decreases guilt over the ingroup misdeeds and strengthens the interpretation of ingroup violence as a form of self-defense.[33] The higher the level of identification with one's own ethnic/religious group becomes lower the identification with the other group. Since self-view as a perpetrator is a threat to the moral identity,[34] forsaking the *real* victim belief/position, becomes a serious threat in itself, thus pushing the group into the "fear-and-justice loop."[35] This makes it even more difficult to uproot competitive victimhood. On the other hand, recognition in the group's being the *real* victim, produces reconciliatory attitudes and optimism,[36] probably because it reassures the moral identity. Thus, in an experiment with Palestinian and Israeli groups,[37] when each of the rival groups were led to believe that it "won" the *real* victim status by a third party (UN and academic research), it softened their antagonism to the adversary group, and expressed more reconciliatory attitudes and less pessimism toward reconciliation.[38]

Realistically however, there is no way that the two groups can be declared "winners" of the victimhood competition. A way, therefore, should be found to remove the competition and to provide the two groups with recognition of their suffering. This is where the model of Superordinate Shared Identity (SOSHI) comes in. The idea behind the SOSHI model is to add a top layer of overarching identity to the separate, even contradicting, identities of two (or more) groups, thus enabling them to share an identity as victims *of the conflict*. This position allows the two adversary groups to maintain their status as the *real* victims while at the same time acknowledging their counterparts' victimhood; it enables each of the rival groups to feel empathy toward the other group's suffering[39] without risking its own moral identity. While the common identity model[40] uses existing overarching identities, such as school, university, town or nation,[41] the SOSHI model is based on creating a *new* shared identity that leans on past traumas to create hope.[42] In this aspect, this is a revolutionary idea, which may be seen as utopic, but as I show below—it is based on the reality of two Palestinian-Israeli grassroots organizations.

The SOSHI model extends the boundaries of Traumatic Collective Memory, bringing together previous enemies, who have been inflicting violence and grief upon each other for decades, under a shared umbrella of the same *real* victimhood, thus transforming their CV into a community of empathy and hope. As I show below, the transformation into a community of hope emerges from the core carriers of the new SOSHI—people from both groups who personally lost loved ones or actively participated in the conflict as combatants. Their mutual recognition creates a sense of catharsis to individuals who used to be both victims and perpetrators, and now recognize that the relevant enemy to fight is the actual conflict itself, which is to blame for the woes of the two groups, and especially of the new SOSHI members. These two groups harness this state of mind to dedicate themselves to stopping the conflict instead of fighting one another.

IV. CAN SUCH SHARED SUPERORDINATE IDENTITY GROUPS BE CREATED?

How and why would the SOSHI achieve its goal? Underlying the process is the fact that even in groups involved in prolonged conflicts there exists a minority of group members that do feel empathy for the victims of the other side. The challenge is to employ this minority as a lever to arouse such feelings in the rest of the community. The success of the initial kernel will have a ripple effect on wider circles and encourage more people to share the new identity thus continuously expanding the circle of the "community of hope."

In this section, I describe impressing cases of success in a courageous effort of implementing SOSHI by two Palestinian-Israeli civil society organizations. These two groups have grown significantly in recent years, spreading their idea of the two nations being victims of the conflict into larger circles. While they did not yet reach a critical mass, they attract substantial and growing support. Below, I trace their expansion and opine on their chances of becoming an influential factor in advancing the prospects of a peaceful resolution to the Palestinian-Israeli conflict.

The Parents Circle: The Bereaved Families' Forum

The Parents Circle-Families Forum (PCFF), established in 1995, is a joint Palestinian-Israeli organization of over 600 families, all of whom have lost a close family member as a result of the prolonged conflict. Joint activities have shown that the reconciliation between individuals and communities from both sides is possible, and it is this insight that they are trying to pass on to both sides of the conflict. Moreover, the PCFF has concluded that the process of reconciliation between individuals is a prerequisite to achieving a sustainable peace, a notion that was also found by researchers.[43] The organization thus utilizes all resources available in education, public meetings and the media, to spread these ideas.

The Parents Circle-Families Forum is registered as an association and is managed jointly by the professional staff, Israelis and Palestinians working in two offices: the Palestinian Office is Beit Jala and the Israeli Office is in Ramat Ef'al, Tel Aviv. Although the PCFF has no stated position on the political solution of the conflict, most of its members agree that the solution must be based on free negotiations between the leadership of both sides to ensure basic human rights, the establishment of two states for two peoples, and the signing of a peace treaty. The historic reconciliation between the two nations is a necessary condition for obtaining a sustainable peace treaty.

It should be noted that without explicitly stating this, the PCFF has embraced a SOSHI of bereaved families that includes family members of Israeli and Palestinian victims that empathize with the suffering of the other side, and are willing to put aside their grievances against each other and concentrate on finding a peaceful solution to the conflict. In this SOSHI group, the focus is on easing the suffering and empathizing with the sufferer be him/her an Israeli or Palestinian.

While participants from each of the old groups in the new joint group might have started from a hostile perspective to members of the other old group that harmed their families, over time deep relationship have emerged between members of the opposing former groups. This relationship is based on the mutual acknowledgment of the grief of the other and binds all participants in the understanding that all of them are victims of the conflict, which is their real common enemy. By adopting this frame of mind, the members of the new group subconsciously have created a shared superordinate identity group of the conflict's victims. They have thus expanded the limits of the Collective (and personal) Traumatic Memory[44] to also include the casualties and victims of the other side.

The number of members in the group has been steadily increasing over time. The rise did not occur because of an increase in the number of victims but due to the ripple effect, a growing circle of victims who decide to join the group.

> The Parents Circle doesn't want new members; we want the cycle of violence to end, but this conflict continues to take innocent lives on both sides. Help us continue our efforts to reach out to the bereaved and invite them to take part in our programs. Our members are our greatest resource in combatting hatred and divisive propaganda, in the pursuit of a lasting peace and an end to the cycle of violence and bereavement.[45]

Within this group there are several attributes which confirm my hypothesis concerning the benefits of the SOSHI. First, the members of this group show increased empathy for the other side. Second, the circle of participants in the group and hence those who share the superordinate identity keeps expanding, and for the above-mentioned good reasons. This expansion is predicated on one or both of the following two factors: group members from both sides feel close to each other since they have changed their self-view from being each other's victims to all of them being victims of a conflict that must be stopped; group members wish to belong to a community based on hope rather than to a community based on victimhood and hate. Whatever the reason members join in, the result is the same—an adoption of a Superordinate Shared Identity of victims of the conflict instead of each other's, and a conviction to struggle for peace. It is important to note here, that whereas re-categorization of the groups unites them as victims aspiring to change the future, this does not imply that they should forget the past, nor does it require that they agree with the other side's narrative. They should however be familiar with it and accept the right of the other side to their own narrative. The only shared narrative, which is the crucial point, is that past traumas are the anchor for the new SOSHI; for understanding and empathizing with the pain and suffering of the outgroup; and for the joint struggle to end the conflict, walking together toward a future of freedom and hope.[46] This shared narrative is exemplified by the following excerpt from the FCFF website:

> I went to Jerusalem. There were Israeli and Palestinian families. All spoke about pain, and of what we had not gained with violence. That influenced me a great deal. I saw that there was a human aspect, which I was to discover more of. As of that moment, I felt that I had a mission, a national duty. The release of land is not done only with rifles. The Israeli community must be able to see in me somebody who holds tightly onto the hand of peace.[47,48]

Combatants for Peace

Combatants for Peace (CFP) is a group of Palestinians and Israelis who have taken an active part in the cycle of violence in the region: Israeli soldiers serving in the IDF and Palestinians who were combatants fighting to be free from the Israeli occupation. This group of former combatants established the organization for peace on the basis of non-violence principles. Whereas not all of the members are strictly victims in the usual sense of the word, all of them are victimized by the unfortunate situation the conflict has placed them in, by what they had to endure, and by the activities it made them participate in. Many of the members of the organization have been wounded in the wars either mentally or physically, quite a few still suffer from PTSD, and some suffer from moral injury.

This group, the same as PCFF, has chosen SOSHI of victims of the conflict, which transcends each side's original perspective of the other as the enemy, into a new perspective of all members—seeing themselves as an expanded group, who shares a common identity of non-violent warriors focusing on ending the conflict.

Combatants for Peace, established in 2006, declares in its website that its vision is to bring peace to both sides

> Through joint nonviolence in the present, we lay the foundations for a nonviolent future. [49]

From the perspective of SOSHI, perhaps the most telling story is that of Suliman al-Khatib from Ramallah, a member of CFP:

> Growing up, my family was badly impacted by the ongoing conflict; there was so much suffering all around me. My heart cried out for my people, and I desperately wanted to help my family and my community. I was determined to make a difference, but there was no peaceful way to do this; the only option was to join the violent struggle – so I did.

> One day I had the opportunity to watch *Schindler's List*. I was deeply moved, and it changed my life forever. I realized that these "enemies" were actually human beings who were suffering profoundly. I reconstructed my worldview. I realized for the first time that I had mistaken the enemy. I had thought it was the Israeli people, but I was wrong. Instead, we had a common enemy: hatred and fear. I knew that if we could somehow unite against these common foes, then together we could end this conflict. [50]

Suliman al-Khatib's words directly reflects the idea of SOSHI. The enlightenment he experienced consists of all the elements of SOSHI: recognizing the trauma and suffering of the outgroup, understanding that the mutual enemy is the conflict itself, and a desire to share his identity as victim with those he now could see as sharing it too. This recognition helped him to overcome his wish for revenge, transforming it into an effort to stop the violent cycle. He found his way as a founding member of Combatants for Peace.

CFP and PCFF join forces in some of their activities. The most prominent of those is the alternative joint Israeli-Palestinian annual memorial ceremony for both Israelis and Palestinians who lost their lives in the conflict. The tradition of holding the ceremony started in 2006 and continues annually on the eve of Israel's Memorial Day (which coincides with the Palestinian day of remembering the Naqba). It is called the alternative memorial ceremony, short for being alternative to the official Israeli ceremony. In the words of CFP's website:

> On this particularly difficult day we call upon both sides to acknowledge the pain and the aspirations of those living on the other side of the fence and for

each of us to strive to prevent the next war. . . . At the ceremony, Israeli and
Palestinian bereaved families speak about their personal pain.[51]

In 2006 it was a small ceremony with few dozens of participants in a
small fringe theater in Tel Aviv. In 2017 the ceremony has been a demonstration of power and defiance to the policy of denying the Palestinians' narrative and suffering. About 4000 participants packed one of Tel Aviv's basket-
ball stadiums, leaving many participants in the parking lot for lack of capacity indoors. Hundreds of participants participated in similar ceremonies in
other cities. Palestinians who were denied entrance to Israel joined it in Beit
Jala by digital technology, together with many Israelis who chose to join
them there. This is the result of the ripple effect. It should be noted that by
contrast to the alternative ceremonies, the official Israeli ceremonies on Independence Day mention only the Israeli victims, and those of the Palestinian
authorities mention just the victims of their own. Moreover, the Israeli authorities did not hide their detest of the group's alternative ceremony, thus
the groups and all those who joined them showed courage in holding and
participating in these ceremonies. Furthermore, the growth in the number of
participants in these ceremonies is not limited to bereaved families. The
overarching superordinate identity of victims of the conflict now embraces
widening circles of Palestinians and Israelis, who are not direct victims of the
conflict, but still feel close to each other on the basis of their SOSHI as two
societies who are victims of the conflict between them, and based on their
determined wish to stop it.

DISCUSSION AND CONCLUSION

This chapter suggests that it is conceivable to transform victimhood into a
positive leverage toward reconciliation and peace not by fighting this powerful emotion but by tolerating it, changing only the perspective as to who
should be blamed for it, and who can be accepted into the ranks of its
casualties.

Recognition of suffering and victimhood has been proven to be an important factor in softening tough attitudes toward the outgroup. Such recognition
is required to ease the impact of the chosen trauma[52] and the traumas evolving from the present conflict. When the group is led to believe that such
recognition is achieved, it softens its attitudes on divisive issues, and when
led to believe that the majority of the outgroup does not acknowledge their
victimhood, the opposite happens.[53] Since each side needs reassurance of it
being the *true* victim, and since the strongest effect of such recognition is
when it comes from the adversary,[54] it seems impossible to achieve. Researchers therefore have been looking for other ways to bypass this dead end.
Vollhardt,[55] for example, suggested that similarities of experiences between

victim groups, defined as "inclusive victim beliefs," may give rise to empathy and prosocial behavior toward outgroups, even toward the other party in the conflict. However, later research found that these inclusive victim beliefs, may have positive effects on intergroup relations only if based on a universal notion of inclusivity, and they may also have negative effects when limited to a selective notion of similarities.[56] While the "inclusive victim beliefs" may—in the above-mentioned conditions—help groups come to terms with past aggression and progress toward forgiveness, they do not change the fundamental perspective of two groups with separate contrasting identities, where each sees the other as the main reason for its suffering and victimhood.

SOSHI, on the other hand, suggests a "game changer"; in addition to arousing empathy to similar experiences of all the groups, it completely transforms the conflicting sense of belonging of each group into a shared belonging. By widening the boundaries of the group and changing the targeted enemy from the outgroup to the conflict itself, it uses "the notion of we-ness that transcends the individuals and leads to collective action,"[57] in a completely new way. The Palestinians and the Israelis who adopt the SOSHI of victims of the conflict, create an active new group with a novel identity, which drives them to act toward achieving peace.

This, however, is not the only effect of the SOSHI. The alternative Memorial Day, the CFP and the PCFF's main activity, attracts an audience of participants far bigger than their own membership. It seems, that at least on the Israeli side, the thousands who joined the ceremonies in 2017 were looking for a ceremony that will reflect their profound need for catharsis to their confused emotion of being both victims and perpetrators, and in being part of an action toward peace. Joining a group that declares its Super Ordinate Shared Identity as victims of the conflict, constitutes an action that not only does not abandon the *true* victim status of all Israelis but also acknowledges the *true* victim status of the Palestinians, thus balancing the need to identify with the Israeli fallen soldiers and their families on the one hand, and the wish to empathize with the suffering of the Palestinians, on the other hand. Moreover, the fact that the core carrier of this message are bereaved individuals and families from both sides, makes their groups into a community of hope, such that wide circles of Israelis wish to be part of.

It is also important to mention the fact that both CFP and PCFF do not forget the past, but build on past traumas to create a better future.[58] This reminds of Rorty's[59] suggestion that in their struggle against racism, Americans adopt the approach that they are successors of a long legacy of freedom and hope which was earned by hard fought, bloody, and terrible struggles that eventually led to the freeing of slaves and to equal rights to blacks and women. To facilitate this approach Americans introduce into their pantheon of the collective American memory icons of history and culture from the opposite groups that in the past held dreadful battles. Today these icons represent one shared community that overcame many crises and to which all citizens can feel loyalty. In other words, Rorty[60] suggests not to forget the past, but to use it as a tool to create a community of freedom and hope. This message aligns with that of the alternative joint Israeli-Palestinian Memorial Day, in which the memory of the fallen previous enemies is honored by both sides, and all are introduced to the common Pantheon of memory.

The CFP and the PCFF groups (and similar groups) are still not very prevalent and are relatively small but they are growing, they attract attention and they show promise. Their existence and success comes however to peril for two reasons. One is financial, their success depends on the good will of volunteers and philanthropists. It is therefore up to NGOs and grass roots organizations to strengthen and support them. The second comes from politics. From the way politicians have regarded the alternative joint Israeli-Palestinian ceremonies it is clear that not only is it unlikely that the community of shared victimhood and hope will get any help from the government and governmental organizations, but that the more this community grows, the more resentment it will probably get from politicians who prefer competitive victimhood that serves their political interests.

Nevertheless, the increased popularity of these two groups and the joint ceremony they are holding, indicates their viability. As Rorty[61] pointed out, there is a struggle between those who believe society should adhere to old collective truths and myths, and those who prefer skepticism toward the consensus, while encouraging individualistic thinking. It is too early to predict who will win, but it is my belief that victimhood can be defeated.

NOTES

1. The author wishes to thank Ori Solomon for excellent research assistance.
2. See Volkan 2001.
3. See Volkan 2001; Volkan 2006.
4. Bar-Tal, Chernyak-Hai, Schori, and Gundar 2009.
5. Bar-tal, Chernyak-Hai, Schori, and Gundar 2009 showed that whereas most of the results of this process are detrimental (they have compiled a list of possible consequences society may suffer as a result of this process) it may be useful sometimes as it can unite members in the face of perceived danger and strengthen the home front in times of conflict.
6. Volkan 2006.
7. Kaufman 2006.
8. Volkan 2001.
9. Pittinsky and Simon 2007.
10. Ibid.
11. Pittinsky and Simon 2007.
12. Gaertner and Schopler 1998.
13. Perceiving the group as pure entity, separated from its individuals.
14. Volkan 2006; Pittinsky and Simon 2007; Keynan 2009.
15. Bar-tal 2007.
16. Bar-tal, Chernyak-Hai, Schori, and Gundar 2009.

17. On self-view as victims and the urge for recognition in this status, see Gan 2014.

18. Noor, Shnabel, Halabi, and Nadler 2012; Simantov-Nachlieli, Shnabel and Halabi 2015.

19. See, e.g., Noor, Shnabel, Halabi, and Nadler 2012.

20. Klar, Schori-Eyal, and Klar 2013; Biran and Bartal 2016; Keynan 2016.

21. Bar-tal, Chernyak-Hai, Schori, and Gundar 2009.

22. Volkan 2006.

23. For such actions and their self-justification, see Peleg 1997.

24. Keynan 2009.

25. For the centrality of the Holocaust and its impact on Israelis' identity, see for example, Ofer 2009.

26. Keynan 2015.

27. Ibid.

28. Ibid.

29. Trauma suffered by soldiers in situations of harmful military activity within a civilian population, Shay 2010.

30. Keynan 2015.

31. Ibid.

32. Bar-Tal 2007.

33. Myers, Hewstone, and Cairns 2009 and Noor 2008—both quoted in Andrighetto, Mari, Volpato and Behluli 2012.

34. Shnabel and Nadler 2008; Hameiri and Nadler 2017.

35. Keynan 2015.

36. Simantov-Nachlieli, Shnabel, and Halabi 2015.

37. Hameiri and Nadler 2017.

38. When led to believe that a majority among the adversary group acknowledges the ingroup's "chosen trauma" (Volkan 2006), the ingroup members expressed more conciliatory attitudes on divisive issues (Jerusalem; the settlements). In contrast, when led to believe that only a minority of the adversary members acknowledged its chosen trauma, their attitudes remained as they were. Recognition by the adversary has a stronger affect than recognition by a third party (e.g., the UN).

39. Keynan 2009.

40. Gaertner and Dovidio 2000.

41. Gaertner and Dovidio 2000 suggest the benefits of recategorization of two separate groups to include both groups in a higher level of category inclusiveness, thus enabling the harness of the two groups to shared goals, and reducing ingroup-outgroup bias. The SOSHI model takes it a step further to enable overcoming the competitive victimhood.

42. Keynan 2009.

43. See, for example, Hewstone et al. 2008.

44. A usual tendency among social categories is exaggeration of differences. The magnitude of distortions and exaggerations increases as the salience of the categorization increases. On the other hand—definition of group categorization at a higher level of category inclusiveness (superordinate category), reduces intergroup bias and conflict. When members of different, even adversary, groups are induced to conceive of themselves within a single group rather than as separate groups, attitudes toward former outgroup members become more positive through the cognitive and motivational processes involving pro-ingroup bias. Common, superordinate, group identity may be achieved by increasing the salience of factors like common goals or fate, that are perceived to be shared.

45. Palestinian Israeli Bereaved Families for Peace. http://www.theparentscircle.com/.

46. Rorty 1989

47. Jalal Khudiari, N.D.

48. Disasters of the War, http://www.theparentscircle.com

49. Combatants for Peace. "Our vision." http://cfpeace.org/about-us/our-vision/

50. Combatants for Peace. "Personal Stories." http://cfpeace.org/personal-stories/suliman-al-khatib/.

51. Combatants for Peace. "Memorial Day." http://cfpeace.org/projects/memorial-day/

52. Volkan 2006.

53. Hameiri and Nadler 2017.
54. Ibid.
55. 2009.
56. Cohrs, McNeill and Vollhardt 2015.
57. David and Bar-Tal 2009, p. 356.
58. Keynan 2009.
59. 1989.
60. Ibid.
61. Ibid.

BIBLIOGRAPHY

Andrighetto, Luca, Silvia Mari, Chiara Volpato, and Burim Behluli. "Reducing competitive victimhood in Kosovo: The role of extended contact and common ingroup identity." *Political Psychology* 33, no. 4 (2012): 513–29.

Bar-Tal, Daniel. "Socio-psychological foundations of intractable conflicts." *American Behavioral Scientist* 50, no. 11 (2007): 1430–53.

Bar-Tal, Daniel, Lily Chernyak-Hai, Noa Schori, and Ayelet Gundar. "A sense of self-perceived collective victimhood in intractable conflicts." *International Review of the Red Cross* 91, no. 874 (2009): 229–58.

Biran, Hadar, and Daniel Bar-Tal. "Expressions of victimhood in Israeli newspapers during operation 'cast lid.'" *Megamot* 51 (1) (2016): 7–37 (in Hebrew).

Cohrs, J. Christopher, Andrew McNeill, and J. Ray Vollhardt. "The two-sided role of inclusive victimhood for intergroup reconciliation: Evidence from Northern Ireland." *Peace and Conflict: Journal of Peace Psychology*, Vol. 21 no. 4 (2015): 634–47.

David, Ohad, and Daniel Bar-Tal. "A sociopsychological conception of collective identity: The case of national identity as an example." *Personality and Social Psychology Review* 13, no. 4 (2009): 354–79.

Gaertner, Lowell, and John Schopler. "Perceived ingroup entitativity and intergroup bias: An interconnection of self and others." *European Journal of Social Psychology* 28, no. 6 (1998): 963–80.

Gaertner, Samuel L., and John F. Dovidio. *Reducing intergroup bias: The common ingroup identity model.* Hove: Psychology Press, 2014.

Gan, Alon. *From Victimhood to Sovereignty: An analysis of the victimization discourse in Israel.* Jerusalem: The Israel Democracy Institute, 2014.

Hameiri, Boaz, and Arie Nadler. "Looking backward to move forward: Effects of acknowledgment of victimhood on readiness to compromise for peace in the protracted Israeli–Palestinian conflict." *Personality and Social Psychology Bulletin* 43, no. 4 (2017): 555–69.

Hewstone, Miles, Jared B. Kenworthy, Ed Cairns, Nicole Tausch, Joanne Hughes, Tania Tam, Alberto Voci, Ulrich von Hecker, and Catherine Pinder, "Steppingstones to reconciliation in Northern Ireland: Intergroup contact, forgiveness and trust," In *The social psychology of intergroup reconciliation*, edited by Areie Nadler, Thomas E. Malloy, and Jeffrey D. Fisher, 199-226. New York: Oxford University Press, 2008.

Kaufman, Stuart J. "Symbolic Politics or Rational Choice? Testing Theories of Extreme Ethnic Violence." *International Security* 30, no. 4 (2006): 45–86.

Keynan, Irit. "Collective Memory and Intergroup Leadership, Israel as a Case Study." In *Crossing the Divides, Intergroup Leadership in a World of Difference,* ed. By Todd L. Pittinsky, 219-230. Boston: Harvard business press, 2009.

Keynan, Irit. *Psychological war trauma and society: Like a hidden wound.* London and New York: Routledge, 2015.

Klar, Yechiel, Noa Schori-Eyal, and Yonat Klar. "The 'Never Again' state of Israel: The emergence of the Holocaust as a core feature of Israeli identity and its four incongruent voices." *Journal of Social Issues* 69, no. 1 (2013): 125–43.

Noor, Masi, Nurit Shnabel, Samer Halabi, and Arie Nadler. "When suffering begets suffering: The psychology of competitive victimhood between adversarial groups in violent conflicts." *Personality and Social Psychology Review* 16, no. 4 (2012): 351–74.

Ofer, Dalia. "The past that does not pass: Israelis and Holocaust memory." *Israel Studies* 14, no. 1 (2009): 1–35.

Peleg, Ilan. "Human Rights in the West Bank and the Gaza Strip: Politics and Law in Transition". In *Middle East and North Africa: Governance, Democratization, Human Rights*, edited by Paul J. Magnarella, 190–208. London and New York: Routledge, 1997

Pittinsky, Todd L., and Stefanie Simon. "Intergroup leadership." *The Leadership Quarterly* 18, no. 6 (2007): 586–605.

Rorty, Richard. *Contingency, irony, and solidarity*. Cambridge: Cambridge University Press, 1989.

Samuel L. Gaertner and John F. Dovidio. *Reducing intergroup bias: the common ingroup identity model*. New-York and East Sussex: Routledge, 2000.

Shay, Jonathan. *Achilles in Vietnam: Combat trauma and the undoing of character*. New York: Simon and Schuster, 2010.

Shnabel, N., & Nadler, A. "A needs-based model of reconciliation: Satisfying the differential needs of victim and perpetrator. "*Journal of personality and social psychology* 94, no.1 (2008): 116–32.

SimanTov-Nachlieli, Ilanit, Nurit Shnabel, and Samer Halabi. "Winning the victim status can open conflicting groups to reconciliation: Evidence from the Israeli-Palestinian Conflict." *European Journal of Social Psychology* 45, no. 2 (2015): 139–45.

Vollhardt, Johanna R. "The role of victim beliefs in the Israeli-Palestinian conflict: Risk or potential for peace?" *Peace and Conflict: Journal of Peace Psychology* 15, no. 2 (2009): 135.DOI 10.1080/10781910802544373.

Volkan, Vamik D. "Transgenerational transmissions and chosen traumas: An aspect of large-group identity." *Group Analysis* 34, no. 1 (2001): 79–97.

Volkan, Vamik. *Killing in the name of identity: A study of bloody conflicts*. Durham NC: Pitchstone Publishing, 2006.

Chapter Eight

The Politics of Victimhood

A Vision of an Apocalypse

Ruth Amir

The breadths of Israel's mantle of victimhood can be captured concisely in Prime Minister's Benjamin Netanyahu's utterance during a Bible study session hosted at his residence. Netanyahu noted that the fabled Hasmonean kingdom only survived for about eighty years before being conquered by the Romans, and that he is working to ensure that modern Israel will surpass that mark and reach its 100th birthday in another three decades (less than a biblical generation).[1] Strictly speaking, Netanyahu suggested that the mounting external and internal threats imperil Israel's existence in the immediate future. This apocalyptic vision is not merely a lesson learned from the Holocaust but rather a deeper representation of Israel's ontology of victimhood.

Netanyahu's apocalyptic vision reminisces Walter Benjamin's *Theses on the Philosophy of History*.[2] The ninth thesis commences with an epigraph from Gerhard (Gershom) Scholem's poem written for Benjamin's birthday in 1921, entitled "Greetings from Angelus." The poem was about a Paul Klee painting, *Angelus Novus,* that Benjamin had purchased. In both Scholem and Benjamin's accounts the angel of history is a melancholic, ineffectual figure that adheres to the same ideology that sustains and fetishizes suffering and catastrophes.[3] Benjamin pictured the angel of history as the angel image in Paul Klee's aquarelle *Angelus Novus*: "Where we perceive a chain of events, he sees one single catastrophe which keeps piling wreckage upon wreckage and hurls it in front of his feet."[4] Netanyahu, like the melancholic angel, is bewildered by the series of accumulating catastrophes, never takes his flight, his wings are entangled in the status quo of catastrophe. For Scholem, "the immanence of history, can only be overcome by a leap that does not save the past of history in an 'eternal image,' but rather in a leap leading out of the

historical continuum into the 'time of now,' whether the latter is revolutionary or messianic."[5] Israel has yet to perform such leap.

This essay engages with Israel's ontology of victimhood, its embedded-
ness in politics, dynamics, and destructive practices. As a matter of political
choice, the ontology of victimhood came to construe both the history of
suffering, establishment of the State of Israel, and the aggression toward its
various Others. I argue that the derived politics of victimhood performs
several roles, and is therefore manifold and dynamic. Like other national
liberation movements, Zionism sought to cast off the burden of passive victimhood associated with the Diaspora and adopted agentive victorious victimhood as an integrative mechanism. Victimhood was collective and exclusive, as victim status was denied from Othered groups such as Diaspora,
Mizrahi, and Yemeni Jews. The politics of victimhood was therefore a means
of suppressing political, ethnic, religious, and economic rivalries by making
a claim for a non-political "objective" space. Since 1967, the boundaries
between victim and victimizer have become increasingly blurry, as it became
increasingly difficult to sustain the role of the victim. This victimhood that I
refer to as victimhood 2.0, turns outwardly and inwardly with disproportionate power toward those who dare to criticize and challenge it.

This essay progresses as follows: the first section engages with Israel's
ontology of victimhood. The second deals with the construction of the politics of victorious agentive victimhood—the offensive ethos—for dealing
with the external and internal Oriental Others. The third section focuses on
victimhood 2.0, Othering, and further crumbling of the universalism of human rights, as part of the politics of victimhood. The concluding section
proposes a rights-based rather than pity-based discourse to promote a trajec-
tory for breaking away from the politics of victimhood.

THE ONTOLOGY OF VICTIMHOOD

Victimhood is the ontological underpinning of the Israeli ethos, identity, and
politics.

This ontology is dynamic; it fluctuates between the objectified victim as a
sufferer, the victorious victim, whose agentive powers are used for making a
greater good for himself, and the martyr, who is touched with transcendence
and is thus owed the duty of care by others.[6]

Israel conveys itself to the world through a history of suffering. Thus, for
example, the Ministry of Foreign Affairs website offers a snippet of this
ontology in the "About" section, in an article on Zionism by Israeli political
scientist Benyamin Neuberger.[7] After describing the historical bond between
the Jewish people and Zion, Neuberger claims that, "modern Zionism might
not have arisen as an active national movement in the nineteenth century

without contemporary antisemitism considered in a continuum of centuries of persecution."[8] Others have gone even farther and alluded to a causal link between the Holocaust and the establishment of the State of Israel.[9] Notwithstanding, the fact that official Israel represents itself exclusively in such terms suggests that the agentive powers of Zionism came to a halt. This seems like the return of the negation of exile narrative that repressed and depreciated the history of two thousand years as an empty time.[10] This narrative of the establishment of the state is a narrative of pity rather than of the right to self-determination. This ontological underpinning retrieves the notion of empty time in the Diaspora as part of the negation off exile.

Israel constituted itself as a victim community encircled by hostile enemies who challenge its right to exist. For Zionism, the ultimate lesson from the Holocaust is the trope "Never again will *Jewish blood* be shed with impunity!"[11] This lesson seeks to overcome the history of suffering through agentive powers. The writings of theologian Emil Fackenheim display a third aspect of victimhood in addition to the victim as an objectified sufferer or agentive victorious victim, that of holiness and transcendence. Fackenheim maintained that when one authentically faces up death, one's life is touched with transcendence.[12] Thus, after the Holocaust, Jewish survival is sacred and authenticates the good against the evil forces in the universe.

This initial ontology can be visualized as several concentric circles around the common core populated by the meta-narrative of victimhood. The distance of each circle from the core reflects the bearing of the narrative. The initial narrative consisted of three circles: the outermost was that of the Gentiles at large, the next was the enemy, the Arabs, and the innermost circle was populated by Others, within the Jewish-Israeli collective. These internal Others perceived as a threat to the purity of the imagined community of European Jews, namely, Mizrahi, Yemeni, and Diaspora Jews in general. In this narrative of victimhood, the victims are encircled by enemies and are locked in this position. The number of surrounding circles and their density may change over time.

As noted, victimhood is dynamic, and transactional. As the politics of victimhood evolved, the threats represented in each of the initial three circles changed. Thus, for examples, the Gentiles circle includes international human rights NGOs, the United Nations, International Criminal Tribunals, and BDS supporters. The Arabs' circle now includes the various terrorist organizations, ISIS, Iran, and global Jihadism. Most disconcerting and destructive is the new circle of Diaspora Jews, and the crowding of the innermost circle that of others from within the Jewish-Israeli collective. The circle of Diaspora Jews currently populates Progressive Jews and organizations such as J Street, Partners for Progressive Israel, and the New Israel Fund, that are critical of Israeli policies. These are stigmatized as auto-anti-Semites and anti-Zionists. The circle of enemies from within signals the deepening of the divisions in Israeli society and the creation of new ones. This circle now includes Israeli human rights NGOs, the Left, Progressive Jews, the mass media, the Justice system, and the Supreme Court.[13] The November 2017 report of the Berl Katznelson Foundation that monitors hate speech in Israeli statuses, tweets, posts, and talkbacks, found a monthly average of 18,214 uses of the word "traitor," and two percent of the contents call for direct violence.

The politics of victimhood draws Israel toward moral particularism.[14] Collective identity is, as Jurgen Habermas suggested, a rickety balance between universalism and particularism.[15] Habermas contextualized collective identity as "much more concrete than the ensemble of moral, legal and political principles around which it crystalizes."[16] The philosophical discussion of universalism and particularism in Europe was provoked by the impasse in the European political community around the dawning of the twentieth century. These inconsistencies have been a source of inexorable cultural conflicts endemic in deeply divided societies dealing with Islamic modernity, the politics of identity associated with new social movements, and the politics of reconciliation.[17] Much of the discussion in the European context is critical of the hegemonic forms of European universalism that depended on the exclusion and domination of Eastern Others and the justification of certain kinds of particularism within ethical universalism.[18] This same critique applies to Zionism's nation-building and what seems now as a perpetual movement toward particularism through the victimhood ontology and the politics it produces.[19]

THE POLITICS OF VICTIMHOOD: THE OFFENSIVE ETHOS AND OTHERING

Zionism sought to establish in Palestine a Jewish nation-state grounded in Western-Liberal ideas. The Zionist movement, which shared Europe's Orientalism, either denied the Arab presence in Palestine, or claimed that no national movement or self-awareness existed among Palestine's Arab population before or even after the rise of Zionism.[20] It insisted on its exclusive victimhood and viewed the Zionist project as a European civilization under threat by Oriental barbarism.[21] One of the representations of this view is the common reference to Israel as a European enclave within the hostile, underdeveloped, and barbaric Levant. Thus, Ehud Barak's reference to Israel as "a villa in the jungle" is not merely a trope. As Eitan Bar-Yosef wrote, in Israeli culture, Africa is a space for exercising or projecting personal, national, racial and territorial fantasies.[22]

Israeli identity was constructed on the negation of the exile and the Othering of European Diaspora Jews, Mizrahi Jews, and Palestinians, and the denial of their pasts.[23] This denial did not draw only on European Orientalist views, it also emanated from the aversion to the use of force in Jewish scripture, and the divisions within the Jewish Settlement over the use of force.

Agentive Victimhood: The Development of the Offensive Ethos

Ever since the loss of Jewish sovereignty in the Land of Israel during the years 132–136 C.E., Jews were exempt from the ethical dilemmas surrounding war. Many Jews conceived of war in temporal terms, it either belonged to the distant past or to the messianic future. It was not considered part of the realm of present.[24]

The foundational ethics of the Bible and Talmud regarding the sanctity of human life also applies to the actions of modern nations.[25] Self-defence was therefore essential for a nation committed to protect its citizens.[26] The establishment of Jewish military power was for Zionism the only means for overcoming the Diasporic helplessness.[27] This helplessness is conveyed in Hayyim Nachman Bialik's poem, "The City of Slaughter," written after the 1903 Kishinev pogrom. Bialik, Israel's national poet, depicted the shame and humiliation of the disgraceful death of the slain Jews who were unable to defend themselves. The Zionist negation of exile projected this image on Diaspora Jews in general.

In this poem, Bialik depicted Diaspora Jews—heirs of the Hasmonaeans and Maccabees—at a state of utmost wretchedness. Dwelling in "privies, jakes and pigpens . . . [they] lay, with trembling knees, [c]oncealed and cowering."[28] Bialik has thus juxtaposed the seed of saints, the scions of the lions who in defiance of their glorious past did not fight back, and rather, fled shamefully. Bialik depicted the Jews as roaches in flight, and further dehumanizes and blames them for dying like dogs. Bialik's contempt toward these Jews is deep. He seems unforgiving as he goes farther to describe their disgraceful wretched death as the death of dogs.[29] This use of bestial images not only dehumanizes Diaspora Jews but also robs them of their glorious ancestry. This serves to dissociate the wretched Diaspora Jews from the heroic Zionist Jews. The powerful metaphors and bestial images serve as a critical charge sheet against the victims of the massacre. The absence of solidarity with the Pogrom's victims is disturbing Their humiliation and disgraceful death serve as both caveat and threat for Diaspora Jews.

Bialik's poem is part of the negation of exile discourse that propagated agentive victorious victimhood. It reprimanded the victims for failing to protect themselves and called for Jewish activism.[30] When read in this context, the poem's mobilization to the Zionist cause is a disturbing precursor to the extensive Othering of groups. The dead, non-agentive bodies are objectified and silenced.

Absorbed in its agentive victorious victimhood, the Zionist movement promoted the idea that the land without people is awaiting the people without land.[31] The first Zionist settlers who arrived in Palestine in the last two decades of the nineteenth century were convinced that Palestine was the land of the Jews.[32] The Jewish settler society in Palestine was therefore in fundamental conflict with the Arab population.[33] Israel Zangwill acknowledged the Arab presence and potential conflict in 1905:

> Palestine proper has already its inhabitants. The pashalik of Jerusalem is already twice as thickly populated as the United States, having fifty-two souls to the square mile, and not 25% of them Jews. . . . [We] must be prepared either to drive out by the sword the [Arab] tribes in possession as our forefathers did or to grapple with the problem of a large alien population, mostly Mohammedan and accustomed for centuries to despise us.[34]

The recourse to Jewish military power was, according to Ehud Luz, the most substantial innovation of modern Jewish history. It was also an agentive liberationist victimhood.[35] For Luz,

> The historical experience of the Jew who in a world in which violence against his person has become almost universal, has been driven to gain power in order to defend himself. Feeling humiliated in exile, and in the face of force exercised against him, the Jew might himself fall into worship of force, believing that the only way by which he can restore his dignity and secure his survival is by enhancing his power.[36]

The Labor movement considered the use of military power a necessity that must be exercised thoughtfully and sparingly. As Laleh Khalili wrote, "[i]n the nations state's telling of the national narrative, the national hero casts off the yoke of passivity and victimhood, and surges forward . . . ."[37] Some Zionist leaders were concerned about the moral implications of such use.[38] Until the mid-1930s the Zionist leadership in Palestine permitted only defensive action and exercised self-restraint even during the Arab Revolt. The "purity of arms" notion allowed the use of limited force in pursuit of military objectives, in keeping with the distinction between combatants and civilians.[39]

The endorsement of military activism and the shift toward the offensive ethos since 1939 replaced the initial Zionist non-belligerence.[40] The atrocities between Arabs and Jews during the 1930s and 1940s were viewed in the wider context of the Jewish experience and signaled *de facto* acceptance of Zeev Jabotinsky's analysis that there was no chance for an agreement with the Arabs prior to the establishment of Jewish sovereignty.[41]

Labor's position was based on flawed underlying assumptions. First was the colonialist *terra nullius* doctrine that had no bearing on reality, and second, the underestimation of the Palestinian opposition.[42] According to Edward Said and others, when the Zionists realized that they could no longer sustain the *terra nullius* myth, they sought to diminish the presence of the indigenes and dehumanize them.[43] The Orientalist image of the Arabs as wild, barbaric, and uncivilized assisted in repudiating their national aspirations.[44]

Notwithstanding, during the 1948 war, Israeli soldiers underwent sociopolitical training, a code word for indoctrination, to convince them that a form of militarism rooted in Judaism was the only way to win the war.[45] One of the significant representations of this militant offensive ethos can be found in a eulogy delivered by Moshe Dayan.[46] Ro'i Rothberg, a young settler and security officer for Kibbutz Nahal Oz near Gaza, was shot off his horse by Palestinian infiltrators on April 29, 1956. Dayan, then IDF chief of staff, delivered this eulogy at his funeral. Mourning the death of the handsome young man, Dayan said: "We are a generation of settlers, and without the steel helmet and the gun's muzzle we will not be able to plant a tree and build a house. . . . The millions of Jews who were annihilated . . . are watching us from the ashes of Israeli history, commanding us to settle and establish a country for their people."[47]

The dead bodies of Ro'i, Uri Ilan, and other fallen soldiers were granted agentive powers that transcended their actual influence during their lifetime.[48] This monumental eulogy is remarkable because it provides one of few rare moments in which Israel acknowledged the swapping of the victim and victimizer roles. Dayan did not blame the assassins, who for eight years had been watching the Israelis cultivating the land that once had been their own. As a farmer he could identify with their agony, yet Dayan pleaded the Israelis to be steadfast to the suffering of others and to continue pursuing their goals. In his words: "[t]his is our choice – to be ready and armed, tough and harsh – or else the sword shall fall from our hand and our lives will be cut short."[49] Two generations later Israel still clings to these two options as if they are mutually exclusive.

The motif of the sea of hatred threatening to engulf Israel is fundamental in Israeli ethos. It conveys the message that offense is the only alternative and that peace is merely an illusion. This pessimistic vision is repeated over and again.

Agentive Victimhood: Oriental Others from Within

Diaspora Jews, Mizrahi, and the Ultra-Orthodox Jews were all considered a menace to the nascent Israeli collective identity, whether culturally, economically, politically, or socially. The Othering of groups within the Jewish collective, evident in Bialik's "In the City of Slaughter" to substantiate Jewish victimhood and its need for self-determination, resonates in Bialik's constitutive poem, "The Last Dead of the Desert." Bialik referred to the forty years of wandering in the desert and the unconceivable death toll of six hundred thousand dead. Referring to the dead victims he shows no compassion or solidarity:

> Deplore them not! Unwept let all those be
> Who fell as slaves, tread o'er them, march as free! [50]

Bialik referred to the biblical desert generation, those doomed to perish in the process of ascending to the Land of Israel. The unfit or unworthy of entering the Promised Land die dishonored.

Zionism internalized the image of Diaspora Jews through the politics of victimhood. Rather than claiming the national aspirations in a discourse of rights, Zionism chose the victim mantle. As Khazzoom noted, this was a historical reaction to Orientalism or internal colonization. [51] The depiction of those sacrificed en route established Zionism as a republican virtue enterprise that consisted in the contribution to the success of the Zionist project, or the upbuilding of the state. [52] The treading over the dead is a powerful metaphor of resilience, insistence and determination but also of cruelty and heartlessness. The dead are so wretched that they are not even buried; they are left to rot in the desert. This is both a caveat and a threat on those who are reluctant of this vision or those who dare to dispute it. The Zionist return is conveyed in the poem as a virtuous end, one that justifies all means. This is a liberationist narrative of reclaiming agency.

The desert imagery depicts Zion as a desolate land, *terra nullius*, awaiting the return of virtuous Jews. This notion of the barren land and the desert imagery, which converges with colonial discourse, is abundant in writings and cultural products of Zionism's founding parents. To assert her argument about the shift to the offensive ethos, Shapira quotes another poem by Bialik titled "The Dead of the Wilderness." While both titles are similar, the poems offer contradictory representations of the Jews en route Zion. In the latter work, the desert generation become agentive. [53] They do not succumb to their fate, but rather, awaken and demand recognition as the mighty, heroic new generation:

> The last Generation of slaves and the first generation of
> Freemen! [54]

This poem captures the revolutionary transformation that Zionism chose as representative of itself. The generation of slaves are again condemned and sacrificed. The liberationist narrative aspires to replace the history of suffering. These two variations of the theme are a telling representation of the abysmal difference between the Zionist self-image and veracity. The injustices perpetrated on Yemeni, Mizrahi, and Balkan Jews, and particularly the policy of the removal of Yemeni children to children's homes, is an example of the active Othering of non-European Jews.

THE YEMENI, MIZRAHI, AND BALKANS' BABIES AFFAIR

The Yemeni, Mizrahi, and Balkans' Babies Affair highlights Israel's initial exclusive agentive victimhood and practices of Othering. Between 1948 and 1954 at least 1,500 children aged between zero and four years had disappeared from hospitals or childcare facilities in the immigrant transit camps and in towns.[55] Among them were about 250 children of other ethnicities that went missing from hospitals.[56] However, only Yemeni children were forcibly separated from their families. Children of other ethnicities disappeared from hospitals or clinics. Whereas in recent years the families of the disappeared children joined forces to inquire the children's whereabouts, this is a primarily Yemeni phenomenon. This prejudicial directive that singled that out the Yemenis was defended by the objective circumstances such as the parents' poor health, and the conditions at the camps.

The mass migration of Yemeni Jews to Israel started out in the late nineteenth century as a pull-work-migration.[57] Arthur Ruppin, the founder of the *Eretz Israel* Office of the World Zionist Organization in Jaffa, encountered Yemenis on his first journey to Palestine in 1908. Ruppin wrote in his memoir:

> There are two thousand Yemenis in Jerusalem. . . . It is easy to recognize them by their shaven head . . . like the Arabs. . . . The trace of Arab blood is evident, and their skin is very dark. They are the most faltering social group among the population in Jerusalem . . . and are almost the only Jews that engage in drudgery such as carrying and stone masonry that successfully compete with the Arabs.[58]

Indeed, the absorption of the Yemenis in Palestine was a typical case of ethnic plantation colonialism.[59] Immigration was selective, limited to men younger than thirty-five years, in perfect health. They dwelled in separate quarters at the outskirts of the larger plantation colonies of the first *Aliyah*. Unselective immigration of families commenced in December 1948.

After years of dwelling in camps in Aden, the Yemeni immigrants were settled in camps. A directive issued by the Executive of the Jewish Agency to the camps' managements had ordered the forced separation of babies and toddlers from their parents and their transfer to children's houses.[60] Like the image of the noble savage, the Yemenis were initially characterized as innocent, trusting, and highly spiritual people, but also primitive and lacking parental skills.[61] Prime Minister David Ben-Gurion's letter to the Army Chief of Staff Yigael Yadin describes Yemeni-Jews as:

backward compared to us by two thousand years, if not more. He is devoid of
the fundamental and primary tenets of civilization (as distinguished from culture). The treatment [by Yemeni man] of the wife and children is that of a
primitive person. [. . .] The Yemeni father does not take care of his children
and family in the manner that we do, and he is not used to feeding his children
to the point of satiation before he feeds himself.[62]

Curiously, in this letter Ben-Gurion suggested that these children are not
likely to thrive without the loving care of Israeli women-soldiers. Giora
Josephthal, Head of the Absorption Department at the Jewish Agency had
instructed to forcibly separate sick children from their families:

Because in some cases Yemeni mothers refused to give their children to hospitals or infants' homes, although the children were to be in danger if untreated
in a medical institution, it is necessary in such cases to take the children by
force. [. . .] [M]ost of the Yemeni mothers are indifferent to the destiny of their
children. They are themselves sick and frail, and they have almost no technical
opportunity to check where their babies were sent and what happened to
them.[63]

A testimony by a nurse at the children's house suggests that the children's
removal actually benefitted them: "All mothers want their children near, but I
explained to them that they needn't worry, that it's for their own good. We
couldn't let the parents in the children's house any time because hygiene had
to be kept."[64]

Rumors and speculations about the kidnappings and the children's whereabouts suggested that the children were trafficked in Israel and abroad, transferred to Christian missions, or were subject to clandestine medical experi-
ments.[65] In 1986, Avigdor Pe'er, Deputy Director of the Ministry of Welfare's Department of Immigrant Care, testified before the Knesset's Interior
Committee that Yemeni Children were allocated to women's organization
based on political affiliation.[66] The children were then transferred to the
United States and adopted by Jewish families. Pe'er explained that the case
workers acted out of benevolent motives, thinking that it was in the child's
best interest.

Over the years, Israeli governments dismissed the grievances of Mizrahi
Jews about their Othering and exclusion. Following several cycles of public
pressure, three commissions of inquiry were established over the years to
investigate the infants' whereabouts.[67] All the commissions denied the
Yemenis' allegations' and found that aside from single cases of adoptions
and several unresolved cases, most of the infants had died.[68] Moreover, all
three commissions justified the overwhelming morbidity and mortality rates
by reference to the medical condition of the immigrants.[69] The State acted in
this matter as though more than the fortunes of the infants were at stake, and

the commissions' protocols and other archival materials were to remain confidential until 2071.

The victimhood ontology of life under constant threat was used to suppress ethnic and economic rivalries. With the Holocaust as a gold standard of suffering and the Jews' endangered existence, grievances of various groups concerning their own suffering and marginalization were suppressed.

VICTIMHOOD 2.0: ACTIVE OTHERING WITHIN THE JEWISH COLLECTIVE

Israel's ontology of victimhood nurtures and perpetuates itself. The subsequent politics of victimhood operates through a heightened threat perception, Othering and exclusion. The agentive victim-turned perpetrator uses his agentive powers by using disproportionate force against the enemy Other. Gabi Siboni, senior researcher at the Institute for National Security Studies, outlined Israel's response to an outbreak of hostilities. Siboni wrote that,

> the IDF will need to act immediately, decisively, and with force that is disproportionate to the enemy's actions and the threat it poses. Such a response aims at inflicting damage and meting out punishment to an extent that will demand long and expensive reconstruction processes. The strike must be carried out as quickly as possible, and must prioritize damaging assets over seeking out each and every launcher. Punishment must be aimed at decision makers and the power elite.[70]

While this is response reflects the frustration of asymmetrical warfare, Israel is becoming increasingly particularistic. The ontology of victimhood defies the ontological basis of human rights and is extended to those supporting it. Thus, Israel's recent politics of victimhood targets, for example, Liberals, Progressive Jews, human rights NGOs, and virtually every Jewish of non-Jewish group or individual who criticize the Israeli Government and its policies. The culprits are punished by exclusion, dehumanization using bestial images, and are accused of treason or declared an existential threat.[71]

Israeli official rhetoric constructs these divisions as overlapping. Both Progressive Jews and human rights NGOs that stand for universalism have come to populate all new concentric circles surrounding the victimhood ontology. The Western Wall egalitarian prayer and private conversions conflict between Progressive and Ultra-Orthodox Jews surrounds the right of Progressive Jews to exercise their freedom of religion. Since 1967, the Western Wall Heritage Foundation has maintained the site under the rules of an ultra-Orthodox synagogue. A presiding rabbi ascertains that all prayer conforms to Orthodox rules, such as separation of men and women with a high fence, forbidding women to pray in loud voices, the use of accessories that are used by men during prayer.[72] In 2003 Israel's Supreme Court affirmed the right to egalitarian prayer at Robinson's Arch situated at the southern end of the wall. In 2009 the Western Wall Heritage Foundation breached the Court's decision and demanded the police to forcibly remove the women of the wall. In 2012 after much protest by Jewish communities in the United States, Prime Minister Netanyahu appointed the Jewish Agency Chairperson, Nathan Sharansky, to negotiate a compromise. The proposal brought before the cabinet secretary was followed by protracted negotiations that culminated in its approval by the government on January 31, 2016. Six months later, the program was halted following pressures by the Ultra-Orthodox coalition members.[73]

The wall conflict with Diaspora Jews is part of the wider issue of the shifting relationships between Israel and American Jewry. A growing number of Diaspora Jews are not only less willing to unconditionally support Israel, but also publicly criticize its government.[74] The conflict is part of the wider campaign in Israel for the de-legitimation of J Street and its critique of Israeli policies.

The wall conflict triggered an all-out disproportionate verbal war against Progressive Jews. Shas chairman and Interior Minister Aryeh Deri strongly denounced non-Orthodox Judaism during a question-and-answer session in the Knesset on November 6, 2017, as he referred to Reform religious practices as "not the Jewish religion."[75] While Deri began by referring to non-Orthodox Jews as "our brothers," he further added that they were causing "incredible damage to Judaism."[76] Deri's attack trailed a particularly ill-tempered committee hearing in the Knesset regarding Israel–Diaspora relations. Shas MK Michael Malkieli allegedly compared non-Orthodox Jews and the women of the wall to dogs.[77] Similarly, MK Gafni referred to Reform Jews as "a group of clowns who stab the holy Torah." Deputy Minister Porush said that "Reform Jews should be sent to the dogs," and threatened to oust the women of the wall: "the Women of the Wall should be put outside the [Jewish] camp with the rest of the garbage." Interior Minister Deri added: "They will not get any recognition. In Judaism there is only one stream."[78]

The former U.S. Ambassador to Israel, Dan Shapiro, warned at a recent conference sponsored by the Anti-Defamation League:

> There is an idea that has some currency in certain circles around the Israeli government that says, "You know what, we can write off that segment of American Jewry because in a couple of generations their children or grandchildren will assimilate. So let's focus on the Orthodox who are an important constituency but smaller. Let's focus on Evangelicals, and we can sustain our support from the American public by focusing on those populations and writing off and being dismissive of Jewish progressives."[79]

It seems that Victimhood 2.0 revived a version of the negation of exile. This view recently voiced by Deputy Foreign Affair Minister Zipi Hotovely, who referred to American Jews as "people that never send their children to fight for their country" and that "most of them are having quite convenient lives."[80] Hotovely, addressed the increased tensions between Israel and U.S. Jewry, on the issue of egalitarian prayer at the wall, and over Israeli policies on Israeli-Arab citizens and the Palestinians. Referring to American Jews she said: "They don't know how it feels to be attacked by rockets, and I think part of it is to actually experience what Israel is dealing with on a daily basis."[81] She accused progressive Jews for using the wall conflict to get recognition and that by so doing they are making a religious, holy place something for political dispute. Hotovely further said she had fallen victim to a "liberal dictatorship" Hillel rescinded her invitation to give a talk at Princeton University.[82]

Hotovely's words defeat the purpose of Zionism. If indeed the situation of Israelis is far worse than that of American Jews, then implicit in her message is the colossal failure of Zionism. Moreover, Hotovely suggest that Israelis are the victims of American Jews who lead convenient life in exile. Her words reminisce Moishe Pipik, Phillip Roth's doppelganger and alter ego in *Operation Shylock, A Confession.*[83] Pipik has been going around Israel impersonating Philip Roth, conducting interviews with reporters, and documenting the trial of suspected Nazi Criminal John Demjanjuk. Pipik tries to raise funds for Diasporism, a plan for the resettlement of Jews in their ancestral countries, because as he claims, "Zionism has outlived its historical function," and a nuclear Catastrophe is waiting to happen in the Middle East.[84] Pipik suggest that Diasporism is "the only way to assure Jewish survival and to achieve 'a historical as well as a spiritual victory over Hitler and Auschwitz.'"[85] He even meets Lech Walesa to convince him to allow Jews to resettle in Poland. This is also linked to Netanyahu's apocalyptic vision.

Israel's perpetual movement toward particularism resulted in the placement of human rights NGOs in the concentric circles of either enemies from within or the Gentiles, contingent on their location. Israel's perceived threat by human rights NGO emanates from the latter's universalism that is opposed to ethnonationalism and victimhood. The politics of victimhood allow no criticism. It is either unconditional support of Israel or the denial or its right to exist.

The promotion of legislation intended to curb human rights organizations and other NGOs is part of an attempt to change the status or rights of Arab-Israeli citizens, attempts to restrict the authority and power of the Supreme Court. While some of these proposed laws died or mellowed in the process, the accompanying statements by legislators and senior political leaders provoke a violent public discourse that delegitimizes universal human rights culture.

Israeli human rights NGOs are often funded by foreign governmental organizations while right-wing organizations typically receive financial support from foreign NGOs, religious communities, and private people. Therefore, any restriction on foreign contribution is likely to be to the detriment of the former.

Since 2011 human rights NGOs have been under attack. A bill proposed by MK Arie Eldad on March 30, 2011, followed proposal by MK Ophir Akunis a year earlier. MK Eldad compared Israeli human rights NGOs to terror organizations such as the ETA, Basque underground, and the IRA.[86] Both proposals prohibited foreign contributions to human rights, and political NGOs by states and international organizations such as the United Nations and the European Union "due to the incitement by many organizations that disguise themselves as 'human rights organizations' and are interested in affecting political discourse, the character, and policies of Israel."[87]

Phrases like "Fifth Column" and "Anti-Israeli NGOs" who seek to destroy everything that is part of the Zionist project have been used. [88] On July 13, 2015, a Private Member Bill was tabled by MKs Yinon Magal, Bezalel Smotrich, Mordechai Yogev, and Nissan Slomianski (Jewish Home) one day after the United Nations published its report on Operation Zuk Eithan in Gaza.[89] Article 83 of the coalition agreement between the Likud and Jewish Home parties guarantees the government's support of the bill.[90] The proposed law subjected Israeli human rights NGOs to taxation of 37 percent of contributions from foreign governments exceeding $50,000. The receipt of such contributions was to result in a change of status to foreign NGO.[91] The implications of this classification are that "Government Ministries and the IDF will be banned from any collaboration with these NGOs, including the transfer of funds, denial of civic service volunteers, conferences and joint publications."[92]

On December 27, 2015, the Ministerial Committee on Legislation voted for a law proposal by Justice Minister Ayelet Shaked. According to this law, NGOs that receive over 50 percent of their funding from foreign sources are to disclose this fact in detail in their official publications.[93] Representatives of these NGOs were to carry a badge that identifies them as such and wear it in the Knesset and in every meeting with public or elected officials.[94] After much protest, the requirement to carry a badge was dismissed and the law was passed. In June 2017, Netanyahu announced that he would like to altogether ban contributions from foreign governments to Israeli NGOs.[95]

This legislation and accompanying discourse, affect the attitudes of the Israeli public toward democracy, human rights, and political, social, and ethnic minorities.[96] The *Democracy Index* published by the Israel Democracy Institute in 2015 and 2016 suggests the right-left divide was mentioned as the second greatest source of tension among Israelis.[97] This reflects the escalation of the rhetoric that associates the political left (and sometimes even the moderate right, and center) with treason, self-antisemitism, and denial of Israel's right to exist. In 2016 there was also a steep rise in the share of Jews (mainly right-wing and center) as 71 percent held that human and civil-rights organizations are harmful to Israel. Correspondingly, an overwhelming majority of Jews (81 percent) and a small majority of Arabs (54 percent) defy the application of international norms in the fight against terror, and agree that Israel should fight terror "any way it sees fit, without taking into consideration the views of other countries about how it conducts this battle."[98] These findings tap the growing particularism in Israeli society.

PROGNOSIS

Can Israel break free from its destructive victim ontology and the derived politics of victimhood? Fifteen years have passed since the Cohen-Kedmi Commission tabled its report on the disappeared Yemeni, Mizrahi, and Balkans' babies. Netanyahu's government was indeed the first to grant recognition to their suffering, lifted some of the confidentiality of the official documents, but did not offer an apology or tangible or symbolic reparations. Thus, recognition was extended to the suffering of the families in a discourse of pity. Missing from this recognition are the terms of a discourse of rights, such as the right to truth, dignity, the right to family, and children's rights. Missing also is the breach of the government's fiduciary duty.[99] Thus the case was used to append their suffering to the dominant narrative of victimhood rather than to address their grievances.

The powerful presence of the past on the present Israeli agenda is overpowering. Walter Benjamin imagines the past as immanent: "As flowers turn toward the sun, by dint of a secret heliotropism the past strives to turn toward the sun which is rising in the sky of history."[100] This imagery is pertinent to the politics of victimhood on the one hand, and hopeful global incidence of transitional justice on the other. For Benjamin, heliotropism represents the revolutionary reflection that enables to break away from a troubled past after dealing with it to its fullness.

Dealing with the fullness of the past invokes the need to balance between the past, present, and future. To break out from the ontology and politics of victimhood Israel should adopt a discourse of rights, and rely less on the less objective element—as Hannah Arendt referred to it—the "little hunchback" who was prominent in Benjamin's life, and whom he blamed for his childhood catastrophes.[101] Israel must not construe every incident as yet another misfortune associated with its victimhood. As Benjamin, noted, redemption occurs through memory, as Jews were prohibited from investigating the future. Our secret agreement with previous generations is the imperative "remember!"[102] Israel should remember the atrocities, but refrain from using them politically. In *Memories of a Bad Year*, J. M. Coetzee deals with the origins of the state with the question of how far back can we remember:

> Every account of the origins of the state starts from the premise that "we"—
> not we the readers but some generic we so wide as to exclude no one—
> participate in its coming into being. But the fact is that the only "we" we
> know—ourselves and the people close to us—are born into the state and our
> forebears too were born into the state as far back as we can trace. The state is
> always there before we are. How far back can we trace? In African thought,
> the consensus is that after the seventh generation we can no longer distinguish
> between history and myth. [103]

NOTES

1. Jonathan Lis, "Netanyahu: Israel Must Cope with Future Security Threats If It Wants to Reach 100." *Haaretz*, October 10, 2017. https://www.haaretz.com/israel-news/.premium-1.816457. Accessed October 12, 2017.

2. Walter Benjamin, *Illuminations* (New York: Schocken Books, 1968).

3. Benjamin, *Illuminations*, 257; See Sharon Ribak, "The Critique of Historicism and Progress: Walter Benjamin's Ethical-Messianic Time Concept" *Protocols: History and Theory* 26 (2012). Online Journal, http://bezalel.secured.co.il/zope/home/he/1349198192/1349563447 (Accessed October 12, 2016) (Hebrew).

4. Benjamin, *Illuminations*, 257. Benjamin purchased the aquarelle in 1920. See Susan Handelman, "Walter Benjamin and the Angel of History." *Cross Currents* 41,3 (1991), 344–52.

5. Gershom Scholem, *On Jews and Judaism in Crisis Selected Essays* Translated by Werner J. Dannhauser. (New York: Schocken Books, 1976.), 234.

6. Henrik Ronsbo and Steffen Jensen, "Introduction: Histories of Victimhood, Assemblages, Transactions, and Figures," in *Histories of Victimhood*, eds. Steffen Jensen and Henrik Rønsbo (Philadelphia: University of Pennsylvania Press, 2014), 4–5.

7. Israel, The Ministry of Foreign Affairs, "About" http://mfa.gov.il/MFA/AboutIsrael/State/Pages/ZIONISM-%20Background.aspx (accessed October 12, 2017).

8. Benyamin Neuberger, "Zionism," Israel Ministry of Foreign Affairs website, posted on October 12, 1999. Available online at http://mfa.gov.il/MFA/AboutIsrael/State/Pages/ZIONISM-%20Background.aspx (accessed October 12, 2017).

9. See the debate between Dan Michman and Yehuda Bauer. Yehuda Bauer, *Rethinking the Holocaust* (New Haven: Yale University Press, 2001), 335.Dan Michman, "From Holocaust to Resurrection! From Holocaust to Resurrection? The Historiography of the Causal Link between the Holocaust and the Establishment of the State of Israel, between Myth and Reality." *Iyunim Bitkumat Israel* 10 (2000), 234–58. See Bauer's comment in Yehuda Bauer, "Did the Holocaust Facilitate the Establishment of Israel? A Reply to Dan Michman's Article," *Iyunim Bitkumat Israel* 12 (2002), 653–54. (Hebrew) See also Evyatar Friesel, *The Holocaust: Factor in the Birth of Israel?* Yad Vashem Shoah Resource Center, The International School for Holocaust Studies. Available online at http://www.yadvashem.org/odot_pdf/Microsoft%20Word%20-%203575.pdf (accessed October 15, 2017).

10. See Benjamines notion of homogenous empty time in Benjamin, *Illuminations*, 261.

11. Leonard Grob, "'Forgetting' the Holocaust: Ethical Dimensions of the Israeli-Palestinian Conflict." In *Anguished Hope: Holocaust Scholars Confront the Palestinian Israeli Conflict*, edited by Leonard Grob and John K. Roth (Grand Rapids, Michigan: William B. Eerdmans Publishing Company, 2008), 11. (Emphasis added) This trope is attributed to Abba Kovner, poet and the organizer of the Vilna Ghetto revolt.

12. Emil L. Fackenheim, *To Mend the World: Foundations of Future Jewish Thought* (New York: Schocken Books, 1982), 362; Emil L. Fackenheim, "Holocaust," in *20th Century Jewish Religious Thought: Original Essays on Critical Concepts, Movements, and Beliefs*, eds. Arthur

Allen Cohen and Paul R. Mendes-Flohr (Philadelphia: Jewish Publication Society, 2009), 399-408.

13. Berl Katznelson Foundation, *Hate Report*, November 25, 2017. Online at http://hasata.berl.co.il/(accessed November 25, 2017) (Hebrew).

14. See discussion of the divide in Alan Gewirth, "Ethical Universalism and Particularism," *The Journal of Philosophy* 85, no. 6 (1988), 283; Yaakov Rozenberg, "Reflections on Universalism and Particularism," *Hagut: Studies in Jewish Educational Thought* 8 (2008), 191-208-208; Iver B. Neumann, *Uses of the Other: "the East" in European Identity Formation* (Minneapolis: University of Minnesota Press, 1999).

15. Gewirth, *Ethical Universalism and Particularism*, 283; Jürgen Habermas, *Between Facts and Norms: Contributions to a Discourse Theory of Law and Democracy* (Cambridge, Mass.: MIT Press, 1996).

16. Jürgen Habermas and Peter Dews, *Autonomy and Solidarity: Interviews with Jürgen Habermas*, Rev ed. (London; New York: Verso, 1992), 241. See also David Held, *Democracy and the Global Order* (Stanford: Stanford University Press, 1995).; Gerard Delanty, "Habermas and Occidental Rationalism: The Politics of Identity, Social Learning, and the Cultural Limits of Moral Universalism," *Sociological Theory* 15, no. 1 (1997), 56.

17. Gewirth, *Ethical Universalism and Particularism*, 283–302; Rozenberg, *Reflections on Universalism and Particularism*, 191–208; Neumann, *Uses of the Other;* Delanty, *Habermas and Occidental Rationalism*, 30–59.

18. Habermas, *Between Facts and Norms*; Jürgen Habermas and Max Pensky, *The Postnational Constellation: Political Essays*, ed. Max Pensky, trans. Max Pensky (Cambridge, UK: Polity Press, 2001); Neumann, *Uses of the Other*, 191–208; Gewirth, *Ethical Universalism and Particularism*, 283–302. This critique is related to the critique of Liberal Democracy's blind spot with respect to its practices of exclusion. See Delanty, *Habermas and Occidental Rationalism*, 30–59.

19. Neumann, *Uses of the Other*; Delanty, *Habermas and Occidental Rationalism*, 30–59.

20. Haim Gerber, "Orientalism, Zionism and the Palestinians," in *Jewish-Arab Relations in Eretz Israel/Palestine*, eds. Haim Gerber and Elie Podeh, Vol. 43, 2002), 27–48.

21. Devorah Hakohen, *Immigrants in Turmoil: Mass Immigration to Israel and its Repercussions in the 1950s and After* (Syracuse New York: Syracuse University Press, 2003), 4.; Sammy Smooha, "The Mass Immigrations to Israel: A Comparison of the Failure of the Mizrahi Immigrants of the 1950s with the Success of the Russian Immigrants of the 1990s," *The Journal of Israeli History* 27, no. 1 (2008), 1–27.

22. Eitan Bar-Yosef, *A Villa in the Jungle: Africa in Israeli Culture*. (Jerusalem, an Leer Jerusalem Institute and Hakibbutz Hameuchad, 2013), 11. (Hebrew)

23. Amnon Raz Krakotzkin, "Exile within Sovereignty: A Critique of the Concept 'Negation of Exile' in Israeli Culture," *Theory and Criticism* 5 (1994), 114–32. (Hebrew); Amnon Raz Krakotzkin, "Exile within Sovereignty: A Critique of the Concept 'Negation of Exile' in Israeli Culture," *Theory and Criticism* 4 (1993), 23–53 (Hebrew).

24. Ehud Luz, *Wrestling with an Angel: Power, Morality, and Jewish Identity* (New Haven: Yale University Press, 2003), 350; Avi Kober, *Israel's Wars of Attrition: Attrition Challenges to Democratic States* (London; New York: Routledge, 2009), 115–16.

25. Gerald J. Bildstein, "The State and the Legitimate Use of Force and Coercion in Modern Halakhic Thought." In *Jews and Violence: Images, Ideologies, Realities*, Edited by Peter Y. Medding. (New York: Oxford University Press, 2002), 3–22, 15.

26. Norman Solomon, "Judaism and the Ethic of War." *International Review of the Red Cross*, 87, no. 858 (2005), 295–309.

27. Amir Bar-Or, "The Making of Israel's Political-Security Culture," in *Militarism and Israeli Society*, eds. Gabriel Sheffer and Oren Barak (Bloomington, IN: Indiana University Press, 2010), 259–279.

28. Hayyim Nahman Bialik and Israel Efros, *Complete Poetic Works of Hayyim Nahman Bialik: Translated from the Hebrew* (New York: Histadruth Ivrit of America, 1948), 129–43 (Vol. I).

29. Ibid.

30. Iris Milner, "'In the City of Slaughter'": The Hidden Voice of the Pogrom Victims," *Prooftexts* 25, no. 1–2 (2005), 60–72.

31. Diana Muir, "A Land without a People for a People without a Land." *Middle East Quarterly* 15, no. 2 (2008), 55–62. Contra, see a thorough discussion in Shapira, *Land and Power*, 41–42, 50–52.

32. Shapira, *Land and Power*, 55.

33. Rashid Khalidi, *Palestinian Identity: The Construction of Modern National Consciousness* (New York: Columbia University Press, 1997). See also Shapira, *Land and Power*, 41; Ghada Karmi, *Married to Another Man: Israel's Dilemma in Palestine* (London and Ann Arbor, Michigan: Pluto Press, 2007).

34. Quoted in Benny Morris, *Righteous Victims: A History of the Zionist-Arab Conflict, 1881–1999* (London: J. Murray, 1999), 140.

35. Laleh Khalili, *Heroes and Martyrs of Palestine: The Politics of National Commemoration* (Cambridge, UK; New York: Cambridge University Press, 2007), 23.

36. Ehud Luz, "The Moral Price of Sovereignty: The Dispute About the Use of Military Power Within Zionism." *Modern Zion*ism 7, no. 1 (1987): 51–98, 57.

37. Khalili, *Heroes and Martyrs of Palestine,* 23.

38. Anita Shapira, *Berl Katznelson: A Biography*, (Tel-Aviv: Am Oved, 1980), 719–20 (Hebrew); Berl Katznelson, "Berl Katznelson." in *Sources: Anthology of Contemporary Jewish Thought*, eds. Eliezer Schweid and David Hardan, vol. 5, (Jerusalem: World Zionist Organization, the Department for Education and Culture in the Diaspora, 1970), 148–49.

39. Kober, *Israel's Wars of Attrition: Attrition Challenges to Democratic States*, 115-116. See criticism of the code in Dan Yahav, *Purity of Arms: Ethos Myth and Reality* 1936-1956, (Tel-Aviv, Tamuz Publishers, 2002). (Hebrew)

40. Anita Shapira, *Land and Power: The Zionist Resort to Force, 1881–1948*, (New York: Oxford University Press, 1992).

41. Stuart A. Cohen, *Israel and Its Army: From Cohesion to Confusion* (New York: Routledge, 2008), 20–22.

42. Avi Shlaim, *The Iron Wall: Israel and the Arab World* (New York: W. W. Norton, 2000), 1–6.

43. Edward W. Said, Ibrahim Abu-Lughod, Janet L. Lughod, Muhammad Hallaj, Elia Zureik, "A Profile of the Palestinian People." In *Blaming the Victims: Spurious Scholarship and the Palestinian Question*, eds. Edward W. Said and Christopher Hitchens (London: Verso, 2001), 241.

44. Edward W. Said, *Orientalism* (New York: Pantheon Books, 1978).

45. Shay Hazkani, "Political Indoctrination of Soldiers in the IDF, 1948–1949." *Israel Studies Review*, 30, 1 (2015): 20–41

46. Moshe Dayan, *Moshe Dayan: Story of My Life* (Tel Aviv: Yedioth Achronoth and Dvir, 1976), 191. (Hebrew)

47. Dayan. *Moshe Dayan: Story of My Life*, 191.

48. Nerina Weiss, "The Power of Dead Bodies," in *Histories of Victimhood*. Edited by Steffen Jensen and Henrik Rønsbo, 161–72 (Philadelphia: University of Pennsylvania Press, 2014), 161–72.

49. Dayan. *Moshe Dayan: Story of My Life*, 191.

50. Bialik and Efros. *Complete Poetic Works of Hayyim Nahman Bialik*, 65–67.

51. Bialik and Efros. *Complete Poetic Works of Hayyim Nahman Bialik*, 482.

52. Shafir and Peled, *Being Israeli: The Dynamics of Multiple Citizenship*, 17; Hakohen, *Immigrants in Turmoil*, 49.

53. Anita, Shapira. *Land and Power: The Zionist Resort to Force, 1881–1948* (New York, Oxford University Press, 1992).

54. Bialik and Efros, *Complete Poetic Works of Hayyim Nahman Bialik*, 115.

55. The numbers are estimated in Boaz Sangero, "Where There Is No Suspicion There Is No Real Investigation: The Report of the Committee of Inquiry into the Disappearance of the Children of Jewish Yemenite Immigrants to Israel in 1948–1954," *Theory and Criticism* 21 (2002), 47–76. (Hebrew)

56. Ruth Amir, *Who Is Afraid of Historical Redress? the Israeli Victim-Perpetrator Dichotomy* (Brighton, MA: Academic Studies Press, 2012); N.A. *Report: State Commission of Inquiry in the Matter of the Disappearance of Children of Yemeni Immigrants between 1948-1954; Commission Chairs: Yehuda Cohen; Yaakov Kedmi.* (Jerusalem, Government Printer, 2001). (Hebrew).

57. Shoshana Madmoni-Gerber, *Israeli Media and the Framing of Internal Conflict: The Yemenite Babies Affair*, 1st ed. (New York, NY: Palgrave Macmillan, 2009); Yosef Meir, *The Zionism Movement and the Yemenite Jews* (Tel-Aviv: Afikim, 1983). (Hebrew).

58. Arthur Ruppin, *My Life* (Tel-Aviv: Am Oved, 1947), 27. (Hebrew).

59. Shafir and Peled, *Being Israeli: The Dynamics of Multiple Citizenship.*

60. N.A. *Report: State Commission of Inquiry in the Matter of the Disappearance of Children of Yemeni Immigrants between 1948–1954;* (Hebrew).

61. N.A. *Report- Commission of Inquiry of the Finding Yemeni Children; Commission Chairs: Joseph Bahaloul and Reuben Minkowski.* (Jerusalem: Government Printer, 1967), 1–2.

62. David Ben-Gurion, "A Letter from David Ben-Gurion to Yigael Yadin." In *David Ben-Gurion: The First Prime Minis*ter. Edited by Yemima Rosenthal and Eli Shealtiel (Jerusalem: The State Archives, 1997), 169. (Hebrew).

63. Haim Zadok, *The Load of Yemen 1946–1951* (Holon: A'Ale Batamar, 1985), 132. (Hebrew).

64. Quoted in Meira Weiss, "The Immigrating Body and the Body Politic: The Yemeni Children Affair and Body Commodification in Israel," *Body and Society* 7, no. 2–3 (2001), 98.

65. Y. Harris, *On the Claws of Eagles: The Whole Truth on the Magic Carpet Affair* (Bnei Brak: Torat Avot, 1988) (Hebrew); Yehoshua Bitzur, "The Lost Yemeni Children Were Transferred to Women's Organizations According to Political Affiliation," *Ma'ariv*, June 22, 1986, 18. (Hebrew). N.A. *Report: State Commission of Inquiry in the Matter of the Disappearance of Children of Yemeni Immigrants between 1948–1954*
Sangero, "Where There Is No Suspicion There Is No Real Investigation," 49.

66. Yehoshua Bitzur, "The Lost Yemeni Children Were Transferred to Women's Organizations According to Political Affiliation."

67. These were the Bahaloul-Minkowski Commission of 1967, the Shalgi Commission of 1988, and the Cohen-Kedmi Commission of 1995.

68. Amram NGO claims that conservative evaluations suggest that one in eight Yemeni children disappeared. Yemeni infants comprised two-thirds of the disappearances, while one third were children of Mizrahi or Balkans' immigrants.

69. *Report: State Commission of Inquiry in the Matter of the Disappearance of Children of Yemeni Immigrants during 1948–1954*, 325–30.

70. Gabi Siboni, "Disproportionate Force: Israel's Concept of Response in Light of the Second Lebanon War." The Institute for National Security Studies, October 2, 2008. http://www.inss.org.il/publication/disproportionate-force-israels-concept-of-response-in-light-of-the-second-lebanon-war/ (accessed November 10, 2017). This doctrine was reaffirmed by Israel's Chief of Staff, Gadi Eisenkot. See Amos Harel, "IDF plans to use disproportionate force in next war," *Haaretz*, October 5, 2008. https://www.haaretz.com/analysis-idf-plans-to-use-disproportionate-force-in-next-war-1.254954 (accessed November 1, 2017).

71. Berl Katznelson Foundation, *Hate Report.*

72. Allison Kaplan Sommer, "Israel's Western Wall Crisis: Why Jews Are Fighting with Each Other over the Jewish Holy Site, Explained," *Haaretz*, June 27, 2017. https://www.haaretz.com/israel-news/1.797925 (accessed October 31, 2017).

73. Kaplan Sommer, "Israel's Western Wall Crisis: Why Jews Are Fighting with Each Other over the Jewish Holy Site, Explained."

74. Dov Waxman, *Trouble in the Tribe: The American Jewish Conflict over Israel*, (Princeton, Princeton University Press, 2016). See also, Dan Shapiro, "Klal Yisrael is an Israeli Strategic Asset," *Jewish Journal*, June 30, 2017, http://jewishjournal.com/opinion/221147/klal-yisrael-israeli-strategic-asset/ (accessed November 18, 2017).

75. Jeremy Sharon, "Deri: Non-Orthodox Jewish Streams Not Judaism," The Jerusalem Post, November 7, 2017. http://www.jpost.com/Israel-News/Politics-And-Diplomacy/Deri-non-Orthodox-Jewish-streams-not-Judaism-471924 (accessed on November 10, 2017).

76. Sharon, "Deri: Non-Orthodox Jewish Streams Not Judaism,"

77. Sharon, "Deri: Non-Orthodox Jewish Streams Not Judaism."

78. Sharon, "Deri: Non-Orthodox Jewish Streams Not Judaism."

79. Judy Maltz, Divorcing the Diaspora: How Netanyahu Finally Writing Off U.S. Jews." *Haaretz*, November 23, 2017. https://www.haaretz.com/israel-news/1.821523 (accessed November 23, 2017).

80. JTA Staff, "Hotovely: US Jews Lead 'Convenient' Lives, Don't Serve in the Military," *Jewish Telegraphic Agency.* November 22, 2017. Available online https://www.jta.org/2017/11/22/news-opinion/united-states/hotovely-us-jews-lead-convenient-lives-dont-serve-in-the-military (accessed November 25, 2017).

81. JTA Staff, "Hotovely: US Jews Lead 'Convenient' Lives, Don't Serve in the Military."

82. i24 News. "Israeli minister: most US Jews don't send their kids to fight for their country." *i24 News*, November 22, 2017. https://www.i24news.tv/en/news/israel/160947-171122-israeli-minister-most-us-jews-don-t-send-their-kids-to-fight-for-their-country (accessed November 25, 2017).

83. Philip Roth, *Operation Shylock: A Confession*, Vintage international ed. (New York: Vintage Books, 1994).

84. Roth, *Operation Shylock*, 32.

85. Roth, *Operation Shylock*, 32.

86. The Knesset, Minutes of the 367th Meeting of the Eighteenth Knesset, Issue 33, 2012, of July 4, 2012, 73-82. https://www.nevo.co.il/law_word/law140/18_ptm_215990.doc (accessed November 1, 2017) (Hebrew).

87. Open Knesset Website, MK Ophir Akunis, Private Member Bill, Issue P/18/3140 Tabled on March 30, 2011. Akunis tabled this proposal together with MK Robert Iltov and Zipi Hotoveli. https://oknesset.org/bill/5881/(accessed October 12, 2017) (Hebrew). The Ministerial Committee on Legislation decided against this proposed legislation on May 29, 2011. The decision was appended to the Minutes of Government Decisions and was validated on June 9, 2011 as 3304 (HK 1831).

88. The Knesset, Minutes of the 367th Meeting of the Eighteenth Knesset, Issue 33, 2012, of July 4, 2012, 73–82, at 74. (Hebrew)

89. Open Knesset Website, MK Yinon Magal, Private Member Bill P/20/1729. https://oknesset.org/bill/9315/ (Accessed October 12, 2017) (Hebrew).

90. The Knesset, Coalition Agreement for Forming the 34th Government, Prepared and Signed on May 7, 2015. http://main.knesset.gov.il/mk/government/Documents/coalition2015_3.pdf (accessed November 1, 2017) (Hebrew).

91. Open Knesset Website, MK Yinon Magal, Private Member Bill P/20/1729)

92. The Knesset, Minutes of the 367th Meeting of the Eighteenth Knesset, Issue 33, 2012, of July 4, 2012, 73–82. https://www.nevo.co.il/law_word/law140/18_ptm_215990.doc (Hebrew).

93. Ruth Eglash and William Booth, "Israeli NGOs decry 'deeply anti-democratic move' as new law approved." *The Washington Post*, July 12, 2016. https://www.washingtonpost.com/world/israeli-ngos-decry-deeply-anti-democratic-move-as-new-law-approved/2016/07/12/a07b1bdb-a431-4fce-b76d-d0a35dfca519_story.html?utm_term=.c4111d1d5a58 (accessed October 31, 2017).

94. TOI Staff, "After contentious debate, Knesset passes NGO law." *Times of Israel*, July 12, 2016. https://www.timesofisrael.com/after-hours-of-debate-controversial-ngo-bill-passes-into-law/ (accessed October 31, 2017).

95. Moran Azoulay, "Netanyahu Demands to Exacerbate the NGO Law: Complete Ban on Foreign Contributions." *Ynet,* June 11, 2017. http://www.ynet.co.il/articles/0,7340,L-4974314,00.html.

96. Tamar, Hermann et al. *The Israeli Democracy Index 2016* (Jerusalem: The Israel Democracy Institute, 2016).

97. Hermann et al. *The Israeli Democracy Index 2016.*

98. Hermann et al. *The Israeli Democracy Index 2016.*

99. See the legal discussion of a forcible child transfer case in Canada in Ruth Amir, Cultural Genocide in Canada? It Did Happen Here! *Aboriginal Policy Studies* 7:2 (forthcoming 2018).

100. Benjamin, *Illuminations*, 257.
101. Hannah Arendt, "Introduction," in *Illuminations*, Walter Benjamin (New York: Schocken Books, 1968), 5–6.
102. Benjamin, Illuminations, 264.
103. J. M. Coetzee, *Memories of a Bad Year* (London: Vintage Books, 2008), 3.

BIBLIOGRAPHY

N.A. *Report- Commission of Inquiry of the Finding Yemeni Children; Commission Chairs: Joseph Bahaloul and Reuben Minkowski*. Jerusalem: Government Printer, 1967.

N.A. *Report: State Commission of Inquiry in the Matter of the Disappearance of Children of Yemeni Immigrants between 1948–1954; Commission Chairs: Yehuda Cohen; Yaakov Kedmi*. Jerusalem, the Government Printer, 2001. (Hebrew)

Amir, Ruth. *Who is Afraid of Historical Redress? The Israeli Victim-Perpetrator Dichotomy*. Brighton, MA, Academic Studies Press, 2011.

———. Cultural Genocide in Canada? It Did Happen Here! *Aboriginal Policy Studies* 7:2 (forthcoming 2018).

Arendt, Hannah. "Introduction." In *Illuminations*, edited by Benjamin, Walter, 1–55. New York: Schocken Books, 1968.

Azoulay, Moran. "Netanyahu Demands to Exacerbate the NGO Law: Complete Ban on Foreign Contributions." *Ynet*, June 11, 2017. http://www.ynet.co.il/articles/0,7340,L-4974314,00.html(accessed November 2, 2017) (Hebrew)

Arendt, Hannah. "Introduction." In *Illuminations*, edited by Benjamin, Walter, 1–55. New York: Schocken Books, 1968.

Bar-Or, Amir. "The Making of Israel's Political-Security Culture." In *Militarism and Israeli Society*, edited by Sheffer, Gabriel and Oren Barak, 259–79. Bloomington, IN: Indiana University Press, 2010.

Bar-Yosef, Eitan. *A Villa in the Jungle: Africa in Israeli Culture*. Jerusalem, Van Leer Jerusalem Institute and Hakibbutz Hameuchad, 2013. (Hebrew)

Bauer, Yehuda. *Rethinking the Holocaust*. New Haven: Yale University Press, 2001.

———. "Did the Holocaust Facilitate the Establishment of Israel? A Reply to Dan Michman's Article," *Iyunim Bitkumat Israel* 12 (2002), 653–54. (Hebrew)

Ben-Gurion, David. "A Letter from David Ben-Gurion to Yigael Yadin." In *David Ben-Gurion: The First Prime Minister*. Edited by Yemima Rosenthal and Eli Shealtiel (Jerusalem: The State Archives, 1997), 169. (Hebrew)

Benjamin, Walter. *Illuminations*. Schocken Paperback. New York: Schocken Books, 1968.

Bialik H. N. and Israel Efros, *Complete Poetic Works of Hayyim Nahman Bialik, Translated from the Hebrew*. New York, Histadruth Ivrit of America, 1948.

Bildstein, Gerald J. "The State and the Legitimate Use of Force and Coercion in Modern Halakhic Thought." In *Jews and Violence: Images, Ideologies, Realities*, Edited by Peter Y. Medding. (New York: Oxford University Press, 2002), 3–22.

Bitzur, Yehoshua. "The Lost Yemeni Children Were Transferred to Women's Organizations According to Political Affiliation," *Ma'ariv*, June 22, 1986, 18. (Hebrew)

Coetzee, J. M. *Diary of a Bad Year*. London: Vintage Press, 2008.

Cohen, Stuart A. *Israel and Its Army: From Cohesion to Confusion*. New York, Routledge, 2008.

Dayan, Moshe. *Moshe Dayan: Story of My Life*. Tel Aviv: Yedioth Achronoth and Dvir, 1976.

Delanty, Gerard. "Habermas and Occidental Rationalism: The Politics of Identity, Social Learning, and the Cultural Limits of Moral Universalism." *Sociological Theory* 15, no. 1 (1997): 30–59.

Eglash, Ruth and William, Booth. "Israeli NGOs Decry 'Deeply Anti-Democratic Move' as New Law Approved." *The Washington Post*, July 12, 2016. https://www.washingtonpost.com/world/israeli-ngos-decry-deeply-anti-democratic-move-as-new-law-approved/2016/07/12/a07b1bdb-a431-4fce-b76d-d0a35dfca519_story.html?utm_term=.c4111d1d5a58(accessed October 31, 2017).

Fackenheim, Emil L. "Holocaust." In *20th Century Jewish Religious Thought: Original Essays on Critical Concepts, Movements, and Beliefs*, edited by Cohen, Arthur Allen and Paul R. Mendes-Flohr, 399–408. Philadelphia: Jewish Publication Society, 2009.

———. *To Mend the World: Foundations of Future Jewish Thought*. New York: Schocken Books, 1982.

Friesel, Evyatar. *The Holocaust: Factor in the Birth of Israel?* Yad Vashem Shoah Resource Center, The International School for Holocaust Studies. Available online at http://www.yadvashem.org/odot_pdf/Microsoft%20Word%20-%203575.pdf (accessed October 15, 2017).

Gerber, Haim. "Orientalism, Zionism and the Palestinians." In *Jewish-Arab Relations in Eretz Israel/Palestine*, edited by Gerber, Haim and Elie Podeh. Vol. 43, 27–48, 2002.

Gewirth, Alan. "Ethical Universalism and Particularism." *The Journal of Philosophy* 85, no. 6 (1988): 283–302.

Habermas, Jürgen. *Between Facts and Norms: Contributions to a Discourse Theory of Law and Democracy*. Studies in Contemporary German Social Thought. Cambridge, Mass.: MIT Press, 1996.

Habermas, Jürgen and Peter Dews. *Autonomy and Solidarity: Interviews with Jürgen Habermas*. Rev ed. London; New York: Verso, 1992.

Habermas, Jürgen and Max Pensky. *The Postnational Constellation: Political Essays*. Translated by Pensky, Max, edited by Pensky, Max. Cambridge, UK: Polity Press, 2001.

Hakohen, Devorah. *Immigrants in Turmoil: Mass Immigration to Israel and Its Repercussions in the 1950s and After*. Modern Jewish History. Syracuse New York: Syracuse University Press, 2003.

Harel, Amos. "IDF Plans to Use Disproportionate Force in Next War," *Haaretz*, October 5, 2008. https://www.haaretz.com/analysis-idf-plans-to-use-disproportionate-force-in-next-war-1.254954 (accessed November 1, 2017).

Harris, Y. *On the Claws of Eagles: The Whole Truth on the Magic Carpet Affair*. Bnei Brak, Torat Avot, 1988. (Hebrew).

Hazkani, Shay. "Political Indoctrination of Soldiers in the IDF, 1948–1949." *Israel Studies Review*, 30, 1 (2015): 20–41.

Held, David. *Democracy and the Global Order*. Stanford: Stanford University Press, 1995.

Hermann, Tamar, et al. *The Israeli Democracy Index 2016* (Jerusalem: The Israel Democracy Institute, 2016).

i24 News. "Israeli Minister: Most US Jews Don't Send Their Kids to Fight for Their Country." *i24 News*, November 22, 2017. https://www.i24news.tv/en/news/israel/160947-171122-israeli-minister-most-us-jews-don-t-send-their-kids-to-fight-for-their-country (accessed November 25, 2017).

Kaplan, Sommer, Alison. "Israel's Western Wall Crisis: Why Jews Are Fighting with Each Other over the Jewish Holy Site, Explained," *Haaretz,* June 27, 2017. https://www.haaretz.com/israel-news/1.797925 (accessed October 31, 2017)

Karmi, Ghada. *Married to Another Man: Israel's Dilemma in Palestine* (London and Ann Arbor, Michigan, Pluto Press, 2007).

Katznelson Berl Foundation. *Hate Report* November 25, 2017. Online at http://hasata.berl.co.il/ (accessed November 25, 2017) (Hebrew).

Katznelson, Berl. "Berl Katznelson." in *Sources: Anthology of Contemporary Jewish Thought*, 148–49. Edited by Eliezer Schweid and David Hardan, vol. 5. Jerusalem, World Zionist Organization, the Department for Education and Culture in the Diaspora, 1970), 148–49.

Khalidi, Rashid. *Palestinian Identity: The Construction of Modern National Consciousness* (New York: Columbia University Press, 1997).

Khalili, Laleh. *Heroes and Martyrs of Palestine: The Politics of National Commemoration*. Cambridge, UK; New York: Cambridge University Press, 2007.

Khazzoom, Aziza. "The Great Chain of Orientalism: Jewish Identity, Stigma Management, and Ethnic Exclusion in Israel." *American Sociological Review* 68, no. 4 (2003): 481–510.

Knesset. Coalition Agreement for Forming the 34th Government, Prepared and Signed on May 7, 2015. http://main.knesset.gov.il/mk/government/Documents/coalition2015_3.pdf (accessed November 1, 2017) (Hebrew).

————. Minutes of the 367th Meeting of the Eighteenth Knesset, Issue 33, 2012, of July 4, 2012, 73–82. https://www.nevo.co.il/law_word/law140/18_ptm_215990.doc (Hebrew).

Kober, Avi. *Israel's Wars of Attrition: Attrition Challenges to Democratic States*. London; New York: Routledge, 2009.

Lis, Jonathan. "Netanyahu: Israel Must Cope with Future Security Threats If It Wants to Reach 100." *Haaretz*, October 10, 2017. https://www.haaretz.com/israel-news/.premium-1.816457. Accessed October 12, 2017.

Luz, Ehud. The Moral Price of Sovereignty: The Dispute about the Use of Military Power within Zionism. *Modern Judaism* 7, no. 1 (1987), 51–98.

————. *Wrestling with an Angel: Power, Morality, and Jewish Identity* New Haven: Yale University Press, 2003.

Madmoni-Gerber, Shoshana. *Israeli Media and the Framing of Internal Conflict: The Yemenite Babies Affair*. New York, Palgrave Macmillan, 2009.

Meir, Yosef. *The Zionist Movement and the Yemenite Jews*. Tel-Aviv, Afikim, 1983. (Hebrew)

Michman, Dan. "From Holocaust to Resurrection! From Holocaust to Resurrection? The Historiography of the Causal Link between the Holocaust and the Establishment of the State of Israel, between Myth and Reality." *Iyunim Bitkumat Israel* 10 (2000), 234–58. (Hebrew).

Milner, Iris. "'In the City of Slaughter': The Hidden Voice of the Pogrom Victims." *Prooftexts* 25, no. 1–2 (2005): 60–72.

Morris, Benny. *Righteous Victims: A History of the Zionist-Arab Conflict, 1881–1999*, London, J. Murray, 1999.

Muir, Diana. "A Land without a People for a People without a Land." *Middle East Quarterly* 15, no. 2 (2008), 55–62.

Neuberger, Benyamin. "Zionism," Israel Ministry of Foreign Affairs website, posted on October 12, 1999. http://mfa.gov.il/MFA/AboutIsrael/State/Pages/ZIONISM-%20Background. aspx (accessed October 12, 2017).

Neumann, Iver B. *Uses of the Other: "The East" in European Identity Formation*. Minneapolis: University of Minnesota Press, 1999.

Open Knesset Website, MK Ophir Akunis, Private Member Bill, Issue P/18/3140 Tabled on March 30, 2011. Available online at https://oknesset.org/bill/5881/ (accessed October 12, 2017) (Hebrew).

————, MK Yinon Magal, Private Member Bill P/20/1729. Available online at: https://oknesset.org/bill/9315/ (Accessed October 12, 2017) (Hebrew).

Raz Krakotzkin, Amnon. "Exile within Sovereignty: A Critique of the Concept 'Negation of Exile' in Israeli Culture." *Theory and Criticism* 5, (1994): 114–32.

————. "Exile within Sovereignty: A Critique of the Concept 'Negation of Exile' in Israeli Culture." *Theory and Criticism* 4, (1993): 23–53.

Ribak, Sharon. "The Critique of Historicism and Progress: Walter Benjamin's Ethical-Messianic Time Concept" *Protocols: History and Theory* 26 (2012). Online Journal, http://bezalel.secured.co.il/zope/home/he/1349198192/1349563447 (Accessed October 12, 2016) (Hebrew).

Ronsbo, Henrik and Steffen Jensen. "Introduction: Histories of Victimhood, Assemblages, Transactions, and Figures." In *Histories of Victimhood*, edited by Jensen, Steffen and Henrik Rønsbo, 1–22. Philadelphia: University of Pennsylvania Press, 2014.

Roth, Philip. *Operation Shylock: A Confession*. Vintage international ed. New York: Vintage Books, 1994.

Rozenberg, Yaakov. "Reflections on Universalism and Particularism." *Hagut: Studies in Jewish Educational Thought* 8, (2008): 191–208.

Ruppin, Arthur. *My Life*. Tel-Aviv: Am Oved, 1947.

Said, Edward W., Ibrahim Abu-Lughod, Janet L. Lughod, Muhammad Hallaj, Elia Zureik, "A Profile of the Palestinian People." In *Blaming the Victims: Spurious Scholarship and the Palestinian Question*. Edited by Edward W. Said and Christopher Hitchens, 235–64. London: Verso, 2001.

Said, Edward W. *Orientalism*. New York: Pantheon Books, 1978.

Sangero, Boaz. "Where there is no Suspicion there is no Real Investigation: The Report of the Committee of Inquiry into the Disappearance of the Children of Jewish Yemenite Immigrants to Israel in 1948–1954," *Theory and Criticism* 21 (2002), 47–76. (Hebrew)

Scholem, Gershom. *On Jews and Judaism in Crisis Selected Essays* Translated by Werner J. Dannhauser. New York, Schocken Books, 1976.

Shafir, Gershon and Yoav Peled. *Being Israeli: The Dynamics of Multiple Citizenship*. Cambridge Middle East Studies. Cambridge: Cambridge University Press, 2002.

Shapira, Anita. *Berl Katznelson: A Biography*, Tel-Aviv, Am Oved, 1980. (Hebrew)

———. *Land and Power: The Zionist Resort to Force, 1881–1948*, New York, Oxford University Press, 1992.

———. *Land and Power: The Zionist Resort to Force, 1881–1948*. New York, Oxford University Press, 1992.

Shapiro, Dan. "Klal Yisrael is an Israeli Strategic Asset." *Jewish Journal*, June 30, 2017, http://jewishjournal.com/opinion/221147/klal-yisrael-israeli-strategic-asset/ (accessed on November 18, 2017).

Sharon, Jeremy. "Deri: Non-Orthodox Jewish Streams Not Judaism," *The Jerusalem Post*, November 7, 2017. http://www.jpost.com/Israel-News/Politics-And-Diplomacy/Deri-non-Orthodox-Jewish-streams-not-Judaism-471924 (accessed on November 10, 2017).

Shlaim, Avi. *The Iron Wall: Israel and the Arab World*. New York, W. W. Norton, 2000.

Shohat, Ella. *Israeli Cinema: EastWest and the Politics of Representation*. London; New York; New York: I.B. Tauris; Distributed in the U.S. and Canada exclusively by Palgrave Macmillan, 2010.

Siboni, Gabi. "Disproportionate Force: Israel's Concept of Response in Light of the Second Lebanon War." The Institute for National Security Studies, October 2, 2008. http://www.inss.org.il/publication/disproportionate-force-israels-concept-of-response-in-light-of-the-second-lebanon-war/(accessed November 10, 2017).

Smooha, Sammy. "The Mass Immigrations to Israel: A Comparison of the Failure of the Mizrahi Immigrants of the 1950s with the Success of the Russian Immigrants of the 1990s." *The Journal of Israeli History* 27, no. 1 (2008): 1–27.

Solomon, Norman. "Judaism and the Ethic of War." *International Review of the Red Cross*, 87, no. 858 (2005): 295–309.

TOI Staff, "After contentious debate, Knesset passes NGO law." Times of Israel, July 12, 2016. https://www.timesofisrael.com/after-hours-of-debate-controversial-ngo-bill-passes-into-law/ (accessed October 31, 2017).

Waxman, Dov. *Trouble in the Tribe: The American Jewish Conflict over Israel*, (Princeton, Princeton University Press, 2016).

Weiss, Meira. "The Immigrating Body and the Body Politic: The Yemeni Children Affair and Body Commodification in Israel." *Body and Society* 7, no. 2–3 (2001), 93–109.

Weiss, Nerina. "The Power of Dead Bodies." In *Histories of Victimhood*. Edited by Steffen Jensen and Henrik Rønsbo (Philadelphia: University of Pennsylvania Press, 2014), 161–72.

Zadok, Haim. *The Load of Yemen 1946–1951*. Holon, A'Ale Batamar, 1985. (Hebrew)

Chapter Nine

Moving beyond the Victim-Victimizer Dichotomy

Reflecting on Palestinian-Israeli Dialogue

Maya Kahanoff, Itamar Lurie, and Shafiq Masalha

It's a Dream
By Olav H Hauge (1966)
Translated by Robin Fulton

> It's the dream we carry in secret
> that something miraculous will happen,
> that it must happen –
> that time will open
> that the heart will open
> that doors will open
> that the mountains will open
> that springs will gush –
> that the dream will open,
> that one morning we will glide into
> some little harbor we didn't know was there.

As three co-authors living amid the Israeli-Palestinian conflict, we have borne witness to the growing hold victimhood has over our societies. The fear of being victimized can narrow perceptions of others, in seeing them as potential enemies and stripping them of their complex humanity. Nevertheless, through our work with individuals and groups we have also observed another process wherein the split between "us" and "them" or "victim" and "victimizer" is bridged. Wherein the negatively perceived "other" may be seen as a complex human being, and one's identity ceases to be defined by traumatic history. We have witnessed how every minor inner shift allows for a significant ontological change, and greater complexity in the perception of one's self and "others." This chapter addresses a process that occasionally occurs and in our view can be facilitated. Throughout this process, the binary split between victim and victimizer, a prevailing phenomenon in situations of prolonged conflict, consisting of a psychological barrier to conflict transformation and peace-building, gives way to a different means of experiencing and understanding the world. It may be said that a new internal social space has been accessed and rediscovered. In Hauge's words, "Some little harbor we didn't know was there."

In this article we present a number of cases in which we witnessed a process of transformation that took place in discourse between Israeli-Jews and Palestinian-Arabs, wherein the exclusive perception of victimhood expanded to contain additional characteristics and nuances. As such, the harsh dichotomy between the personal/collective sense of victimhood, typified by "us-them," and "victim-perpetrator" ebbs to create room for the discernment of more nuances, in recognition of the complexities inherent in the identities of both oneself and the "other," within each group, and without.

The cases presented are drawn from different spheres in which the authors of the article work, with a focus on the means through which victimization ceases to be central to one's identity, emotional reactions, and perception of the world. The first theoretical section offers a background on the phenomenon of victimhood and its severe social and psychological impact and implications, especially among members of groups in conflict.

The second section, based on research conducted by co-author Maya Kahanoff, analyzes the development of discourse between Israeli-Jews and Palestinian-Arabs throughout structured intergroup encounters. The first study was conducted during an Arab and Jewish teachers' seminar on the Holocaust held at the Van Leer Jerusalem Institute (Kahanoff, 2018). The second study was conducted during a year-long dialogue encounter between Jewish and Arab students at Hebrew University (Kahanoff 2016). Kahanoff examines the dynamics that take place between and within each group, as well as those that occur within individual participants' consciousness. Kahanoff demonstrates the unsettling nature of dialogue in crafting a space wherein individuals not only encounter the image or narrative of the "other," but also the image or narrative of one's self, arguing that therein lies dialogue's potential for transformation. Her study ultimately demonstrates the value of creating an internal "third space," in which it is possible to openly examine victim-victimizer processes, transforming dichotomies into more complex perceptions of self and others.

The third section, based on the work of co-authors Itamar Lurie and Shafiq Masalha, analyzes the discourse of a supervision group on child psychotherapy conducted during a training program for Palestinian and Israeli mental health professionals. The specific case, involving a child from a refugee camp, demonstrates how empathy often recedes when conflict surfaces, evoking profound feelings related to the victim-victimizer dichotomy. The training program offered a joint framework within which to work together on a common task (in this case, learning psychotherapy) as an anchor for group cooperation, combined with concerted efforts to avail opportunities for truthful communication, thus giving meaning and value to affects related to victimization.

The fourth section addresses two respective cases that exemplify the powerful impact of unconscious guilt and shame on victimhood. The first is a psychotherapy case from Lurie's private clinic, wherein as an Israeli-Jewish therapist he treated a post-traumatic Palestinian man, suggesting that by verbally processing unconscious guilt, his patient was able stop seeking out situations in which he was victimized. The second highlights a vignette that took place at the Psychoanalytic Institute in Jerusalem, which suggests that the Israeli-Palestinian victim victimizer complex may be processed by acknowledging the past and reconciling with unconscious guilt and shame over historic wrongs. Throughout the chapter, all identifying data has been adjusted to maintain confidentiality.

The fifth and final section presents insights gathered from analyses of the various cases, offering suggestions for overcoming a sense of victimhood in moving forward with an emphasis on interpersonal and group work. We conclude with recommendations for relevant forms of leadership.

I. I AM THE VICTIM, YOU ARE THE VICTIMIZER

I.a. Theoretical Background on Adversarial Discourse Trapped in Conflict

One of the most significant components of the national ethos of societies in prolonged conflict is the belief in each society's own victimization.[1]

Bar-Tal et al.[2] define self-perceived collective victimhood as "a mindset shared by group members that results from perceived intentional harm with severe and lasting consequences inflicted on a collective by another group or groups, as harm that is viewed as undeserved, unjust, and immoral and one that the group was not able to prevent." This belief is complemented by viewing one's own society as just, moral, and humane. Feelings of being victimized, explains Bar-Tal,[3] lead society to believe that the conflict was imposed by an adversary who fights for unjust goals and uses immoral means to achieve them. He further argues that with time, as a result of prolonged suffering and loss, these beliefs become ingrained in the society and are held on both individual and collective levels.

Staub and Bar-Tal note that a collective sense of victimhood in a conflict may also have roots in the distant past.[4] As such, incidents that occur during periods of intractable conflict, even within different contexts, feed the sense of victimhood in present confrontations. A salient example of this perception is Jews' collective sense of victimhood within the framework of the Israeli-Arab conflict, which has been fueled by their collective memory of the 2,000-year Jewish diaspora, characterized as an ongoing period of persecution culminating in the Holocaust.[5]

The implications of such self-perceived collective victimhood is the exclusive focus on one society's own suffering, disregarding, or even delegitimizing, others' suffering. A collective state of victimhood impedes empathy for an adversarial group's suffering and acceptance of responsibility for harm inflicted by one's own group.[6] It becomes a paralyzing force, providing rationale for the persistence of a struggle despite its costs.

Groups involved in prolonged, violent conflicts tend to view their own group as the victim of the conflict, and compete with one another over their status of victimhood.[7] This phenomenon has been termed "intergroup competitive victimhood," the tendency of adversarial groups to perceive their ingroup as being subjected to more injustice and suffering at the hands of the out-group than the other way around.[8] This has been found to be a dominant and destructive feature of relations between Israeli Jews and Palestinians.[9]

Nadler and Liviatan[10] argue that the "victimhood competition" between Palestinians and Israelis may be understood as a fight over moral social identity. Palestinians portray Israel as an imperialist power, sometimes comparing Jewish soldiers to Nazis. Israeli Jews, on the other hand, insist they are the victims of Arab aggression.[11] This is likely the case, as recognition of the victimhood of the other side of a conflict implies one's society's moral responsibility and wrongdoing. This discussion has far-reaching implications for processes intended to transform the victim-victimizer dichotomy. In this article we explore corrective processes whereby both sides learn to expand their own self-perception along with that of the "other."

I.b. Personal, Social, and Political Dynamics That Entrench Conflict

It is important to highlight three central views regarding reasons why victimization is powerfully instilled within people's psychology, namely the personal, the social, and the political. We concur with Gratch's[12] conceptual view of the interplay between intrapsychic and object-relation perspectives in psychoanalysis. In relation to our discussion, the adherence to the victim-victimizer dichotomy should be examined as reflecting both intrapersonal subjective processes and contextual dynamics (familial and social) that are central in shaping one's attitude toward victimhood.

The personal view posits that personal and familial trauma is central, whether consciously or unconsciously, in determining reactions to one's environment. Traumatic experiences create a great sensitivity to the possibility of re-traumatization. This is evident post-traumatically in bodily reactions and somatic memories, from perceptual biases to evocative stimuli, diminished trust in others, and exaggerated perception of external threats.[13] Laub and Lee,[14] Fraimberg,[15] and Gampel[16] describe how parental trauma impacts the foundation of a child's sense of safety and trust in others. This posttraumatic position, which at times also affects the next generation, responds to the world as a potentially traumatizing agent. The unconscious fear of re-traumatization may lead to an unconscious identification with a past aggressor, so as not to fall to into victimhood again.[17] Such identification is characterized by a sense of justification of one's own aggression and lack of empathy toward the other victim.

The social view regarding the powerful psychological instillment of victimhood, suggests that social membership is defined through identification with the narrative of victimization. Holding on to memories and experiences of victimhood becomes a centerpiece in one's membership to one's family and society. According to Vamik Volkan,[18] disasters experienced by groups cause its members traumas whose effects last for years after the traumatic conditions pass. Volkan argues that the mental representation of trauma in the group's collective memory becomes a strong indication of its identity and a mobilizing factor. Thus, the impact of trauma echoes beyond those who experienced it firsthand, generating intergenerational transmission of the trauma that impacts anyone who is "under the ethnic or national tent."[19] Thus, members of the traumatized group, including those with no direct connection to the people who experienced the trauma personally, may display post-traumatic symptoms due to the incident's imprint on their psyches. Volkan coined the term "chosen trauma," which is the group's unconscious choice to define its identity, in part, through the intergenerational transmission of the victimized self, carrying the memory of their ancestors' trauma.[20]

Israeli and Palestinian societies alike attribute a great deal of value to those who have sacrificed their lives and health for their national cause. Here, fallen combatants are remembered with the same sorrow as civilian victims. Holding on to the victimization discourse is often perceived as sensitivity to the personal loss of those who died, and loyalty to the bereaved families who were left scarred by the conflict. Deviating from this discourse runs the risk of severing one's membership from the mainstream of a society united by its losses.

The political view entails leaders' conceptualization of social and political realities in terms of threats of victimization. Social, religious and political leaders have great impact on the construction and interpretation of reality in terms of victimization. The role of leadership in the "social construction of reality,"[21] has been explored since the beginning of sociology. In psychoanalysis too, Bion was first to describe how unconscious group processes interact with the leader's position.[22] He labeled one of these processes as "fight-flight," wherein the group's collective anxiety expects the leader to assume the role of clearly discerning reality, identifying enemies, and taking protective measures. This role, which is part and parcel of any leadership, becomes skewed when such unconscious dynamics surface, and group members demand group cohesion and conformity. The leader then sees enemies everywhere, identifying them from without and from within.

I.c. Coping with Victimhood: Escapism Versus Processing

It is important to start by indicating that there are two notable avenues to move beyond victimhood, the escapist solution and the processing solution. The more common mode is the escapist response to the victimization, which is present in both Israeli and Palestinian societies. It involves turning away from social and political issues through focused attention on professional and lifestyle matters. The Israeli-Palestinian conflict is experienced as dictated by others and cannot be changed by anyone. Most people in this sphere were born into the reality of occupation, the presence of vastly differing economic and political rights, recurrent rounds of violence, and have witnessed leaders' inability to offer a negotiated solution. Such conditions seem to underlie many people's motivation to maintain a distance from the daily news with its insistent reportage of violence, suffering, and trauma. Refuge is offered in focusing on a high quality of life through rich recreational activities. This coping mechanism is perhaps more present in Israeli society wherein the reality of the conflict is felt less on a daily basis.

The interest in recreational activities gains new meaning if seen in the perspective of the overall context. The hedonistic reality of Tel Aviv once juxtaposed with the parallel reality that Palestinians experience, highlights its avoidant quality. Palestinian suffering is present through its negation and conscious omission of disturbing facts. This solution, despite its pseudo-qualities, does renounce implied guilt and responsibility regarding disparate human realities. It is interesting to note that in Israel both hospitals and shopping malls have become zones wherein the discourse of victimization is left behind once one passes the guard (usually an Israeli-Jew) at the gate. These two public spaces enjoy professionals and consumers from both nations, an island of humanity usually free of the external political conflict. These spaces are akin to the borderless global culture, where medical routines and protocols cross borders, along with the aesthetics of hospital interiors and shopping areas. These spaces allow for a sense of disconnection from one's political and ethnic reality, and membership in the global consumer society. Here one's humanity and membership merely requires willingness to participate and a credit card.

A milder version of the escapist solution to victimhood, involves choosing to concern oneself solely with issues over which one has some measure of agency and control. Here there is a focus on professional development, the advancement of family members, and establishing safe and secure living conditions for oneself, immediate family, and social network. This focus on the immediate tasks of living, requires ongoing monitoring of the political reality, with an internal attempt to downgrade and minimize powerful affective reactions that may surface.

The second avenue, for moving beyond victimhood, lends itself to this chapter's undertaking, namely, to process and transform victimization through an internal process. The division between victim and victimizer is often accompanied by a sense of one's own moral superiority, since victimhood is self-perceived as devoid of bad intentions. In order to maintain this mental paradigm, there is a proclivity to perceive confirmatory "evidence" and to reject challenging data.

Psychoanalytic and psychodynamic theorists provide useful insights into the underlying mental states that characterize members of groups in prolonged conflict and offer means of considering the processes involved in the transformation of relations from mutual negation to recognition and conciliation. Melanie Klein[23] describes two psychic layers that exist within a person. She dubs the more primitive one "schizoid-paranoid," noting that this layer is threatened by the complex reality and therefore splits into "good" vs. "bad," "safe" vs. "persecutory." She labels the more developed layer the "depressive" layer. Here, the treatment of ambivalence is different: complexity is accepted, and the "good" and "bad" can be seen within oneself and in others. This depressive position is accompanied with a capacity for guilt and remorse, since one's condition is not blamed on another, but rather sought out within oneself.

According to Klein,[24] the paranoid-schizoid position (PSP) in adults is a reaction in certain situations to the anxiety felt toward internally destructive impulses, from which they escape so as not to perceive themselves as evil, and that they project upon an external object (the "other"). Upon projecting internally destructive impulses on an external object, one may see oneself as a good and righteous victim while viewing the "other" as a mal-intentioned aggressor.

For Klein, psychological development entails a transition from a split emotional state into a more integrated position, namely the aforementioned "depressive position," in which an individual recognizes that the supposed absolute good also contains evil, and vice versa. That transition is reflected in one's ability to see the world's complexities more holistically. Therein the "other" ceases to be the perfect friend or the ideal enemy to persecute.

In summary, the desired transformation required to make dialogue with the "other" possible, involves a transition from a paranoid-schizoid mental state (wherein reality is seen in terms of black and white) to a depressive state (wherein reality is more nuanced). In the depressive state, members of groups in conflict do not project the blame for the situation on the "other," but rather look within to fully experience their internal complexity. The transformation thus entails the development of a capacity to relate differently to both the "other" and oneself.

II. IMPASSE AND TRANSFORMATION IN ISRAELI-PALESTINIAN INTERGROUP DIALOGUE

Studies indicate that adversarial victimhood has a dramatic impact on the dynamics of intergroup dialogue in the Israeli-Palestinian context.[25] Co-author Maya Kahanoff,[26] as a Jewish-Israeli, focused on comprehending the Jewish-Israeli participants' experiences during such encounters, highlighting processes of potential transformation.

II.a. Intergroup Dialogue Trapped in Binary Discourse

In her research, Kahanoff[27] found that discourse among intergroup encounters between Palestinians and Israelis is split by two mutually exclusive oppositional frames of interpretation. Kahanoff describes how in the intergroup dialogue that took place on center stage, each side portrayed the other as the powerful aggressor and itself as the victim. The resulting discourse was thus flattened, stuck between supposedly mutually exclusive contrasts: rulers and subjects, oppressors and oppressed, strong and weak. At the same time, both sides maintained silence and concealment regarding the aggressive and immoral aspects of their own camp. For example, the Jewish participants repelled, as a rule, any discussion of the oppression and violence involved in the Israeli occupation, while resisting any attempt to perceive themselves as occupiers; the Arab participants, for their part, avoided discussing Palestinian violence and the militant attacks against the Jewish population, and rejected being deemed terrorists.

The intergroup dialogue distinguishes between aggressor and victim. The "victim" discourse ignores the face and complexity of the other, which is portrayed as one-dimensional, dominant, strong, and aggressive. It is a narrow unilateral discourse that aggressively obliterates the other, while also repressing one's own aggressive traits, ultimately leading toward a discursive dead end.

The following scenario that Kahanoff analyzes sheds light on the aforementioned phenomenon.[28] As part of a seminar of Arab and Jewish teachers on the Holocaust, held at the Jerusalem Van-Leer institute, the group visited Yad Vashem (Israel's Holocaust memorial museum). In the discussion held afterwards, an Israeli participant shared her difficulty in hearing Palestinians compare the Holocaust with their current situation today, and challenge aggressive Israeli behavior toward them. Another Israeli participant, Merav, further describes these difficulties empathically:

> As soon as you hear stories of villages being depopulated in 1947, or check-points, arrests [of Palestinians] . . . you are shocked. It shakes your view of your morality, of the morality of the society you live in – on both sides. You hear someone else's story and identify with it and it shakes the entire picture you had constructed for yourself. What do you do with this?[29]

Yet another Israeli, Shoshana, expresses a more existential concern:

> When you recognize the trauma, the picture becomes more complicated and hard to handle, and the fear that if we see all of the complexity we would be weakened by it and could no longer stand up for ourselves – and we mustn't, because we have to be strong! People's feeling that we have to be strong, because if we aren't strong we won't exist . . . that is the Jewish experience, in my eyes. It's a basic existential fear that also ruins us.[30]

Identification with the other is problematic for Jewish participants as they see their image reflected in the eyes of "the other," who perceives them as oppressive and aggressive rather than persecuted, which is how they often see themselves. In this phase, Jewish participants experience a forced transformation from victims who deserve compassion to objects of hatred.

On the other hand, it seems that Palestinian participants' difficulty feeling the "other's" pain and recognizing their collective trauma, arises from the disempowered and unstable place they occupy today. Recognition of the "strong party's," or oppressor's, pain is perceived by them as a threat in blurring their fluid boundaries, confusing and defacing their yet unrealized national identity. As the awareness and identity of the members of the "sub-jugated" group is constituted in contrast to the Jewish "other," it is threatened by revelatory humane encounters.

The encounter with the "other" as a subject, in revealing humane and vulnerable aspects, requires new, unfamiliar treatment of both the "other" and the self.[31] This might undermine the one-dimensional image of the Jew as an oppressor, while also undermining the image of the Palestinian as righteous.

At this point, Palestinian participants experience ambivalence toward their Jewish counterparts. They are conflicted between the desire to more intimately engage with Jews' positive humane traits, and the will to maintain their completely negative perception of Jews, against which their own distinct victim identity may be preserved. Thus anger and desire for recognition and separation exist alongside yearning for acceptance and belonging.

This interpretation provides a certain explanation for the lack of listening observed in most intergroup conversations, and for the struggle over speech as an expression of the struggle for life and death. Waiving speech and listening to the other in silence, is experienced as helplessness or nonexistence. Conversely, by speaking the individual places one's group and story at the center, silencing the "other's" narrative. Thus, the salient question at this juncture is how to promote such a desired transformation in discourse between groups in conflict?

II.b. Intragroup Discourse: Transcending Binaries within a Safe Space

In order to move beyond existing binaries, a "potential space," in Donald Winnicott's words, may serve to facilitate a space within which individuals may reflect more freely.[32] The potential, or transitional, space offers an intermediate safe zone in which experimentation and play occurs without the risk of adverse consequence. Here, thoughts, spontaneous gestures, emotional states, and imagination, may be explored without a price or commitment. It is a mental state, and offers necessary background to allow for discovery of one's authentic, or in Winnicott's terms "true self."[33]

The following "backstage dialogues," as Kahanoff[34] refers to other realms of dialogue that open up within intragroup encounters, may constitute transitional spheres that promote the desired transformation processes. First, the sphere within which intragroup dialogue takes places is addressed, wherein multiple positions may unfold and transcend the binary pattern. Then, the realm of individual internal dialogue is explored, wherein one develops a symbolic moral space of sorts, which loosens a conflictual knot as a result of self-reflection in opening up toward the "other." This movement gives rise to new possibilities for relationship building based on mutual recognition and cooperation.

The following are excerpts from internal dialogues that took place within the Israeli group after visiting the demolished village of Lifta on the outskirts of Jerusalem.[35] The facilitator of the dialogue within the uni-national framework, invites the group to "enter the shoes of the other"—to imagine what the village previously looked like, how people lived there, how they saw things, and so forth, and to try and empathize with feelings that may arise among Palestinians who visit such sites today. Meira shares her attempt to feel the experience of loss from the other side:

> I asked myself, what do they feel there at the spring? I try to go beyond the story we know . . . I had my memory of going to a German city in the 1980s, and feeling moved to see the destroyed Jewish quarter. Imagine yourself there. Looking through the houses at the view, the [Jewish] neighborhood of Givat Shaul, a landscape that is familiar to me, but they look at it with completely different eyes. We will never agree on a single truth, but it helped me understand where they're coming from.[36]

Another participant, Ilana adds:

> What moved me the most was at the end, when the Palestinian guide in Lifta said: now we have 30,000 refugees from Lifta. I tried to think about myself saying, what does it feel like to be a refugee, to be considered part of a village where nobody lives anymore? It touched me in terms of understanding where they are today. Real, essential refugeehood, over generations.

And Yael:

> I don't care what percentage were expelled or fled. I'm not interested in counting. Maybe historically it's inaccurate, but it doesn't change the story that there were people here, on whose land another people built its country. It helps to understand where they're coming from, and then I can talk to them. [37]

In the conversation with her Israeli counterpart, Yael repeated her memory of picking figs and prickly pears in Lifta as a girl, and how only during the encounter with the Palestinians did she realize that made her feel like "an occupier." In this light, Ilana shared her concern that listening to the other would be interpreted as consenting to accusations and suggests, "We will have to explain to them. We are listening to you, but it doesn't mean that silence is consent. . . . As if we expelled [innocent] people who were [just] picking leaves. I will not accept that."

From a psychoanalytic point of view, as Benjamin explained, the act of recognition involves lifting dissociation, a concerted effort to overcome denial. In cases of collective trauma, Benjamin suggests, this action is especially difficult (and risky), as uncomfortable "truths" that others wish to deny are exposed. This not only elicits scorn or condemnation, but also imposes the burden of anxiety and anger, which may be incurred throughout the process of shedding dissociation upon witnessing. [38]

Thus, an Israeli participant expressed her inner turmoil after witnessing the demolished village of Lifta and watching a documentary of Palestinian testimonies of the Nakba:

> It's hard for us [Israelis] to digest what we just heard. I was raised on the story that the Arabs ran away, not that they were expelled. I was raised on all kinds of other stories. And suddenly to see a movie about . . . people who were murdered when they went out to the fields. You have to put it all out there in detail and see that it's an atrocity, and that we are human beings. [39]

Benjamin suggests that the challenge of witnessing suffering in being an agent of violence, while also being an object of it, involves merging together different parts of oneself that are normally dissociated and split. [40] She further argues that acknowledging the suffering caused by one's own wrongdoing raises the fear of losing one's own goodness, and an inability to bear guilt and remorse, and to free oneself from a feeling of "badness."[41]

In the protected confines of the separate intra-group one may give and receive recognition and soothe the anxiety that feelings of "badness" will take over. In this space, Israeli participants developed the ability to contain different parts of themselves (vulnerability and aggression), and as a result could recognize the other's trauma and their own group's responsibility for it, without destroying or erasing their self-identity.

In intra-group dialogue, a third symbolic space opened that allowed for some processing of the Israeli participants' pain and anxiety, experiences or memories of collective trauma, and a sense of existential threat, which they carry even though they belong to the group perceived as "strong." In most Israeli-Palestinian dialogue groups, these experiences and feelings do not receive recognition by the members of the group perceived as "weak." Developing recognition and even compassion toward shared trauma by members of their own group, may enable them to expose vulnerability and expand beyond the knee-jerk one-sided perspective of self-justifying and blaming the other.

Moreover, the uni-national framework enables the development of plurivocality, which is flattened and reduced in the conflict discourse. It is demonstrated in the examples below, giving space and legitimacy to vulnerable voices that have been silenced on the one hand, and making it possible to encounter the aggressive sides of one's group, on the other. Plurivocality forms the basis for integration of opposing sides in one's self and group, which then enables the transformation of the relationship between the rival groups from binary to complementary, in transcending beyond the victim-victimizer interlock toward mutual recognition.

II.c. Between Persecutor and Persecuted: Internal Subjective Dialogues amid Intergroup Dialogue

The following section relates to inner dialogues that arose during intergroup encounters conducted between Arab and Jewish Hebrew University of Jerusalem students.[42] Participants' inner dialogues compelled them to contend with different aspects of themselves; between their aggressive and vulnerable sides, strengths and weaknesses, and shades of identity as victims versus victimizers. The spectrum of perception was further unraveled in one-on-one sessions conducted throughout a longer process of intergroup dialogue.

During these dialogues, participants attempted to cope with the aggressive images projected on them in the intergroup conversation, as well as with the fissures that were formed in their worldviews. The following examples highlight such internal dialogues.[43] The internal struggle of one participant, referred to as Idit, focused on her inner struggle between pride for serving her country as a soldier and others' accusation of her being an oppressor. Another participant, Yariv, struggles with his pacifist convictions that were challenged by explosive aggressive reactions.

Idit was hurt and shocked by the intensity of the Arab participants' anger and the accusations directed at her in the intergroup dialogue, upon being called an occupier, brute, and murderer. Above all, she did not understand others' desire to hurt, inflict pain on, and even kill her. In her attempts to fathom their extreme rage, she tried to recall or imagine experiences of persecution or victimhood. Sure enough, from the position of the persecuted victim, she felt the pain, insult, and anger.

Idit saw her image reflected back to her from the eyes of the "other" as a persecutor and oppressor, rather than as the persecuted victim, as she had previously perceived herself. As she became aware of others' perception of her as the object of hatred, her identification with the "other" started to feel problematic. Her inner dialogue reached a painful culmination. The two faces—the persecuted victim and the oppressive perpetrator met within her, and Idit struggled to distinguish herself both from the oppressed and persecuted Arabs, and the German persecutors who came to mind:

> I thought about it in the context of Jews and Nazis . . . that we Jews are still angry at them [the Nazis]. We always feel they should be sorry for what they did. And I thought about it. I don't know, maybe it's my egoistic drive as a Jew, as a people, but I won't let others think about me that way. You can blow up, as far as I'm concerned. No way! But I thought about it from our side – we were treated badly too, we were abused, as a nation, exploited, trampled, and we feel [anger] constantly . . . but if I try to put myself in the shoes of . . . the victim, and I understand they're hurt, then . . . the biggest and most shocking thing in my collective historic memory is . . . that case. . . . So, I can understand it, I can . . . they can hate me . . . but to be glad to see me killed?[44]

Idit fluctuates between two positions. In the first, she has a great deal of understanding and empathy for the Arab participants as those oppressed by Jews. In the second position, she is rigidly intolerant when she feels accused of being the oppressor. During the encounter with the Arab "other," Jewish participants' conceptions of morality and justice are shaken. The prevailing Jewish discourse is challenged by the Arab discourse: The Israeli Jewish narrative that describes Jews as those persecuted and Arabs as perpetrators, is confronted by the Arab discourse presenting Palestinians as the persecuted and vulnerable minority.

In Palestinian participants' stories about the personal and collective tragedies that they and their families suffered, a conflation of sorts is formed between the discriminated, humiliated, and banished Palestinians, and Jewish refugees. The internalization of the other as an aspect of the self undermines one's confidence in one's just and stable identity. Thus the conflict itself is internalized: Am I the morally sound victim, or perhaps the aggressive wrongdoer?

Yariv's internal dialogue was comprised of tension between embodying the personas of a "military" and "spiritual" man—in his own words, "two clashing extremes."[45] In his personal interview, Yariv voiced an inner conflict between two different value systems that guide him: On the one hand, the military value system that he acquired during his four years of his service in an elite paratrooper unit; and on the other hand, a pacifist value system that he adopted during an extended trip to the Far East immediately following his military service. Yair describes these two periods as the most significant of his life, during which his identity was forged between clashing influences.

For Yariv the army is charged with positive identification and pride. Like most Israeli youth for whom military service is mandatory, Yariv perceives his service as a valuable and patriotic act. Yet during the intergroup encounter, the very same act became a source of embarrassment and doubt. It is difficult to separate criticism of the army, or soldiers' actions in the occupied territories, from personal identity.

Yariv's text exposes an ongoing inner dialogue that started long before the current encounter, with his aggressive violent face that came to the fore in the intergroup context. The text expresses Yariv's dilemma between his loyalty to the IDF and its soldiers, colleagues and subordinates, and his moral worldview. In his inner dialogue, he struggled to reclaim his humanity on two levels: On one, he faced an external opponent, while on the other he faced an internal one. His struggles with both opponents occurred simultaneously and fed off one other.

On one level, he appeared to be a Jewish participant defending himself against the accusations of an Arab intergroup dialogue participant, whom we will call Ramzi, to prevent the stigmatization of Jews as murderers. On the other level, Yariv struggled with his own memories, with pictures and voices that broke through his repression. In his internal dialogue, his pacifist ideologies confronted the violent aggressor he saw in the mirror. Yariv fluctuated between trying to shake off guilt and shame in trying to reclaim his humanity, and offensively, attempting to justify his actions. In retrospect, he recounts:

> There were all kinds of very serious accusations, of . . . "occupiers" and "everyone who served in the IDF is a murderer by definition," or things like that. . . . And I felt that in terms of the group, some kind of offensive started to form on the Israeli side, the Jewish Israeli. . . . So I waited for the moment I could give him [Ramzi] a piece of my mind, but in the same language as his. In the same language of power and of . . . ruler and ruled . . . As someone who never killed anyone and who has a very pacifistic ideology and . . . When someone calls me a murderer, even before I had a chance to say anything . . . I couldn't just sit there. . . . And besides, no one really gave him a good enough

answer. He just attacked and attacked, without being hit back. . . . You can't just turn the other cheek. . . . I mean . . . You can't just go on taking punches without hitting back. . . . That's not my tactic. No way. . . . There's a certain limit, I can take just so much but no more. . . . So he crossed that limit and I had to answer him. I felt I was obliged to reply on behalf of all the Jewish guys. . . .[46]

Yariv was referring to his blunt reply to Ramzi, wherein he confessed to having been an army commander who oppressed and will likely oppress Arabs again, if needed. Embarrassed by his own violent response, Yariv first tries to explain it by his need to protect himself from further harm. However, Yariv's panic at the sight of his own shades of aggression reflected in that encounter, encouraged him to take responsibility.

Ramzi's words penetrated Yariv to the core, touching upon tender unresolved questions dating back to his military service: Is it possible to be moral and just while being an occupier? The boundary between the individual and the collective was breached, implying that occupying people entails an occupying self. In response, Yariv limited his participation in the remaining intergroup meetings. He shut in his feelings and his confusion, and entrenched himself behind a thick wall that he erected between himself, the Jewish participant, and Ramzi, the Arab participant. He tried to re-establish clear identities that prescribe predictable relations—ruler versus ruled, weak versus strong.

However, Yariv's own internal identity and sense of self had already been subverted. The tension inherent in confronting the polarities of his identity: the universal human pacifist, on the one hand, and the proud aggressive Israeli officer, on the other hand. Yariv confessed that he could, "no longer carry both that identity and my normal one."[47] In turn, Yariv, like Idit, was compelled to reconcile his own internal conflicting sides, in order to create space for reconciling with the external other.

The cases presented above demonstrate the potential for transformation and expansion of awareness of the "other's" sense of victimhood, which takes place in intragroup and internal dialogues within the consciousness of individual participants. Participants' subjective "hidden dialogues" enabled movement between opposing poles of victim-victimizer; movement that led to a new and creative sense of self.

III. GETTING A GRIP ON LATENT VICTIM-VICTIMIZER DYNAMICS IN AN ISRAELI-PALESTINIAN TRAINING GROUP

Co-authors, Itamar Lurie and Shafiq Masalha, were among the Israeli and Palestinian mental health workers who formed The Bi-National School for Psychotherapy with Children in 2016, at Hadassah Hospital. This program was conducted in English, and its participants came from Israel, the West Bank, and Gaza. There was equal representation of both nations among the student body, lecturers, and steering committee. A vignette from a group supervision session is analyzed below, with special attention given to shifts in the positions of victim-victimizer, accused-accuser and their negative impact on participants' empathy.

Meissner's definition of empathy is that "Empathy . . . is a cognitive-affective form of experiencing that attunes the subject to communications from another person, leading to some intimation of the state of mind or inner experience of that other."[48] Empathy is a state of immersing oneself into the subjectivity of the other. According to this model, failures in empathy usually relate to anxiety that arises from an inner threat evoked by opening up to the subjective experience of another person, which impedes psychological attunement.

One example that Masalha and Lurie discussed[49] involved cross-cultural insensitivities that led to strong affective responses, specifically with Israelis' strong negative reaction to Palestinians' use of the term "shaheed," and Palestinians' categorical objection to Israelis' use of the term "terrorist." These terms have different connotations in each society and are perceived by both groups as a symbol of the other's cruelty. The word "shaheed" literally means "witness" and "martyr" and is used as an honorific title for Muslims killed in a struggle connected to the Islamic faith. Palestinians use the term to recognize those who died in the context of their struggle with Israel, whether innocent civilian bystanders killed by stray bullets or bombs, armed combatants, or suicide bombers killed in action.

Many Israelis take issue with the word "shaheed's" reference to martyrdom, as for them it signifies that Palestinians revere, valorize, and condone suicide bombers who ruthlessly kill innocent civilians. In contrast, Palestinians are often offended by Israelis use of the term "terrorist." This word symbolizes the stigmatization of Palestinian armed struggle and ongoing resistance as unethical, calling into question why the Israeli army's destructive occupation-related conduct is not deemed terrorism. Use of the term "terrorist" in the Israeli media is perceived as an indication of Palestinian defeat, demonstrating that their struggle and plight is viewed negatively and de-legitimized.

We have found that in intergroup dialogue, use of the terms "shaheed" and "terrorist," respectively, elicit profound gaps between Israeli-Jewish and Palestinian participants who often perceive of the terms as offensive. These empathic failures may lead, given the appropriate setting and receptiveness, to recognition of profound existential fears shared by both groups. Once articulated, they can often lead to greater empathic understanding.

There were five participants in the group supervision: two Israeli Jews, a man (Avi) and woman (Nava); along with two Palestinian women (Laila and Reema) and an Israeli Jewish supervisor (I):

Laila: This second case is also very difficult. I ran into this case through my work at this school in the refugee camp. It is very bad there, In every respect. . . . So, I am told about a nine-year-old girl who comes to school with a clear mark of a hand on her cheek. I saw her and it seemed like she was slapped hard on the face. I asked her what happened. She said that she just fell and it doesn't bother her. We were standing next to my room and I invited her in. I told her that the mark on her cheek has the shape of a hand and that I was concerned. She avoided this question and asked me something about the room, and I went along hoping to make her comfortable. I suspected that she was covering up what happened, protecting her father. No one in the school has ever met him. I talked to the principal and she said she cannot confront or force the father to come—the school is vulnerable. Has no protection. There are clans that are suspicious of the school, there is the fear that the public school reports to the Israeli authorities and secret services. There are no social services and the police do not enter the camp. The principal said—report if you need to but no one is going to deal with it. I don't know what to do!

I: We have heard this brief synopsis and there is so much in it, and of course, there is much more that she knows, but let us continue our discussion on the basis of this brief description. In any case, 1 suggest that we proceed as we've done in the past, that we bring our thoughts and reactions to Laila and see how this will help us understand more about what can be done here.

Avi: I listen to the case and to your description of this girl and the absence of any support system in the school, and I don't think that I would know what to do there if I were there. And I think about you.

It is important to emphasize that during this specific interaction, it was clear to the supervisor that Avi ended with a focus on the girl's feelings. This focus introduced a slight deviation from the setting intended for the group, wherein the supervisor discouraged "clarifying" questions, and encouraged, at least in the first round of responses, associations from other participants. Though the supervisor was rather passive in letting Avi continue, in retrospect he believed he should have intervened. Somehow, perhaps in reaction to Avi's tone of voice and open-ended summary, he seemed to be assuming the role of the supervisor:

Avi: How does it make you feel?

Laila: When I think about this girl who got physically assaulted I am very concerned. I am motivated to do something to help her. She looks depressed, is quiet in class and is not producing much at school. I think she is the "good girl" who can go undetected as having difficulties. I cannot see her formally without her parents' consent. I don't see it as possible.

Avi: You describe again how hopeless it is to work there. But you somehow push your feelings aside. It must be very difficult.

Laila: You are right. That is why I do everything I can to advance my skills so I can do something about it.

At this point the supervisor perceived a conflict between Avi and Laila in that Avi pressures Laila to become emotional, and she insists that she is seeking help on a practical interventional level:

I: Avi, I want us to examine what's going on now. Twice you suggested that Laila focus on her own pain, frustration, and helplessness, and twice she gently indicated that she does not want to focus on her own feelings but rather discuss issues that relate to the management of the case.

Avi: I see your point.

Reema: There is so much pressure that there is no use of crying over what you can't help.

Avi: But isn't the counter-transference here the key to the work? I think that the helplessness of Laila marks the central presence of the theme of helplessness. The principal can't do anything, the school, the social workers, the mother and the child. This is really depressing.

Laila: What I need now is practical advice regarding what to do in this situation. The fact that the situation in the refugee camp is horrendous, is no news. I live right there, next to it. And in this particular school, there are so many difficult cases, and the system cannot help either.

Avi: This is why —

I: — We need to listen to what Laila is saying. She is in the middle of a battlefield, in a crisis zone, needing guidance, needing to find pathways to effective interventions with the children and the families from this refugee camp. Your insistence on her discussing her feelings seems, at this moment, removed from her needs.

Avi: Probably. This is the essence of my supervision group in Tel Aviv. I can see that this is not what is critical to talk about now.

Nava: I simply don't know what you (Laila) can do.

Laila: Neither do I.

I: I suggest that we study together what you have described to us about this girl. We need to look at the various details that Laila described and open our minds and imagine what could be important for us to investigate further. What are the steps that we can take, in this situation, to find out with whom, and how to intervene. Perhaps this situation reminds you of something from your clinical or personal past.

We will now examine shifts in empathic attunement during the group's discussion, from the vantage point of an experiential gap that surfaced unconscious guilt and anger.

Laila was in the throes of an overwhelming situation. She works in one of the most deprived, neglected, and unrepresented Palestinian refugee camps; and the only one within Israel's expanded sovereign territory. An article titled "Shuafat: A Mark of Shame on All Israelis," by former defense minister Moshe Arens, describes the Shuafat Refugee Camp as follows:

> Most of its 80,000 residents have Israeli residency permits and have the option of obtaining Israeli citizenship. That is where any resemblance to Israel ceases. It is a slum, with no sidewalks, no functioning sewage system, no garbage collection, no postal service, no open spaces, no parks, and no playgrounds, and no police protection to keep order and provide security for its residents. It is infested with criminal gangs in possession of automatic weapons and there are pushers selling drugs to adults and children. Killings are almost weekly occurrences. In Shoafat there is no law and there is no order. [50]

As a young professional working in a refugee camp, addressing multiple cases with little support, she herself was likely in crisis mode. Overwhelmed, she had the inner strength to tackle, the situation. Fight rather than flight. Use of functional coping and defensive strategies to meet the threats, such as denial in the service of the ego, focused attention to facilitate problem-solving, suppression of emotion in favor of clear rational observation, and priority to external needs.

Yet, there is an additional layer to her description. Laila chose a case that highlights the horrendous conditions in the refugee camp under Israeli rule and neglect. It can be interpreted that she covertly confronted the Jews in the group, including the supervisor, with the message, "Face the terrible reality that you have created." As with the Committees for Truth and Reconciliation in South Africa, in this setting the Israelis assumed the role of the white South Africans who listened and learned about the human misery for which they were responsible.[51] After a semester together, Laila may have felt confident in accusing, even if subtly, the Israeli Jewish group members, including the supervisor.

It appears that Avi responded to her implicit accusation by suggesting an exploration of the complicated counter-transference that she must experience. Here Avi seems to empathically fail to read her needs, and applies the kind of personal exploration onto her that he himself has found helpful in his own supervision. He sought to be kind and engage with her personally, but could not take into consideration that she is in the midst of a crisis. Here we see the presence of pseudo-empathy wherein one's superior position is defined by one's ability to empathize with the "other." In this light, Avi's statement, "It must be very difficult," may have served to reinstate his dominance through expression of human concern, reconstituting his power versus her vulnerability.

In retrospect, it appeared to the supervisor that Avi might have felt that he was unconsciously accused. As someone very committed to bridging the gap between Israeli and Palestinian societies, he may have felt uncomfortably implicated upon hearing Laila imply accusation of Israel. Avi's replies may be perceived as retaliation through subtle forms of aggression: directing the focus of the discussion onto Laila's zone of discomfort, sense of helplessness, and dysphoria, by which she would have returned to being a helpless victim. Laila resisted this, insisting that she wanted greater agency, and directed the group toward what she really needed. Laila managed to break out of her victim identity as a member of the subjugated group, and assume agency. Yet in asserting herself and challenging existing power relations, she was greeted with aggressive counter reactions by representatives of the Israeli group who pushed her back to her position of inferiority and victimhood.

Moreover, by describing her reality in the refugee camp, Laila broke a fantasized arrangement wherein she was supposed to appreciate the Israelis in the group and not direct hate evoked by Israel's actions toward them, thus separating Israel as an entity from individual Israelis. Avi does not respond with blatant aggression like the ex-officer in Kahanoff's case study. Rather, he uses a psychological measure to regain control. The question he asks is psychological, and appears legitimate, but it can also be seen as diverting the emphasis back onto Laila's intra-psychic responses and not to her implied cry for help over her experiences in the refugee camp under Israeli rule. Laila stood firm against these covert pressures holding onto her functional priorities and barring entry into her personal realm. Phrased differently, she would not allow "the triumph of the therapeutic," that allows avoidance of the disturbance of social and political truths.[52] We see this development as pivotal in the group's progress toward transformation. If the rift is worked through under the guidance of the grop leaders, then it may serve to deepen understanding. Otherwise, the conflict may lead to a deep impasse.

In retrospect, the supervisor, too, reacted with intense emotions to Laila's description, through becoming somewhat passive. Only upon realizing this, was the supervisor able to resume his role as the facilitator of the group, in addressing group dynamics, creating an openness to respond to Laila's needs. In hindsight, the supervisor expressed difficulty in listening to the implications of Laila's initial description, making him very aware of his separateness in being an Israeli Jew. It conjured desires to free part of himself from national belonging, to be able to lead the group as an open vessel responding to whatever arises. This irrational thought represented a wish to avoid the added complexities of being an Israeli instructor in an Israeli-Palestinian group, by assuming the role of a moral "psychoanalyst without borders" (as in Doctors without Borders). This was important as it was central to Laila's work and significant for the supervisory group that was forced to face the disparate realities of Palestinian and Jewish Israelis. It brought the group's bi-nationality to the fore.

The supervisor's passive stance was a result of realizing that the inner emotions that arose compromised his understanding. Following this line of thought, the withdrawal was not only external, but also experienced as a withdrawal of leadership. Avi stepped in and did his best to salvage the situation. In many ways, he emulated the supervisor's usual approach with an interest in countertransference reactions in the service of understanding therapeutic needs. Avi served the group's needs, but as Bion notes, the underlying current in the group is directed toward the leader, and Avi appears to have voiced the group's need for guidance and containment. Through criticizing Avi for pressuring Laila to talk about her inner reactions, the supervisor shook off his passivity and more clearly perceived Laila's needs in supervision.

The supervisor and group members were eventually able to transcend the impasse, and the superordinate collective goal of studying together united the group through a common task: rekindling a sense of partnership in a learning process. As Gaetner et al.[53] aptly described, while working on a superordinate goal, group members re-categorized their membership as belonging to the joint supervisory group. Now they could listen and learn from one another, while benefiting from group members' emotional and experiential depth. As the leader of the group, the supervisor carries the responsibility to identify the detrimental presence of underlying tension that relates to the conflict, and must recognize and name the emotions. This recognition allows for a new kind of receptivity to evolve. It reduces the urge to stubbornly hold onto one's position in fear of having it go unrecognized. Following recognition, safety is instilled in the group process and the leader should offer these emotions new meaning in terms of understanding oneself and the other, keeping the group's focus on task.

Upon consulting with a Palestinian supervisor who guided a parallel group, he affirmed that from experience, upon conducting intergroup dialogue between Israeli and Palestinian participants, Palestinians often unconsciously use the forum to express anger and frustration as the victims of Israelis. Such messages, as indicated above, unconsciously provoke reactionary mirroring of anger and frustration among Israeli partners. Israelis often feel the implicit message directed toward them, resulting in guilty sentiments, to which they typically react by swallowing anger or through passive-aggression. These responses generally take place subconsciously.

Encounters with Israelis on equal grounds are unusual from most Palestinians' point of view, such that when they occur, Palestinians often find themselves expressing anger and frustration. After all, in most other settings, Palestinians meet Israelis in situations where the dynamic is that of the occupier versus the occupied, or ruler versus subject. In such settings, Palestinians have no means of expressing the frustration and humiliation they experience. Hence, upon having the opportunity to meet Israelis in a more egalitarian and accessible situation, Palestinians' negative feelings surface and are expressed through various, mostly unconscious, fashions.

Processing this victim-victimizer dynamic within group settings transformed the aforementioned emotional residue. Throughout the process Palestinians were able to recognize pain and anger, and to symbolically and unconsciously challenge, confront, or punish Israelis. These aggressive sentiments that accompany victimhood surfaced in the group context as an attempt to affect Israelis. Palestinians' awareness of how Israelis are influenced upon listening to them helps them experience a sense of justice in that they do not bear the burden of history's traumatic consequences alone. Upon listening and processing such latent accusations, Israeli partners' discourse ceased to remain focused on blame and guilt. Israelis' awareness of Palestinian motives to express frustration, and insights into the feelings that arise within them, may offer a way out of the complex dynamics of victimhood entrenched in intergroup dialogue. As such, Israelis may be more attentive to their Palestinian colleagues and to themselves, upon being freed from the diminishing sense of being accused or accusing, attacked or attacking. At this stage, the dialogue opens up, with attention directed toward the "other," beyond the dynamics of victimhood.

IV. THE LATENT IMPACT OF UNCONSCIOUS GUILT AND SHAME ON VICTIMHOOD

IV.a A Clinical Case Summary: Unconscious Repentance through Self-Victimization

Unconscious guilt and shame have a powerful long-term impact on both victims and victimizers. The shame is usually related to the subjective experience in a social context wherein people are pained by the critical external eye that saw them, or could have seen them, violating either social standards or their own ideals.[54] Guilt, in contrast, is more of an internal process of remorse and regret. Traumatic events inherently evoke guilt and shame, and are often hidden and kept within in secret. Both have the capacity to impact perceptions and behaviors. One example is presented here, taken from a psychotherapeutic process, wherein such affects were dealt with and overcome.

Co-author, Itamar Lurie, treated a Palestinian man who suffered from impotence for which no organic reasons were found. His wife berated him continuously for his impotence and made it clear that she wished to annul the marriage and seek a "real man" who can function in every sphere. He felt victimized and humiliated in every social interaction, seeing himself as underappreciated, used, and exploited at work. He could never do enough to please his mother. He fantasized about lashing out, confronting Palestinian police officers, shouting at an Israeli soldier at a checkpoint, stating his value explicitly to his bosses at work, and telling his wife that he will not tolerate her ongoing belittling comments. With time, Lurie pointed out to him that he talks about himself as someone condemned to be punished, seemingly responsible for creating these dynamics. The patient thought about it and eventually said:

> There is something that I haven't told anybody and I know that it haunts me. When I was in high school, as you know, I was a good boy. The Second Intifada was all around but I kept to my studies and athletic activities. My mother was very protective of me and I did what she wanted. One day as I returned from school I could see that there was action in the neighborhood with soldiers and policemen, and smoke coming from all directions. From a distance a soldier motioned to me to come. I turned around and started running. I was fast. I knew the area and arrived home without being caught. The neighborhood was put under curfew and the IDF banged on the door. My mother answered and the soldier said that they needed to question me. My mother screamed and said that I have nothing to do with the whole mess that was happening. But I was taken for three months for interrogation, kept in solitary confinement. They didn't do too much to me. And at one point in the interrogation I told them everything I knew. Now, I did not know much because I was outside of the "inner group." But I said, "So and so brags about his

stone throwing. . . . They say that so and so is active in the Popular Front [for the Liberation of Palestine]," and so on. When they released me I heard that all the people I mentioned were arrested.

He carried various layers of guilt over his behavior under interrogation, and lingering shame for fearing that his "betrayal" disgraced his reputation forever. Only now could he see that he put himself in submissive masochistic relationships as an unconscious means of punishing himself. He was guilty and ashamed of betraying his fellow Palestinians, and particularly tormented by self-loathing and ethical hypocrisy. He now realized that he cast his demeaning wife in the role of punisher. She carried his projected self-hate, as she delivered the punishment while he experienced himself as the innocent victim. This dichotomy changed when he began describing for the first time in his life the months of interrogation and incarceration, and the years of dissociating himself from that experience. Once he could view the complexity of this situation, and also look retrospectively with more kindness at himself as a teenager in the interrogation room, he started changing his outlook and behavior. He looked at his wife more kindly, and was more open with the therapist, an Israeli Jew, about his anger toward Israel and his expectations of their dynamic. The old dichotomies faded away, particularly between himself as good versus the bad others, the virtue in suffering versus the sin in joy, fear of aggression versus discovering his own assertive and aggressive qualities.

This brief clinical summary exemplifies the powerful impact of unconscious guilt and shame on victimization. Unconscious guilt drove the patient to seek punishment and humiliation. In the aforementioned supervision group, unconscious guilt in reaction to the case regarding the girl from the refugee camp caused the Israeli supervisor to react passively, and the Israeli trainee patronizingly. There are of course other ways in which this powerful unconscious motif emerges. For example, one may try to punish oneself through high-risk behaviors or inflexible militant reactions that overcompensate for passive and cowardly past behavior.

IV.b The Encounter with Psychoanalysts in Talbiye, Jerusalem: Reconciliation through Recognition of Repressed Denial

Recently two co-authors of this chapter, Itamar Lurie and Shafiq Masalha, lectured at the Israel Psychoanalytic Society in the Talbiye neighborhood of Jerusalem, which was an Arab neighborhood until 1948. Masalha, as a Palestinian, drew the audience's attention to the fact that the building and hall in which the lecture was held is a Palestinian house; the original owners' decorated tiled floors still ornament the spacious room in which the lecture was held. He wondered aloud whether this fact had crossed their minds, and how they relate to the visibly Palestinian architecture of the building that tells the story of a refugee family that once inhabited this space. Many of the psycho-analysts smiled upon realizing their active denial in dissociating from the building's history and immersing themselves in the present function of the building. Denial takes place even among psychoanalysts. Masalha proceeded to wonder aloud where the Palestinian family that built and lived in the house currently resides. An immediate reply imbued with relief was offered from the audience: "The family lives in England." It seemed that this fact lessened guilt regarding both the exile and appropriation of the Palestinian family's property, as well as the Israel Psychoanalytic Society's use of the space as a center for their activities. They would likely have felt much worse if the family had been displaced to one of the poor Palestinian refugee camps.

The major adverse consequences of denial as a defense, involve avoiding facing reality and resolving the conflict. Denial in psychoanalysis, is a de-fense mechanism in which reality is acknowledged and then given a new meaning to eradicate the discomfort evoked. Jewish Israelis' ongoing denial of their role as "victimizers" has several ramifications. Not only do they avoid confronting the reality, but they also adversely cope with it through strengthening their sense of victimhood. Along this line of thinking, Masalha addressed the audience saying:

> I believe that Palestinians, especially the refugees among them, need your acknowledgement of what you did to them. They need you to acknowledge their suffering and your role in causing it. Most Palestinians realize that after all these years, facts on the ground will not make it possible for them to return to their homes. They, however, need your acknowledgement, evidence of ethi-cal ownership over the consequences of past events, in order to start to nego-tiate a potential compromise. No reconciliation can take place before this step is taken by your side.

Upon sensing some relief in the audience, Masalha interpreted the com-fort they may have felt as a physiological response to his statement address-ing their deep-seated anxiety that Palestinians will not relent until they re-verse the 1948 war. He provided an outlet for an unresolved conflict hidden in the psyche of most Israelis. Jewish Israelis cannot live peacefully with the idea that they acted as victimizers toward Palestinians upon establishing the state of Israel. This notion does not correspond with the fact that they were victims of the Holocaust shortly before 1948, and carry the burden of a long history of anti-Semitism and persecution. Shedding the binary perspective deeming people either "all good" or "all bad," is central to effectively ad-dressing such hard conflicts and disputes. Masalha asserted that Palestinians' exile and defeat in 1948 should not be resolved by infliction of a similar tragedy over Jews in Israel. Rather, reconciling the past needs to occur as a

psychological, social, and political process, wherein the human consequences of past events are owned up to.

Ultimately, examining the above vignette that took place at the Israeli
Psychoanalytic Society in Jerusalem, may lead to the following understanding: the victim-victimizer complex in the Israeli Palestinian case may be
eased through encouraging Jewish Israelis, on both public and leadership
levels, to acknowledge their role in causing harm and pain to Palestinians
who suffered trauma from the 1948 incident. On their part, Palestinians need
to honestly assure Israelis that they do not wish to reverse reality by turning
Jews back into victims. This approach keeps in mind that Jewish Israelis also
contend with trauma. Palestinians need not give up their dream of returning
to their homes, though they face the difficult process of accepting the tragedies of the past in order to go on living with the present reality.

V. TRANSFORMING VICTIMHOOD: INSIGHTS FOR CHANGE

This article addressed instances from the authors' experiences with groups
and individuals, wherein the binary division between victim and victimizer
was transformed. In conclusion, several factors are highlighted that help
facilitate these processes of moving beyond the dominance of victimhood.

Transformation of the binary victim-victimizer positions begins through
enabling a *more complex perception* of oneself and others. This change in
perspective, entails a shift in the perception of oneself, or, in other words, in
fundamental factors related to the way one's identity is constructed. Can
Israelis or Palestinians broaden their own views to see the human plight of
their counterparts? Change occurs when conditions allow for people to loos-
en their grip on self-serving reactions that solely confirm their perspective
and moral superiority.

Overcoming split perspectives requires a *safe environment* to allow for
exploration of intimate themes intricately woven into one's self-definition,
and personal and familial history. Any challenge to the existing perspective
is experienced as unsettling, or even as an assault on a fundamental existential level. In the public sphere, when fear, humiliation, and trauma are
evoked, there is a great risk for emotional or aggressive volatile reactions. In
contrast, in a contained group setting with leadership to facilitate and ensure
ongoing dialogue, we see time and again how difficult affects and experiences form the basis for broadening perspectives of self and others. An
empathic context for listening must exist to facilitate a process of recognizing the suffering and wrongdoings inflicted upon members of the collective,
through intimate appreciation and respect for the exposure of painful truths.

Uni-national group settings can be of great value, particularly when coupled with inter-group encounters. Such settings enable exploration of issues

related to one's identity and morals, without the obstacle posed by facing members of the other group. For example, in an Arab uni-national group, a Palestinian may explore his/her appreciation of, or even attraction to, certain elements of Israeli-Jewish society, thereby introducing a more complex attitude toward Israel and Israelis. In this setting, such an expression is less likely to be experienced as betrayal or flattery of Jews. Similarly, in a Jewish uni-national group, an ex-Israeli soldier may describe his/her moral qualms over contending with civilians while serving in the occupied territories, exploring conflicting emotions in the intimate group milieu. In the intergroup framework, the very same discussion is likely to be interpreted as a plea for forgiveness from Palestinians. Processes worked through in the uni-national group framework often facilitate exploration of charged themes that arise in intergroup dialogue.

The *guidance of leadership* is critically important in transforming the victim-victimizer dichotomy. In discussing leaders' responsibilities in various contexts, we focused on the following characteristics: the ability to identify, articulate, and create room for underlying emotions connected to the experience of victimization. Leaders on all levels must appreciate the role of the underlying emotions, while insisting on verbal exchange and a listening process. We posit that leaders' responsibility involves offering new meaning to past events and acknowledging the painful emotional dimension. Shame and guilt, in particular, which are characteristically inherent to victims' experiences, must be integrated into a new narrative that offers depth and possible hope for those who have suffered.

Transformative group leaders demonstrate through their own personal example in which it is possible to transcend the split between us-them and victim-victimizer, without denial of the past and with a willingness to envision positive future scenarios. This can be exemplified by their cooperative respectful and open attitude maintained with one another and with their members of the group.

While this is beyond the scope of our present paper, it is important to note that *political, cultural and religious leaders* have had a tremendous impact on alleviating hate, diminishing stigmatization, and transcending binary views. Many nations have experienced a significant shift in their relation to intergroup rifts through leaders who offered powerful, positive, unifying visions that value the "other's" humanity with respect to historical narratives. Figures such as Desmond Tutu, Nelson Mandela, Yasser Arafat, Yitzhak Rabin, and Martin Luther King Jr. have been leaders in shifting narratives, transforming years of traumatic struggling and loss into healing processes that recognize collective wounds and humanity.

Last, on a personal note, this chapter was written during a period in which the schism between Jews and Arabs in Israel has been exacerbated. Extremism is rampant while there is a scarcity of tolerant voices that respect differences. The very study of moving beyond victimization, recovering from trauma, and transforming conflict, serves as a signpost for an alternate route.

NOTES

1. Volkan 1997; Caplan 1999.
2. 2009, p. 238.
3. 2013.
4. 2003, p. 722.
5. Bar-Tal 2007.
6. Staub 2006; Bar-Tal 2013.
7. Kelman 2008.
8. Noor et al. 2008; Noor et al. 2012.
9. Shnabel et al. 2013; Sullivan et al. 2012.
10. 2006.
11. Bar Tal 2013.
12. 2014.
13. Van der Kolk 2014.
14. 2003.
15. 1988.
16. 2010.
17. Ibid.
18. 1997; 2001.
19. Volkan 1997, 45.
20. Ibid., 48.
21. To use Berger and Luckman's term, 1966.
22. 1961.
23. 1946.
24. Ibid.
25. Bar-On 2008; Halperin and Bar-Tal 2011; Kahanoff 2016.
26. Ibid.
27. 2016.
28. Kahanoff 2018.
29. Ibid., p. 75.
30. Ibid.
31. Kahanoff 2015.
32. 1971.
33. 1960.
34. 2016.
35. Kahanoff 2018.
36. Kahanoff 2018, 84.
37. Ibid.
38. Benjamin 2011, 209.
39. Kahanoff 2018, p. 85.
40. Benjamin 2011.
41. Ibid.
42. Kahanoff 2016, p. 172–181
43. Kahanoff 2016, p. 172–81.
44. Ibid., p. 72.
45. Ibid., p. 76.
46. Ibid., pp. 179–180.
47. Ibid., p. 181.
48. Meissner 2010, p. 424.
49. Lurie and Masalha 2007.

50. Moshe Arens, Haaretz, Dec. 13, 2016.
51. Krog 1998.
52. Illouz 2008.
53. 2000.
54. Steiner 2011.

BIBLIOGRAPHY

Bar-Tal, D. (2014). *Intractable Conflicts: Socio-Psychological Foundations and Dynamics.* New York: Cambridge University Press.

Bar-Tal, D. and Antebi, D. (1992). Siege mentality in Israel, *International Journal of Intercultural Relations,* 16, 251–75.

Benjamin, J. (2011) Acknowledgment of collective trauma in light of dissociation and dehumanization, *Psychoanalytic Perspectives* 8(2): 207–14.

Berger, P.L. and Luckman, T. (1966). *The Social construction of Reality.* New York: Penguin Books.

Bion, W. R. (1961). *Experiences in Groups and Other Papers.* London: Tavistock.

Böhm, T. (2006). Psychoanalytic Aspects on Perpetrators in Genocide. *Scand. Psychoanalysis Review,* 29(1):22–32.

Caplan, N. (1999). Victimhood and identity: psychological obstacles to Israeli reconciliation with the Palestinians, in K. Abdel-Malek and D.Jacobson (Eds.), *Israeli and Palestinian Identities in History and Literature,* 63-86, New York: St. Martin's Press.

Cohen, S. (2001). *States of Denial: Knowing About Atrocities and Suffering.* Cambridge, UK: Polity Press.

Faimberg, H. (1988). The Telescoping of Generations: Geneology of Certain Identifications. *Contemporary Psychoanalysis,* 24: 99–117.

Fonagy, P., Gergely, G., Jurist, E., and Target, M. (2002). *Affect regulation, Mentalization and the Development of the Self.* New York: Other Press.

Gaertner, S.I., Dovodio, J.F., Banker, B.S., Houlette, M., Johnson, K.M., and McGlynn, E.A. (2000). Reducing Intergroup Conflict: From Superordinate Goals to Decategorization, Recategorization, and Mutual Differentiation. *Group Dynamics,* 4(1) 98–114.

Galron, N. (1989). "After Us the Great Flood." A song from the album *After Us the Deluge,* NMC, 1989.

Gampel, Y. (2010). *Hahorim Shehayim Darki* (In Hebrew: The Parents that live through me), Tel Aviv: Keter.

Gratch, A. (2012). The psychodynamics of Peace, in C. Peter and M. Deutsch (Eds.), *Psychological Components of Sustainable Peace,* Springer, 205–25.

Hauge, O. (1966). It's the Dream. *Olav Gauge: Selected Poems* translated by Robin Fulton. White Pine Press, Buffalo NY: 1990.

Kahanoff, M. (2018). Collective Trauma, Recognition and Reconciliation: Reflections on the Israeli-Palestinian Conflict, in P. Rayman and Y. Meital (Eds.), *Recognition as Key for Reconciliation: Israel/Palestine and Beyond,* 59–92, Brill Press, USA.

Kahanoff, M. (2016). *Jews and Arabs Encountering Their Identities: Transformations in Dialogue.* New York: Lexington Books.

Kelman, H. C. (2018). Reconciliation from a social-psychological perspective, In: A.Nadler, T. Malloy and J.D. Fisher (Eds.), *Social Psychology of Intergroup Reconciliation,* 15–32, Oxford, UK: Oxford University Press.

Kelman, H. C. (2010). Conflict Resolution and Reconciliation: A Social-psychological Perspective on ending Violent Conflict between Identity Groups, *Landscapes of Violence,* Vol. 1: No.1, article 5. Available at: http://scholarworks.umass.edu/lov/vol1/iss1/5

Krog, A. (1998). *Country of My Skull: Guilt, Sorrow, and the Limits of Forgiveness in the New South Africa.* Random House.

Laub, D. (1991). Truth and testimony: The process and the struggle. American Imago, 48(1), 75–91.

Laub, D. and Lee, S. (2003). Thanatos and Massive Psychic trauma: The impact of the death instinct on knowing, remembering and forgetting. *J. Amer. Psychoanal. Assn.*, 51:433–63.

Lurie, I., and Masalha, S. (2007*). Hidden Expectations and sensitivities in a meeting between Jewish Israelis and Palestinians.* Paper presented at the European Society for Child and Adolescent Psychiatry 13th International Congress, Florence, Italy.

Meissner, W. W. (2010). Some Notes on the Epistemology of Empathy. *Psychoanal. Q.*, 79(2):421–69.

Moses, R. (2002). Unconscious defence mechanisms and social mechanisms used in national and political conflicts, in Bunzl, J. & Beit-Halahmi, B, (Eds.), *Psychoanalysis, Identity and Ideology: Critical Essays on the Isreal/Palestine Case,* New York, Kluwer Academic Publishers.

Nadler, A. & Liviatan, I. (2006). Intergroup reconciliation: Effects of adversary's expressions of empathy, responsibility, and recipients' trust, *Personality and Social Psychology Bulletin*, 32, April 2006: 459.

Noor, M., Brown, R., Gonzalez, R., Manzi, J., and Lewis, C. (2008). On positive psychological outcomes: what helps groups with a history of conflict to forgive and reconcile with each other? *Personality and Social Psychology Bulletin*, 34, 819–32.

Noor, M., Shnabel, N., Halabi, S., and Nadler, A. (2012). When suffering begets suffering: the psychology of competitive victimhood between adversarial groups in violent conflicts. *Personality and Social Psychology Review* 16 (4): 351–74.

Ogden, T.H. (1979). On Projective Identification. *Int. J. Psycho-Anal.*, 60: 357–73.

Shnabel, N., Halabi, S., and Noor, M. (2013). Overcoming competitive victimhood and facilitating forgiveness through re-categorization into a common victim and perpetrator identity. *Journal of Experimental Social Psychology* 49, 867–77.

Staub, E. (2006). Reconciliation after Genocide, Mass Killing, or Intractable Conflicts: Understanding the Roots of Violence, Psychological Recovery and Steps toward a General theory. *Political Psychology* 27, 867–94.

Staub, E., and Bar-Tal, D. (2003). Genocide, mass killing and intractable conflict: Roots, evolution, prevention and reconciliation, in D.O. Sears, L. Huddy, R. Jervis (Eds.), *Oxford Handbook of Political Psychology*, 710–51, New York: Oxford University Press.

Sullivan, D., Landau, M., Branscombe, N., and Rothschild, Z. (2012). Competitive Victimhood as a Response to Accusations of Ingroup Harm Doing, *Journal of Personality and Social Psychology* 102 (4), 778–95.

Van Der Kolk, B. (2014). *The Body Keeps the Score: Brain Mind, and Body in the Healing of Trauma.* Penguin Books.

Volkan, V. D. (2001). Transgenerational Transmissions and Chosen Traumas: An Aspect of Large-Group Identity, *Group Analysis,* 34 (1): 79–97.

Volkan, V.D. (1991). On chosen trauma. *Mind and Human Interaction*, 4: 3–19.

Volhardt, J. R. (2012). Collective victimization. in L.R. Tropp (Ed.), *Oxford handbook of intergroup conflict,* 136–57, New York: Oxford University Press.

Winnicott, D.W. (1986). *Holding and Interpretation*, New York: Grove Press.

Winnicott, D.W. (1971). *Playing and Reality*. London: Tavistock.

Index

About the Editor and Contributors

The Editor

Ilan Peleg (PhD, Northwestern, 1974) has served as President of the Association for Israel Studies and is the Founding Editor-in-Chief of *Israel Studies Forum*, the scholarly journal of the Association (published now under the title *Israel Studies Review*). Currently the Charles A. Dana Professor of Government and Law at Lafayette College, he has taught courses on Israel in the Reconstructionist Rabbinical College in suburban Philadelphia for about twenty years. A visiting scholar at Cambridge (St. Antony), Harvard (Human Rights Program), Penn (Jewish Studies), and Princeton (Middle East), and a scholar at the Middle East Institute in Washington, DC, Peleg is the author or editor of ten volumes including *Begin's Foreign Policy, 1977–1983: Israel's Move to the Right* (1987), *The Emergence of Bi-National Israel: The Second Republic in the Making* (with Ofira Seliktar, 1989), and *Patterns of Censorship Around the world* (1993). His more recent books include two volumes published by Cambridge University Press, *Democratizing the Hegemonic State* (2007) and *Israel's Palestinians: The Conflict Within* (2011, with Dov Waxman). Professor Peleg's expertise includes Israeli politics (especially foreign policy), US foreign and security politics, and international relations in general (especially conflict and human rights). He is a frequent speaker in a variety of forums on these issues.

The Contributors

Ruth Amir is Senior Lecturer at the Department of Political Science and Multi-Disciplinary Social Science at Yezreel Valley College. Ruth's research focuses on the intersection of law, history, politics, and society. She has authored books and articles on the politics of victimhood, transitional justice, and genocidal forcible child transfers. Among her most recent publications are the volumes titled *Who is Afraid of Historical Redress: The Israeli Victim-Perpetrator Dichotomy* (2012); *The Politics of Victimhood: Historical Redress in Israel* (2012, in Hebrew); *Critical Insights: Anne Frank, the Diary of a Young Girl* (co-edited, 2017); and *Forcible Child Transfers in the Twentieth Century: Killing them Softly* (forthcoming). Among her recent articles are "Transitional Justice Accountability and Memorialization: The Yemeni Children Affair and the Indian Residential Schools" (2014); "Killing them Softly: The Forcible Transfer of Indigenous Children," (2015); "Suppression and Dispossession of the Armenian Village of Athlit: A *Différend*" (2017); "Canada and Cultural Genocide: It Did Happen Here!" (forthcoming 2018); and "Law Meets Literature: Raphael Lemkin: the Totally Unofficial Man" (forthcoming 2018).

Yael S. Aronoff (PhD, Columbia University; Political Science) is the Michael and Elaine Serling and Friends Chair of Israel Studies and the Director of the Jewish Studies Program at Michigan State University, as well as an associate professor of international relations in MSU's James Madison College. Dr. Aronoff's book, *The Political Psychology of Israeli Prime Ministers: When Hard-Liners Opt for Peace* (Cambridge University Press, 2014) has received positive reviews. Her current book project is *The Dilemmas of Asymmetric Conflicts: Navigating Deterrence and Democratic Constraints.* This book, focusing on the experiences of Israel and of the United States, explores the tensions faced by democracies fighting long-standing asymmetric wars, as they juggle traditional military doctrines with the restraint needed to maintain domestic and international legitimacy.

Moshe Berent (PhD, Cambridge University, 1994, where he studied, among others, with Ernst Gellner) teaches Political Science at the Open University of Israel. He is writing on Israeli identity and the history of Zionism. Among is publications are *A Nation like all Nations: Towards the Establishment of an Israeli Republic* (2015), published originally in Hebrew and translated into English, and *The Interest of the Jews: An Introduction to a Different Israeli History* (forthcoming in Hebrew by Carmel Publishing House, Jerusalem, 2018). He also co-authored a book with Professor Joseph Agassi and Professor Judith Buber Agassi under the title of *Who is an Israeli*, published by Kivunim in Rehovot, Israel.

Maya Kahanoff has over a decade's experience as an academic consultant and evaluator for conflict transformation, dialogue, and reconciliation-aimed programs run by various institutions and peace-building NGOs. Her fields of interest include: psychological aspects of prolonged conflicts; dialogue and recognition in social conflicts; reconciliation and peace education. Her book,

"Jews and Arabs Encounter their Identities: Transformations in Dialogue," was published in April 2016, by Lexington Books, in cooperation with the Jerusalem Van-Leer Institute Press. Kahanoff's study takes us beyond the surface level of intergroup encounters to examine the dynamics that take place between and within each group, as well as those that occur within individual participants' consciousness. Her analysis demonstrates dialogue's potential for transformation as well as its limitations.

Irit Keynan chairs the graduate program for Education, Society and Culture, and the Institute for Civic Responsibility, at the College for Academic Studies in Or Yehuda, Israel. She previously taught at Tel Aviv University and at Haifa University, was a visiting professor at UCLA, and a research scholar at NYU, UMass Lowell, and UCL. Irit is the author of four books, two of them award-winning. Her book *Like a hidden wound – war trauma in Israeli society* won the Association for Jewish Studies' Shapira award for best book in Israel Study for 2012. Irit's teaching and research interests combine interdisciplinary aspects of historical and current dilemmas in the fields of war trauma, collective memory, social justice and ethnic reconciliation. She has published extensively in both academic and professional journals. She holds a PhD in History from Tel Aviv University.

Yechiel Klar is the Head of the Social Psychology Program at the School for Psychological Sciences at Tel Aviv University. He has taught and conducted research at several universities in North America (including the University of Connecticut, the University of Kansas, Carleton University, and Lehigh University). He has won research awards from the Society for Experimental Social Psychology (SESP) and the Society for Judgment and Decision Making (JDM). He has also worked on "Social Psychological Dynamics of Historical Representations in the Enlarged European Union." His main research interests center on judgment, choice and decision making, as well as moral and political discourse in societies affected by enduring ethno-political conflicts (such as in Israel and Palestine) and the roles of historical memory in these conflicts. Yonat Klar (1953–2016), to whom this chapter is dedicated, was a performing artist, stage director, activist, Holocaust educator, and beloved life-long partner. Her precious insights on the presence of the Holocaust in life in Israel today (e.g., Klar, Y., Schori-Eyal, N. & Klar Yonat, 2013) permeate this chapter.

Itamar Lurie (PhD) is a training psychoanalyst and a teacher at the Israeli Psychoanalytic Society. His clinical practice involves treating people of the various communities in Jerusalem. He was involved in introducing certain aspects of psychoanalytic thinking and training practices into the Israeli educational system. He is also one of the founders of the Bi-National Psychotherapy School at the Hadassah Hospital in Jerusalem where Palestinian and Israeli mental health professionals are trained in psychotherapeutic interventions with children and their families. He has co-authored several books with Flora Mor, among them *The Bearers of the Trauma: Long Term Interventions with Trauma Victims in Schools* (in Hebrew, 2008) and *Growing Within Relationships: Psychodynamic Education in Schools.* Ashalim Press (in Hebrew, 2014)

Shafiq Masalha (PhD) is a clinical psychologist and supervisor. He is one of the first Arab clinical psychologists in Israel. He is a senior lecturer at the College for Academic Studies in Or-Yehuda and at the Hebrew University in Jerusalem. Dr. Masalha has researched several areas including: Children and War, Cross-Cultural Parenting, and Cross Cultural Psychopathology and Psychotherapy. He serves as the president of ERICE, an NGO that aims to advance mental health of children in war areas, especially in the Middle East. He and Dr. Esti Galilee of Hadassah have been running a training program in psychotherapy as part of the Bi-National School of Psychotherapy. His training in psychotherapy and in group work helps him in performing mediation using professional skills. Leading groups in conflict has taken place in many of his work areas, including in academic and in clinical settings. He has been teaching a course on group processes at the Hebrew University for fifteen years.

Daniel Navon is Assistant Professor of Sociology at the University of California, San Diego, where he is also a faculty affiliate in Science Studies. He received his PhD in sociology from Columbia University in 2013 and was a Robert Wood Johnson Foundation Scholar at Harvard University from 2013 to 2015. His work focuses on the social studies of science and medicine, comparative-historical sociology and social theory. Recent papers include "Looping genomes: Diagnostic change and the genetic makeup of the autism population" (*American Journal of Sociology*, 2016 (with Gil Eyal)) and "Truth in Advertising: Rationalizing ads and knowing consumers in the early twentieth century US" (*Theory & Society*, 2017). His book *Mobilizing Mutations: Human Genetics in the Age of Patient Advocacy* (2019) examines the way researchers and advocates have used knowledge about genetic mutations to carve out novel categories of human disease and difference over the last half-century.

Ido Zelkovitz is the Head of Middle East Studies Division in the Max Stern Yezreel Valley College and a Policy Fellow at Mitvim- the Israeli Institute for Regional Foreign Policy. Dr Zelkovitz is also a Research Fellow at the Ezri Centre for Iran and the Persian Gulf Studies in the University of Haifa and teaches at IDC Herzliya. Dr. Zelkovitz was the Schusterman Visiting

Professor in the Department of Political Science at the University of Minnesota for the Academic Year of 2014/15. Dr. Zelkovitz won the prestigious Erasmus Mundus Post-doctorate fellowship and in the academic year of 2011–2012 he was a postdoc research fellow in The Institute of Sociology at the Georg-August-Universität Göttingen, Germany. His research, academic courses, and public lectures reflect a focus on cross-disciplinary analysis of Palestinian history and politics and the Arab-Israeli conflict, Israel's geopolitical situation in the Middle East and the role of higher education and students in building national identities in the Middle East. He is the author of two books; the latest is *Students and Resistance In Palestine: Books, Guns, and Politics* (2015).

Made in the USA
Middletown, DE
28 August 2023

37516718R00132